Introduction to the Conventions, Expositions, and Meetings Industry

Introduction to the Conventions, Expositions, and Meetings Industry

Denney G. Rutherford

VNR VAN NOSTRAND REINHOLD
New York

Copyright © 1990 by Van Nostrand Reinhold
Library of Congress Catalog Card Number 89-21454
ISBN 0-442-23495-3

Printed in the United States of America.

Van Nostrand Reinhold
115 Fifth Avenue
New York, New York 10003

Van Nostrand Reinhold International Company Limited
11 New Fetter Lane
London EC4P 4EE, England

Van Nostrand Reinhold
480 La Trobe Street
Melbourne, Victoria 3000, Australia

Nelson Canada
1120 Birchmount Road
Scarborough, Ontario M1K 5G4, Canada

16 15 14 13 12 11 10 9 8 7 6 5 4 3 2 1

Library of Congress Cataloging-in-Publication Data

Rutherford, Denney G., 1942–
    Introduction to the conventions, expositions, and meetings
industry/Denney G. Rutherford.
        p. cm.
    Includes bibliographical references.
    ISBN 0-442-23495-3
    1. Congresses and conventions—Planning—Handbooks, manuals, etc.
2. Meetings—Planning—Handbooks, manuals, etc.   3. Convention
facilities—Handbooks, manuals, etc.   I. Title.
    AS6-R88   1990
    658.4'56–dc20   89-21454
                                                        CIP

To Missy for the strength *and* the freedom . . .

Preface

In 1984 when the late Jerry Lowery, then new president of the Washington State Convention and Trade Center, started suggesting we collaborate on a new course in convention center management, I had no idea it would lead to a project such as this book. Although familiar with some aspects of the conventions, expositions, and meetings industry (CEMI), as I went about researching and designing such a course I became very impressed with the complexity and sophistication of this industry. It seemed as though every time I met an industry professional or learned about a new aspect of the industry, the opportunity for even more knowledge presented itself.

Consequently, we began to teach a class that provided an industry overview. In conjunction with the course in convention centers, it proved a popular introduction to the professional employment possibilities of the CEMI. It had the additional benefit of highlighting for the majority of our students the vast impacts and importance of the CEMI to the hospitality industry in general and hotels in particular. A course such as this also provided an excellent vehicle to better prepare our students interested in hotel marketing or operations in what to expect and how to serve what is arguably the single most valuable market segment in hospitality.

While there exist several outstanding books about aspects of the CEMI, most were written from a specific viewpoint such as that of the meeting planner or hotel sales manager. While these were and are valuable, and several of them have contributed mightily to this book, none by itself covered the whole industry. It was out of that need that this project had its genesis—a project that has been a continual learning and discovery process. During this process I met scores of CEMI professionals and was constantly refreshed and impressed by their enthusiastic support of the concept of a book such as this. The most memorable and deep support was by those listed in the acknowledgments.

This book, therefore, is intended to provide an introductory overview to the CEMI. Eleven separately identifiable segments are introduced, and described and analyzed in the depth necessary to gain an accurate perspective on the people, management, and intra-industry interactions of each.

Some segments of the industry, because of the breadth and depth of their influence or the scope of their operation, are examined in considerable depth. Associations, for example, are examined in some detail because of the economic importance the association market holds for other segments of the CEMI. The same is true for trade shows, conventions centers, meeting planners, exhibitors, and foodservice.

This is not to diminish the importance of the segments that are not covered in such detail. In some cases there was little literature available, and some aspects of the CEMI are so specialized that detailed functional coverage would have exceeded the introductory and overview scope of the book.

The book, therefore, is not a "how-to" text designed for the new practitioner. It is written to be used in the following circumstances:

- A text for an introductory course in college and university meetings management programs
- A comprehensive industry overview for the employees and managers in the CEMI
- A reference review for industry professionals
- Management training programs in hotel sales and convention services management
- Reference and adjunct reading for hotel marketing courses
- Reference or text for CEMI training programs
- A text to support an elective course in hotel, restaurant, and institutional management programs

The parallels and interactions between the CEMI and the hospitality industry are so close that their study together seems to be natural. The importance of the CEMI market to hotels and hotels to the CEMI is so great in some markets that continued linkage will be as intense as it is inevitable.

The conventions, expositions, and meetings industry is a structure of friendly, enthusiastic, and professional men and women who are strong supporters of education and its processes. It has been fun to learn and write about the CEMI and its people and I hope this book will be a positive contribution to the industry and its quest for continued professional growth.

Acknowledgments

I've learned a great deal from the research and inquiry that resulted in this book. Acquiring that knowledge is due in no small part to the members of the conventions, expositions and meetings industry itself. Without the enthusiastic support, encouragement, and generosity of the following people and organizations, this project would have been at best, no fun, and at worst, impossible. These professionals and the organizations they represent deserve the gratitude of the educational community for their commitment to education and professionalism throughout the industry.

Mr. Don Walter, CEM
National Association of Exposition
Managers

Ms. Elissa Matelis Myers, CAE
American Society of Association
Executives
Association Management Magazine

Mr. Bill Mee
Trade Show Bureau

Mr. Roy B. Evans, Jr., CAE
Mr. Ed Polivka
Professional Convention Management
Association

Ms. Helen Zia
Meetings and Conventions Magazine

Dr. Art Jones
Georgia State University

Mr. Kanellos J. Astor
Formerly President/CEO
Washington State Convention and
Trade Center
Group 2+ International Inc.

Mr. Egil "Bud" Krogh, J.D.
Partner
Culp, Guterson, Grader; and
Corporate Counsel
Washington State Convention and
Trade Center

Mr. William Just, CMP
Association for Convention
Operations Management

Ms. Deborah Dupar, CMP
Convention Services Northwest

Mr. Tom Corcoran
Convention Manager
National Restaurant Association

Mr. Lynn Thompson
Anaheim Convention Center

Professor Patti Shock
University of Nevada/Las Vegas

Mr. John Farquharson
Mr. Todd Wickner
Mr. Larry Taylor
ARA Services, Inc.

Mr. George A. Muro
Rowan Northwestern Decorators, Inc.

Ms. Pam Dronberger
Northwestern Exhibit Drayage

Mr. Tom Liegler, CFE
San Diego Convention Center

Dr. Terry Umbreit
Dr. Rom Markin
Dr. Carl Riegel
Washington State University

Mr. Jerry Burtenshaw
ABC Services, Inc.

Mr. David Peterson
Laventhol and Horwath

The Convention Liaison Council

Mr. Michael T. McQuade
Washington State Convention and
Trade Center

Ms. Lillian Sugahara
Greendale Associates

Ms. Jenny Mason
Ms. Diane Iverson
Washington State University

Mr. Chris Matson
Mr. Roy Deaver
Convention Consultants, Ltd.

Ms. Tina Berres Filipski
Editor
The Meeting Manager

Ms. Darlene Gudea
Tradeshow Week

Contents

Introduction to the Conventions, Expositions, and Meetings Industry

1

Introduction to the Conventions, Expositions, and Meetings Industry (CEMI)

The conventions, expositions, and meetings industry (CEMI) is a broadly based, multifaceted collection of endeavors and functions that together orchestrate an economic machine of multibillion-dollar proportions. The various people and organizations responsible for the activities attendant to this industry will be the focus of this book. An industry that is so decentralized as the CEMI does not lend itself to a singular or linear analysis. Each of these entities, however, has as a central part of its focus the concept and execution of a successful convention or meeting.

Webster's defines *convention* as: "An assembly, often periodical, of members or delegates, as of a political, social, professional or religious group" (*Webster's* 1974, 310). The word *meeting* is similarly defined (*Webster's* 1974, 883) as: "A coming together of persons or things (or) an assembly; gathering of people, especially to discuss or decide on matters." These definitions would work for classifying such events to the layperson but for purposes of this book need to be examined in a broader context in order that we might erect a framework to investigate the major segments of the CEMI industry.

To more accurately define a modern meeting or convention, we must also pay attention to the fact that such assemblies may often:

• Occur at specific places called facilities
• Involve food and beverage service
• Provide for specialized technical support such as audiovisual equipment
• Require transportation
• Require housing
• Involve exhibition of products
• Require convention or meeting delegate entertainment

In a way, conventions and meetings may be compared to a theatrical or entertainment production wherein many details and specialists in their execution have to coordinate for the production to be a success. For the rest of this chapter, we will examine CEMI productions by introducing the major actors in the CEMI.

WHO ARE THE ACTORS?

In a number of presentations in the last few years, Mr. Donald Walter, executive director of the National Association of Exposition Managers (NAEM), has likened the CEMI to a large wagon wheel, with the exposition or trade show manager at the hub and the various other specialists that service the production arranged around that professional (Exhibit 1.1). The adaptation of that structure displayed here leaves the hub blank, suggesting that at any given point during a specific production, one or more of the actors may assume a more central importance to the completion and success of the event. In this instance, delegates have also been arrayed on the circumference of the wheel, suggesting that in a greater or lesser way, each delegate's experience is influenced by each of the actors in the CEMI production.

ASSOCIATIONS

Associations are defined as some organized or structured group of people who have an interest, activity, or purpose in common. These may involve professional and technical interests, religious, fraternal, social, educational, or avocational (or hobbyist) activities that have as a central issue the purpose of enhancing or protecting that common interest for the membership of the association. The importance of associations to the CEMI is nested in the fact that virtually every association has regularly scheduled (and ad hoc) meetings and conventions designed to further their interests, exchange information, and promote membership activities.

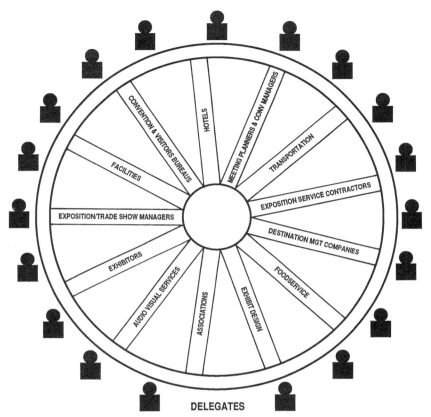

Exhibit 1.1   CEMI wheel. *Source:* Courtesy of Don Walter, National Association of Exposition Managers (NAEM) (1989).

The American Society of Association Executives (ASAE), which is an association of staff leaders of various volunteer association groups, reports over 6000 member-associations whose total individual memberships represent in excess of 55 million people nationwide (ASAE 1987). The fact that many Americans have multiple association memberships suggests that we are a nation of association joiners, and that when these groups gather to meet in convention facilities and hotels, they generate an economic impact that in turn generates significant activity among the other actors in the CEMI.

A capsule description of this importance can be visualized by thinking of a typical convention delegate who purchases airline tickets, hotel rooms, food and beverage, local transportation, entertainment activities, and other services relative to his or her attendance at the meeting. Delegates also patronize retail establishments in those cities and may make purchasing decisions for

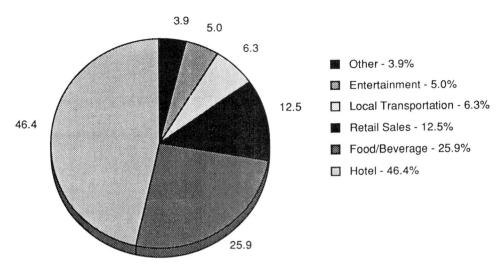

Exhibit 1.2 Breakdown of convention delegate spending in Seattle–King County. *Source:* Seattle–King County Convention and Visitors Bureau.

their companies or groups at trade shows attendant to their convention. They may include their spouses, families, or friends in pre- and postconvention activities in the vicinity of the host city.

In 1986, the Seattle–King County (Washington) Convention and Visitors Bureau predicted convention delegate spending distributed in the Seattle area as displayed in Exhibit 1.2. Each of the delegates visiting Seattle will stay an average of three to four days and spend US$160–$170 each day. Economic data such as these underscore the importance of the meetings and convention delegates to communities, facilities, and other components of the CEMI. It therefore should come as no surprise that communities encourage associations and similar groups to convene in their locale because such meetings are a major economic prize. Chapter 2 will deal with associations in greater depth and analyze their activities and the importance of their role in the CEMI.

TRADE SHOWS

When the association that represents restaurateurs, foodservice executives, and other hospitality industry professionals across the United States has its annual convention, educational meetings, and trade exposition in Chicago in May, the National Restaurant Association (NRA) attracts a vast number of manufacturers and vendors who make and sell products of special and particular interest to people in the foodservice industry. The resulting trade show is one of the biggest in the nation, utilizing nearly 600,000 square feet at

McCormick Place exhibition halls and attracting in excess of 100,000 delegates and attendees.

The 1800 exhibitors at the NRA trade show accomplish major portions of their marketing objectives by participation in this trade show, which in essence is a very carefully managed and orchestrated artificial marketplace for buyers and sellers to interact. The key to understanding the relationship between trade shows and conventions is the recognition that in gathering and convening such meetings, the memberships of those associations and other groups are congregating in a centralized location offering vendors who make their living selling to members of that profession or group a unique opportunity to interact with highly qualified potential customers. Trade shows then become a significant actor in the CEMI.

Tongren and Thompson (1981, 31) identify three types of events that fall under the general rubric of *trade show:*

1. "**Industrial Shows** are used by manufacturers to exhibit their products to other manufacturers, and to provide educational sessions describing new techniques in the industry and demonstrating new products."
2. "**Trade Shows,** in the strict sense, are where sellers of goods and services contact all types of buyers" (1981, 31). Most of these shows are for members of the *trade* as in the example of the National Restaurant Association. These shows may or may not be in conjunction with a convention or meeting.
3. "**Professional or Scientific Exhibitions** are usually adjuncts to the annual meetings of professional or specialized organizations" (1981, 31). A convention of the American College of Cardiac Surgeons, for example, would likely attract large numbers of exhibitors who have specialized products or equipment used by heart surgeons.

It should be noted that the trade show events defined above are not open to the public at large, but only to those who have a specific and demonstrable relationship to the event as a member of the industry, the trade association, or the professional society.

There are, however, large-scale exhibit presentations that are open to the public properly termed public *consumer shows.* At these events, exhibitors who market products relative to a central theme display their goods to a wide variety of people who have a common consumer interest in (for instance) boats, automobiles, homes, or gardening. These shows are usually held annually in large venues (stadiums, convention centers) and typically charge a modest admission fee. Their impact differs from the other types of shows discussed above in that they attract a local clientele, do not account for large numbers of hotel room nights and only minimally impact local retailers and foodservice.

The National Association of Exposition Managers (NAEM) is an association that represents the professional people who manage the various intricate details of a modern trade show or exposition. NAEM reports over 3000 members who are responsible annually for nearly 4000 shows and expositions (Walter 1989). This actor in the CEMI will be further analyzed in Chapter 3 where we will discuss the financial relationships between trade shows and other members of the CEMI; management issues; and the details of show management and execution.

FACILITIES

Because of the economic impact of conventions on host communities in the last 15–20 years, there has been a veritable explosion in the building of special-purpose facilities designed to make the planning and execution of conventions and trade shows convenient and attractive to their managers and attendees. This was not always the case.

Prior to 1970 there were very few buildings that could be classified as comprehensive convention centers. In most instances, they were large public assembly facilities that did double or triple duty as auditoriums, basketball arenas, or hockey rinks. Many were cavernous, dark, and noisy buildings in undesirable parts of town that were neither functional nor more than unidimensional in terms of use. According to Walter of NAEM (Hosansky et al. 1986, 56), all that changed with the opening in the late 1960s of Detroit's Cobo Hall.

Cobo was designed to offer not only a large, divisible exhibit space, but also incorporated a second story for meeting rooms and a large corridor on the exhibit level that could be used for receptions, registration, or additional exhibit space.

The breadth of demand from meeting planners, trade show managers, exhibitors, and others is currently such that modern convention centers have to be responsive to specialized needs. Communities or municipalities embarking on siting, design, construction, and management of such buildings are finding they have to pay attention to what these market segments are demanding, or they risk expending tax dollars for a facility that will be resisted or underutilized by its intended market. Robert Black (1986, 11) cites a "conservative construction cost of US$125 a square foot" in discussing the economic dimensions of the capital cost of such buildings and notes that halls planned or under construction in 1986 represented a US$5 billion capital investment exclusive of land acquisition.

Taxpayers and their representatives need to be convinced that such capital outlays will repay their investment and generate the sort of economic activity the feasibility studies and promoters promise. It is no longer the case that such facilities need be *loss leaders;* they are under increasing pressure to be cost-effective at least to the point of breaking even (Hosansky 1986, 57). Chapter 4 will trace the development of convention facilities, define and identify other types of facilities, and discuss their interactive relationships with the actors in the CEMI. Center management and selected issues will also be addressed.

MEETING PLANNERS AND CONVENTION MANAGERS

Conventions and meetings don't just happen. The myriad of details need to be carefully inventoried, assessed, and executed by an ever-increasingly professional group of people now referred to as meeting planners or convention or event managers. According to Hosansky (1986, 65), "Of all aspects of the (CEMI), the profession of meeting planning is, in a sense, the most bewildering." What he means by this is that as recently as 20 years ago, the term *meeting planner* was not in common usage, and in the ensuing time, a true profession has grown up that has many elements, operates in many venues, and has spurred technological advances in computer equipment, audiovisual equipment, and professional meeting management thought and inquiry. Chapter 5 will introduce and describe the kinds and types of meeting planners and analyze the dimensions of their activities relative to their primary function, and link their activities to other components of the CEMI.

HOTELS

No convention hosting out-of-town delegates would be successful without comfortable, safe, and modern lodging arrangements. Many hotels recognize the importance of the CEMI to their sales mix in such a way that on any given day a significant portion of their rooms may be rented to people and groups who are gathered at meetings in conventions in the area. Hotels also are major providers of meeting facilities, either in conjunction or in competition with municipal convention centers. Hotels provide significant amounts of food and beverage and entertainment services to convention delgates. Chapter 6 will outline the role of hotels to the CEMI and discuss in some depth the ways in which hotels and their organizations have changed to recognize the importance of the CEMI to their marketing and sales mix.

CONVENTION AND VISITORS BUREAUS

The primary purpose of a municipality's convention and visitors bureau (CVB) to the CEMI is to provide the hotels and convention facilities of that community with long-term marketing leads and contacts regarding potential convention and meetings business. To this end, CVBs are organized to employ sales staffs who are aware of the national conventions market, do research regarding that market, and generally serve as the initial contact regarding the capabilities of the host community to execute conventions and meetings.

CVBs are operated and funded under a wide variety of formulas, but most have some association with a taxing authority in addition to private sector funds generated through memberships.

Contrary to past practices, when many bureaus were staffed through political patronage with no clear mandate, CVBs have learned that the most successful such entities are staffed by professional marketing and hospitality people who know the market and command the effective marketing and sales strategies to "sell" their destination as a convention host community. This change was mandated when "communities began to recognize the economic benefits that tourism—as well as meeting and conventions—could bring" (Hosansky 1986, 58).

CVBs may also offer a variety of services and functions that enhance the capabilities of groups and associations planning and executing details of their meetings. Chapter 7 will outline the organizational structures of typical CVBs and discuss the roles, responsibilities, and activities of their organizational components. We will also pay attention to the interactive role of CVBs with convention centers, hotels, and other public assembly facilities for which they may have marketing responsibility.

EXHIBITORS AND EXHIBIT DESIGN

Exhibitors are those participants in trade shows who represent companies with goods, products, and services to sell to convention, meeting, and trade show attendees. They represent those companies that have chosen trade shows and expositions as a one of the major focuses of their marketing efforts. These are companies that have recognized the benefits of being able to market in a controlled environment to highly qualified potential buyers. They work very closely with exhibit design personnel to conceive, design, and maybe even construct the exhibit chosen to demonstrate and display the exhibitor's or manufacturer's product. Exhibitors are represented by their own association, the International Exhibitors Association (IEA), and people who conceive and design exhibits are also represented by the Exhibit Designers and Producers Association (EDPA). Chapter 8 will trace the interaction between exhibitors and exhibit designers, trade shows, and other elements of the CEMI.

TRANSPORTATION

At first glance one would assume that analyzing the role of a transportation company relative to the CEMI would be fairly simple. It is easy to recognize that airlines and car rental companies play a major role in assisting people in getting to and from conventions and meetings.

Since the final deregulation of domestic airlines in the early 1980s, the relationship between air carriers and the CEMI has changed substantially. Airline mergers, *hub-spoke* air terminals, lively competition, route expansion, frequent flyer programs, and a need for increasingly sophisticated and aggressive marketing efforts have combined to forge a new relationship between carriers and the CEMI, especially meeting planners.

Airlines now have account executives who specialize in the meetings and convention market. In a deregulated atmosphere, fare prices have been substantially reduced, and meeting planners and airlines can negotiate attractive rates for an airline to be the *designated* or official carrier for a given convention. Airlines may also provide complimentary fares for planners and association executives on site inspection and familiarization trips. Planners can also negotiate complimentary fares based on a designated number of paid convention fares. A typical arrangement may be one complimentary fare for every 40 to 50 convention fares. Planners may then use the complimentary tickets for speakers, VIPs, or association executives.

Other modes of transportation can also play major roles relative to the event. During the convention itself there is almost always a major requirement for ground transportation for large groups of convention attendees. The meeting planners and trade show managers may be responsible for arranging bus transportation between lodging and convention facilities. Similarly, delegates will require transportation from convention or lodging facilities to entertainment functions in other parts of the convention region.

A little-known element of the transportation industry also plays a major role in the execution of a convention or meeting event that has associated with it a trade show or exhibition. The exhibitors have to arrange for transportation of their exhibits from trade show to trade show and region to region. Several transportation companies have dedicated divisions or parts of divisions that exclusively transport crated and packaged exhibits from one trade show to the next. Chapter 9 will examine in greater depth the roles of the various transportation modes in executing a convention event.

EXPOSITION SERVICE CONTRACTORS

Once called *general contractors,* the people and firms who provide special event services are now becoming more commonly known as *exposition ser-*

vice contractors. As such, these professionals provide services for the trade show, exhibitors, and meeting planners that help the event take place. Among these services may be drayage, booth and exhibit setup and takedown, crating, erection of pipe and drape, and other services under the general rubric of *decorating.* These may also include rental of furniture, logistics assistance, rental of floor coverings, booth cleaning, and labor planning and supervision.

This segment of the CEMI, through their professional association, the Exposition Service Contractors Association (ESCA), represent both national and local firms that provide these sorts of services. They will be discussed in Chapter 10.

DESTINATION MANAGEMENT COMPANIES

The suppliers of on-site meeting services, now known as *destination management companies (DMCs),* have grown out of the companies that in the past arranged for buses and local transportation. They contract with meeting planners or associations to arrange for locally oriented events and services that may include providing interface with transportation companies, planning and executing special parties, and assisting meeting planners and convention managers in making full use of the potential services of the host community.

In recent times, it has become less possible to draw clear distinctions between some of the services the CEMI actors may provide. For instance, DMCs may arrange for transportation or the meeting and convention planners may arrange for transportation themselves. Some DMCs may provide decorating services that traditionally have been the province of exposition service contractors. Audiovisual service may be provided by a company that is dedicated specifically to those sorts of activities, or it may be a function of a DMC or a specialty service contractor. Increasingly, convention facilities may be absorbing some of these activities and renting them to meeting planners and convention managers as separate profit-making activities on behalf of the facility. Chapter 11, devoted to DMCs, will put these activities in perspective and link them to the CEMI segment with which they are most often associated.

FOODSERVICE

In the not-too-distant past, foodservice at convention sites often meant beer, popcorn, and hot dog-type concession food in the exhibit area and the infamous "rubber chicken" banquet food in the ballroom for convention delegates. Convention foodservices have become so critically important, however, that foodservice operators and convention facilities have had to totally and completely rethink the management of this aspect of the CEMI. As reported by *Meetings and Conventions Magazine* in their 1987 study, "The Meetings Market '87," quality of foodservice was considered the most important factor by 80% of the corporate planners responding to the 1987 survey of all factors considered important in the selection of a facility or a hotel. Given this finding, foodservice companies, convention facilities, and hotel banquet and catering departments have had to respond with new levels of professionalism, creativity, food quality, and service. Because so many meeting and convention planning professionals network and interact within their professional associations, facilities and hotels that gain a reputation for mediocre or poor food and service quickly have those reputations spread throughout the meeting planners' grapevine.

Chapter 12 will track how the foodservice operators of various facilities have responded to these challenges and will provide some examples of how a positive reputation for food and beverage service can enhance a facility's reputation, sales, and marketing efforts. We will also examine how foodservice contractors' relationships with convention facilities are structured.

CONCLUSION

The foregoing introduction of the major actors of the CEMI strongly suggests that the definitions offered by *Webster's* are too simplistic for an industry that embodies the mix of capital, people, and ideas that the CEMI does. As we go about seeking an umbrella definition, we will accomplish an analysis and in-depth examination of the various components and elements of the CEMI.

REFERENCES

American Society of Association Executives (ASAE). 1987. *Membership Literature*. Washington, D.C.: ASAE.

Black, Robert. 1986. The Trade Show Industry: Mangement and Marketing Career Opportunities. Paper read at lecture at Cornell University Department of Communications. Reprint permission by Trade Show Bureau, E. Orleans, Massachusetts.

Hosansky, Mel, et al. 1986. The Evolution of an Industry. *Meetings and Conventions Magazine* June:48–67.

Seattle–King County Convention and Visitors Bureau. 1986. Internal document.

Tongren, Hale N., and James P. Thompson. 1981. The Trade Show in Marketing Education. *Journal of Marketing Education* Fall 3(2):28–35.

Walter, Don. 1989. Private communication. Seattle.

Webster's New World Dictionary, Second College Edition. 1974. Cleveland and New York: World.

2

Associations

CHAPTER OBJECTIVES

1. To define what associations are
2. To identify the types of associations
3. To describe the ways in which associations are organized
4. To identify the kinds and types of meetings that associations hold
5. To introduce basic association data and meeting statistics
6. To explain the importance of associations to the conventions and meetings industry

INTRODUCTION

A common thread that runs through the rules, regulations, bylaws, and constitutions of all types of associations is a requirement for various numbers and types of meetings on an annual or other periodic basis. The importance, therefore, of associations as an area of study is exemplified by the number and kinds of meetings these groups hold and the requirements these meeting activities generate throughout the CEMI and hospitality industries.

This chapter will analyze the modern voluntary association. Information will be presented on the background of voluntary associations, definitions and concepts, what associations do, and how the voluntary and staff organizations act and interact, and the association's relation and importance to the conventions and meetings industry will be discussed in depth.

DEFINITIONS

Intuitively, most people will have a basic understanding of what an association is, because most of us belong to some sort of an association in its broadest sense. These association memberships we enjoy may range from trade and professional groups to social, fraternal, religious, and service associations to recreational, hobby, or cultural/ethnic organizations. What all of these groups have in common is that they, in the words of Webster, are "an organization of persons with a common interest." Understanding how individual groups are structured to provide and promote that common interest is what the diversity, breadth, and depth of the association market is all about.

An association, therefore, may be considered an organized body that exhibits some variety of volunteer leadership structure, which may employ a staff, and that serves a group of people who have some interest, activity, or purpose that they share in common. The association is generally organized to promote and enhance that common interest, activity, or purpose.

ASSOCIATION ANTECEDENTS: A BRIEF HISTORY OF VOLUNTARY ORGANIZATIONS

No discussion of the background of what we now refer to as associations would be complete without mentioning that there is a unifying theme that runs through their history. That theme is the voluntary nature of these activities. In other words, people or groups who have identified common interests have come together voluntarily and given of their own free time to promote these common interests. A relatively recent phenomenon is the addition of a paid staff to execute the wishes and policies of the voluntary structure of the organization.

According to Ernstthal and Jefferson (1988, xxvi), modern organizations we know as associations probably can trace their roots to groups formed around common concerns and interests regarding aspects of their work. These have evolved into what we now know as trade associations. References to these sorts of activities have been traced to ancient Egyptians, Chinese, Roman, and biblical societies.

Similar developments can be traced through medieval guilds and the industrial revolution to relatively modern times with the establishment of "The Chamber of Commerce of the State of New York, formed by twenty merchants in 1768. The New York Stock Exchange, established in 1792, is the second oldest existing association" (Ernstthal and Jefferson 1988, xi).

From the turn of the century through the 1920's, trade associations underwent antitrust and other government scrutiny and then began to evolve "into the modern, effective, well-equipped and well-staffed organizations that exist today." (Ernstthal and Jefferson 1988, xiii)

A parallel development with trade associations has been the rise of professional societies. These represent groups of individuals practicing the same professions, such as physicians, lawyers, and scientists (ASAE 1979). Whereas trade associations are represented by individual company members of entire industries, professional societies and associations are groups of individual members who share in common similar education, training, and background. A society of chemists, for instance, may have members from such industries as petroleum, rubber, nuclear power, medicine, and education, but a petroleum engineers' association would all be associated with the oil industry.

Professional societies serve their memberships by acting as forums for debate and dissemination of information and ideas. They also serve to develop and maintain professional standards and ethics. Through professional journals and other media, members of professional societies share their ideas with peers, industry, and society in general.

Other types of individual membership groups, societies, or associations represent the common personal interest or objectives of their memberships. Examples include the American Philatelic Society, whose membership includes people who share a common interest in stamps, and the American Association of Retired Persons. Other societies are established to promote and represent the interest of religious, cultural, charitable, public service, or fraternal groups (Ernstthal and Jefferson 1988, xiv–xv).

At this point in the historical evolution of these types of organizations we can see that the United States is a nation of associations and association joiners. Nowhere is this better illustrated than in Exhibit 2.1.

Most readers would be hard-pressed not to find some specific personal affiliation from among this inventory, and one thing that all or most of the 20,884 have in common is annual meetings and conventions. One measure of the economic value of these meetings and conventions, according to a recent survey (Meetings and Conventions Magazine [M&C] 1988, 51), exceeds US$21 billion based on responses of subscribers to the *Meetings and Conventions Magazine* "Bi-Annual Survey of Corporate and Association Meeting Planners."

At this stage, the future of volunteer associations appears to be consistent with their history. As long as people find common interests to enhance and promote, they will associate in one form or another to promote those interests. As interests, society, and commercial activities grow and change, so will associations. One theme will be consistent in those changes, and that is the requirement for meetings and conventions.

Type	Number
Trade, Business, Commercial	3,927
Agriculture, Commodity Exchange	912
Government, Public Administration, Military, Legal	711
Scientific, Engineering, Technical	1,377
Educational	1,217
Cultural	1,759
Social Welfare	1,641
Health and Medical	2,045
Public Affairs	2,217
Fraternal, Foreign Interest, Nationality, Ethnic	539
Religious	1,066
Veteran, Hereditary, Patriotic	340
Hobby and Avocational	1,366
Athletic and Sports	798
Greek and Non-Greek Letter Societies, Associations and Federations	335
Labor Unions, Associations and Federations	234
Chambers of Commerce, Trade and Tourism	159
Fan Clubs	241
TOTAL	**20,884**

Exhibit 2.1 National associations in the United States (1988). *Source: Encyclopedia of Associations* 1988. Detroit, Michigan. Quoted in Ernstthal (1988, xv).

THE WORK OF ASSOCIATIONS

Most trade, professional, or other voluntary individual membership associations are organized as nonprofit operations and enjoy tax-exempt status from the Internal Revenue Service (IRS). While there are a number of sections of the Internal Revenue Code that apply to not-for-profit organizations, the two main ones under which most associations claim tax-exempt status are Section 501(C)(6), which applies to not-for-profit "business leagues," and Section 501(C)(3), which generally applies to scientific or educational associations.

According to Jacobs (1988, 71–72), to qualify as a "business league" under the Internal Revenue Code administered by the Internal Revenue Service a number of criteria must be met. A review of these criteria is set forth in Exhibit

2.2, because in many ways they dictate what an association may or may not do on behalf of its membership and still maintain its tax-exempt status.

Jacobs goes on to point out (1988, 72) that there are a number of "benefits for an association that receives a tax exemption as a business league." Among these are the ability to receive revenues and income from other association activities without paying taxes on that income. Additionally, being exempt from taxes on a federal level will probably also help the association meet local or state requirements for tax exemption.

Those groups that enjoy tax-exempt status under Internal Revenue Code 501(C)(3) must respond to similar criteria that "business leagues" do and are similarly prohibited from having any net earnings benefitting any private individual among the association's membership. These groups, however, have three other criteria to which they must adhere:

- The association must be organized and operated exclusively for one or more exempt public, rather than private, purposes. (According to Jacobs 1988, 72, "the group can, for example, be scientific, educational, religious and charitable at the same time.")
- No substantial part of the activities of the association may constitute to carry on propaganda or otherwise attempt to influence legislation.
- The group must not participate in or intervene in any political campaign on behalf of any candidate for public office.

- An association seeking tax-exempt status as a business league must not be organized for profit;

- No part of the association's net earnings can inure to the benefit of any private shareholder or individual;

- The organization must be an association of persons having a common business interest;

- The association's purpose must be to promote that common business interest of its members;

- The association's activities must be directed to the improvement of conditions in one or more lines of business;

- The association must not be engaged regularly in a business of a kind ordinarily carried on for profit;

- The association's activities must not be confined to the performance of particular services or individual members;

- The association must be a "business league" and in the same general class as a chamber of commerce or board of trade.

Exhibit 2.2 Internal Revenue Code—Section 501(C)(6) criteria.

Therefore, regarding their membership, 501(C)(3) organizations have to have a more inward looking, insular set of activities, and in the words of Jacobs "must limit lobbying activities and avoid political activities" (1988, 72). If they adhere to these criteria, they will come to enjoy the highest level or "most favored" tax-exempt status similar to that of churches, schools, and other charities. A direct benefit of this status is that in addition to the exemption of income from association activities, donations to these organizations by others qualify as tax deductible in the same way that charitable contributions are tax deductible from individual and corporate income taxes.

So how do the provisions of the Internal Revenue Code as administered by the IRS affect the activities of an association? Or, put another way, how do our associations organize to provide services to their members in a way that is consistent with the Internal Revenue Code and simultaneously fulfill their obligation as set forth in the bylaws or articles of incorporation of the association itself?

To accomplish this, associations generally do a number, or all, of the following general categories of activities on behalf of their memberships:

1. To influence legislation
2. To offer professional education to members
3. To provide opportunities for peer interaction and networking
4. To extend career and professional development
5. To maintain social relationships
6. To disseminate general information
7. To disseminate political information
8. To make available research and statistical data
9. To provide better purchasing power through group discounts
10. To distribute specialized publications
11. To perform public relations activities
12. To handle legal affairs
13. To insure industry standardization
14. To offer group travel opportunities
15. To perform public service activities
16. To improve employer/employee relations

Exhibit 2.3   Purposes of associations. *Source:* Hoyle, Dorf, and Jones (1989, 15). Used with permission.

- Government affairs or relations
- Membership communications and publicity
- Educational programs
- Certification of products or services
- Professionalism activities
- Social awareness/public relations activities

These general categories were developed from surveys done by the American Society of Association Executives and the Chamber of Commerce of the United States covering a respondent group that "approximates the characteristics of all associations" (ASAE 1975, 40–45).

A more comprehensive and detailed list of association purposes is proposed by Hoyle, Dorf, and Jones (1989, 15). These more finely detailed activities are presented in Exhibit 2.3, and the authors suggest that it is within these details that hospitality industry executives should find ample reason to place high value on association activities as generators of potential business for "hotels, conference centers, transportation companies and many other industry enterprises."

Such a comprehensive list serves well the hotel marketer, but for the most part these details are subsumed in the ASAE list of categories.

Government Relations

The vast majority of voluntary associations that are not specifically prohibited from participating in government affairs are very likely do so to a greater or lesser extent. These activities may range from the grass roots level, which encourages memberships to write to various legislative bodies that are considering legislation, rules, and regulations that impact their memberships, to large professionally staffed government affairs organizational units that include research personnel, political officers, professional lobbyists, legislative liaisons, and political action and political education committees (PACs and PECs).

The larger, more sophisticated government affairs segments of association organizations may also include staff people who do legal issue analysis and participate in writing model legislation for consideration by Congress or state legislatures. Other staffers may perform the functions of identifying issues that may be important to association membership and formulating strategy to deal with those issues.

Government relations or government affairs staff also carefully monitor the regulatory environment of the executive branches of government for rules and regulations that may impact the way in which the association's membership can operate.

Membership Communications and Publicity

Because associations are formed to give their memberships the strength of one voice speaking for many, communications is a vital function in most associations. Typically, an association will publish a newsletter and a directory of the membership. The newsletter will be published periodically; the membership directory will usually be published annually. Large associations may also publish magazines or professional journals that carry articles of general interest to the membership. They may also issue technical bulletins, textbooks, legislative reports, regulatory warnings, and legal updates.

Communication among the membership also occurs at conventions and regional or subject-specific meetings via the presentation of professional papers. This, in turn, has a direct bearing on the CEMI, as these conventions and meetings require facilities and support services. The greater the need for any association to meet, the greater its impact on the CEMI. As more and more associations at all levels (national to local) increase their meeting requirements, the more the CEMI industry is challenged to compete within itself for this lucrative business or simply to meet the challenge by being able to supply the necessary space and facilities.

In this age of nearly instantaneous communication via facsimile transmission (FAX), electronic (computer network) mail, and overnight package and letter service, associations' communications with their memberships have become simultaneously easier and more complex. Because of the development of these technologies, memberships may be easily contacted through a variety of means. At the same time, careful management is required to assure that the right message reaches the right audience and through the most appropriate medium. General-interest, low-priority, membership-wide information is probably best suited for the regular newsletter, but vitally important technical data or political news may mandate the impact and expense of FAX.

Associations, like all businesses, have to manage this potentially expensive process to maximize membership service and control a potentially critical cost center. In the words of Maynard H. Benjamin (1988, 105): "Information has always been important to associations, and computer support to this process is sure to become even more important. Members are demanding a greater array of services from their associations, unfortunately without a corresponding increase in staff size." In predicting that associations will offer more of their services to members through computer networks, Benjamin also foresees new forms of training technologies that will be available to members and staffs. Predictions such as this and our recent experience in the "information explosion" strongly suggest that this is an area of association activities that must be carefully managed in the future.

Education

One way in which associations can fulfill the criterion of the Internal Revenue Code that directs them to "improve conditions in one or more lines of business" is to offer to its membership a variety of educational programs and opportunities.

A typical association will have a staff function that conceives, researches, designs, and sponsors seminars, clinics, workshops, or institutes for its membership (ASAE 1975, 41). Through participation in these educational programs, association members may qualify for certificates or diplomas that attest to their participation. It is through programs such as these that associations contribute to the improvement of the conditions for their members and their membership in general.

Such activities are on a significant increase in many associations across the country. Again, this directly relates to the CEMI as the need for education-related meeting space and services increases. Referring ahead to Exhibit 2.11, this is especially important for downtown hotels and suburban hotels.

To support educational services, many associations establish, maintain, and update libraries, databanks, information retrieval services, and other databases of information about areas of interest to the association's membership. Typically, members access these library and informational services in many of the ways discussed in the previous section. The association staff will respond to specific requests or questions by either doing the appropriate research for members or directing members to where they may find the answers to their questions.

Certification of Products or Services

According to ASAE (1975, 42), "consumer demand for sound decision criteria has prompted the development of quality standards, certifications or seals of approval" from professional and trade associations that represent the various industries and service providers. Many associations have responded to this consumer demand by making provision for their memberships to participate in the development of product standards that represent broadly based industry goals. Product standards also satisfy consumer demand for points of comparison among competing products.

According to Jacobs (1988, 68) the development of product standards and certification are among the activities of associations that assist in avoiding government regulation. Self-regulation also includes:

- Professional certification and educational accreditation to assure qualifications and competence in individuals and institutions (see Education and Professionalism Activities)

- Business and professional codes to assure integrity and accountability in industries and professions (see Professionalism Activities)

Accreditation activities can also mean significant use of meetings to provide the accredited courses. In associations for professionals such as accountants or attorneys, where large numbers of annual credits are required, the number of accreditation meetings can be substantial. This again has obvious implications for the CEMI. In this instance, university-based conference facilities can be significant competitors for a portion of the accreditation meeting business.

Many associations spend substantial amounts of time and effort on standardization programs for products. These standardization programs may:

> . . . include setting the physical standards of weight, strength and size. Or standards may specify quantities of ingredients in food products or proprietary drugs. Standards may be written in terms of performance. For example, a performance standard for insulating material may specify the amount of heat transmission permissible to meet the standard. (ASAE, 43)

Commonly recognized industry-wide standards of household appliances, light bulbs, and electrical wire are things that are familiar to most consumers, and in many ways, these standard aspects of products are the result of activities of an industry association. The most common recent example of the failure of industry-wide standards was the parallel development of both VHS and Beta videocassette formats.

The Federal Trade Commission generally approves certification programs if they meet the following criteria:

- Access to the program is in no way restricted or discriminatory.
- Accreditation is not favored or determined by membership in the sponsoring association and services rendered to members are equally available to nonmembers.
- All who qualify receive a uniform certification mark.
- The responsibility of rewarding certification is on a representative, nondiscriminatory committee.

It is through the establishment of strict high quality certification standards that associations avoid unwanted legislative and regulatory scrutiny. Indeed, Jacobs (1988, 68) states that self-regulation by trade and professional associations will be ". . . foremost among the antidotes for regulation by big government in the decades ahead."

Professionalism Activities

Most trade and professional associations have as one of their central tenets the quest for increased professionalism among their individual memberships, companies, and industries. Activities previously mentioned relative to certification of products and services are elements of professionalism activities. Similarly, the results of educational programs certifying members also contributes to increased professionalism among membership ranks.

If an association develops, proposes, and adopts ethics, business, and professional codes for its members, it is also encouraging higher standards of professionalism. By providing self-developed standards by which professionals regulate themselves, associations can further insulate themselves and their members from regulatory security and criticism. A member's knowledge about and ability to adhere to these codes may also play a role in individual certification.

Another important aspect of professionalism is labor relations and human resources management. It is in the best interest of most members of trade associations to have available to them the highest-quality people as employees at all levels in their associated industry. It is only through promoting professionalism activities in these arenas that entire industries may benefit from the activities, expertise, and work of their trade associations.

Social Awareness/Public Relations

It has become increasingly important in the modern era for businesses and professions to be seen as sensitive public-spirited corporate citizens who, in addition to making profits from their activities and providing jobs, also exhibit a social awareness that contributes to the society that makes possible the environment in which to succeed in business endeavors. Associations play out their roles in the social arena in a number of different ways, but the key ones seem to be from among the following:

- Aid in programs for the disadvantaged
- Consumer and consumerism issues
- Ecology and the environment
- Programs for handicapped or developmentally disabled individuals
- Programs for minorities
- Establishment of educational, social, or charitable foundations

Not-for-profit associations often have revenue in excess of expenses from operations that cannot be considered profits, nor distributed in ways that such monies are normally distributed in corporations. They may, on vote of membership through its board of directors, transfer some or all of these monies to a separate foundation which is set up under Internal Revenue Code 501(C)(3) regulations. The foundation then becomes an organization to which other individuals, corporations, or entities may donate money and receive a tax deduction.

These foundations support the social and public relations missions and goals of the associations with which they are affiliated. Foundations distribute funds to support programs in education, research, and training (Whittemore 1984, 192).

It is the work of foundations such as these that helps the association promote socially oriented goals and concomitantly garner for the association positive public relations.

ASSOCIATION ORGANIZATION

If the foregoing discussion of what associations do delineates the activities of voluntary organizations, the next question to answer is how do they go about doing this? The best way in which to answer that question is to look at the organizational structure of associations.

Probably the most fundamental thing to understand about the organization of associations is the concept that the association *is* its membership. The organizational structure of the association will reflect that membership in its richness and diversity of purposes, goals, and the constituencies that the structure represents. Because the strength of the association is in its membership, it is through the leadership of that membership that the association's organization attains its focus. Typically, leadership identity is accomplished by the election of directors. These directors will represent various regions, constituencies, and interests of the association from its entire national or international membership.

According to Imming (1988, 10–12), there are a number of qualifications for an ideal director or board member. Among the most critical are:

- The director must be interested in more than the honor of the position. Serving as a board member represents a serious commitment of time and effort, and should not be viewed as merely a reward.
- The member must be able to devote to the job the kind of time that is required. In many instances this means using his or her own money for travel and living expenses to support board meetings and conventions, and working on behalf of the association for no tangible reward.
- The prospective director should have well-developed communication skills. He or she has to work and communicate effectively with other directors, association staff members, and constituencies.

• The board member must be able to put aside personal interests, regional biases, and other parochial issues in order that the health of the association as a whole is best served.

It is through the voluntary commitments of people who exhibit these and other qualities that associations successfully set about tasks on behalf of their memberships.

Board members or directors are subsequently assigned, or volunteer, for committee activities that represent their interests, or where they can use

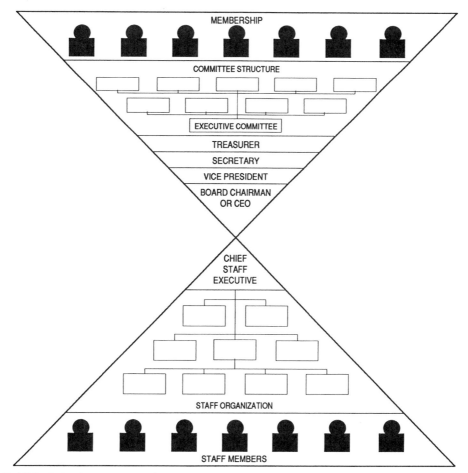

Exhibit 2.4 Association voluntary and staff organization. Adapted by permission of the publisher, from *Fundamentals of Association Management: Organization.* (Washington, D.C.: American Society of Association Executives, 1984), p. 299.

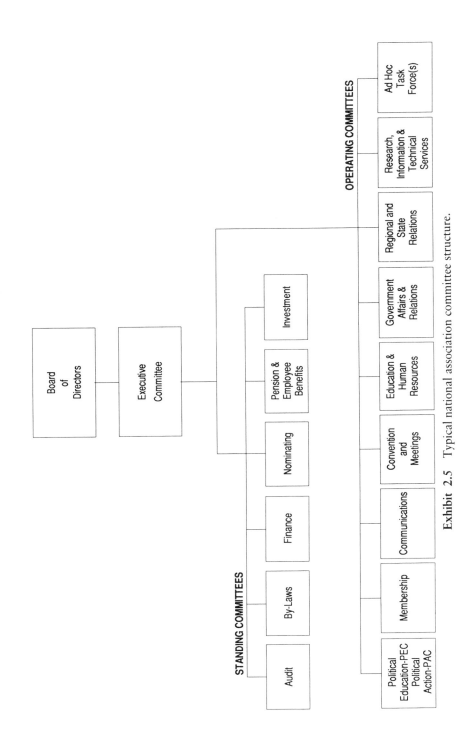

Exhibit 2.5 Typical national association committee structure.

specialized skills or knowledge they may possess. While we are all familiar with the typical pyramid-shaped, hierarchical organizational structure of all modern organizations, perhaps a better way to view the structure relationships in a modern association is to look at the entire organization as two triangles balanced at their peaks, as shown in Exhibit 2.4.

In actual practice, the staff organizational structure will mirror that of the association voluntary committee structure. The important relationship to observe in this particular context of Exhibit 2.4 is the relationship between the chief executive officer (CEO) of the voluntary structure and the chief staff executive (CSE) of the paid staff. It is this relationship that is the key to the translating policy developed by the board into actions and activities by the staff on behalf of the association membership as a whole. It is only through the efficiency of this interactive relationship that the association can achieve its policy goals.

Those policy goals and tasks on behalf of the association membership are primarily developed through discussion, analysis, and implementation of activities in the association voluntary committee structure. Exhibit 2.5 outlines a typical committee structure for a national association that serves a wide variety of members in a diverse industry. While committee structures such as this are typical, this is not representative of any one association. It should be noted, however, that most of the functions that are outlined here and discussed below will have their place in nearly every association; it may be, though, that they do not have a separate committee or staff function assigned. Many associations may combine a number of these activities. They are shown here for illustration and clarification purposes.

Standing Committees

Most association bylaws will provide for a committee to oversee the financial health of the association. One of these functions is performed by the **audit committee**. Specifically, this committee's activity amounts to hiring outside auditing firms to oversee financial records and reports of the association. The committee will analyze the report of the accounting firm and, based on that, make recommendations to the board.

The **bylaws committee** is an important committee for members because it is through these rules and regulations that the association governs itself. Among the policy points debated and recommended by the bylaws committee are:

• Qualifications for membership and forms of membership
• Dues structure
• General and special meeting dates

- Convention and assembly rooms
- Committee descriptions
- Accounting and fiscal details
- List of offices, terms, powers, duties, and definition of the role of the chief staff executive (CSE)

The **finance committee** will typically concern itself with the fiscal period of the association, budgets, trusts, and surety bonds that may be required by the association membership. This committee reports to the board and membership on the financial health of the association.

The **nominating committee** has as its central function the task of identifying and nominating candidates to the board whenever vacancies occur according to the terms of office as outlined in the bylaws. Another function of the nominating committee is to nominate board member directors to be considered as elected officers of the association. The nominating committee will design ballots and conduct elections with the help of association staff members and in accordance with association bylaws.

The increase in the number of associations nationally means an increase in the demand for qualified, experienced, and effective staff members. Because association management is a well-founded career, it is important for the most effective associations to hire and retain top-quality employees. It is increasingly important for associations to establish pension and employee benefit plans that will assist the association's CSE in hiring and retaining top-quality people. It is the function of the **pension and employee benefits committee** to see that these plans are adopted, well funded, and well managed.

Any association that has revenues in excess of expenses will probably make a provision for investment of those monies to fund a number of association activities, foundation work, and provision for reserve funds to cover shortfalls during economic downturns. The **investment committee** will interview and approve fund management, analyze fund performance, set strategy for future performance, and direct changes in investment guidelines. This is a critical committee for directors, for it is through careful, successful investments that the association is able to serve its membership in achieving all of its goals.

Operating Committees

Any large national association that has significant interest in legislation and regulatory activity as it relates to their constituent businesses will have, as a committee function, political action and political education committees. **Political action committees (PACs)** raise private monies from among the membership that are used to contribute to and support the candidacies of prospective members of Congress and legislatures who support the points of view consistent with association activities. PACs are limited by federal and state regulations in the amounts and kinds of contributions they can make, but if an association is politically active, it is important that it have a well-developed policy strategy formulated by a committee of directors who have the knowledge and expertise to guide staff activities in this area.

Political education committees (PECs) also involve the raising of private monies from among association and industry membership, but these monies are limited to activities that are not directly related to political candidacies and campaigns. Typically, PECs will expend donated monies to pay honoraria (lecture fees) to members of Congress and legislators to learn from those politicians about legislation and activities that may affect either positively or negatively the abilities of the association membership to do business. In many instances, these funds are not only expended upon honoraria for people who share the association's view, but very often upon members of Congress or legislators on the opposing side in order that the association membership can learn about challenges to their activities; hence, the name *political education*.

Because the strength of any association lies in its membership, the **membership committee** of the board is one that provides crucial and strategic policy formulation for the long-term health of the association. The board committee on membership will typically set membership policies, direct staff in membership activities and drives, work on dues structures, and work closely with state and/or regional units of the association in developing and maintaining healthy memberships at all levels. It is through a broadly based and actively involved membership that an association and the industries or professions it represents survives in the long term.

In large associations, the strength of the membership and the association's relations with its membership is in many ways directly related to the ability of the association to communicate internally and externally. It is through the **communications committee** of the board of directors that policy and procedures for this communications process are designed and implemented by staff. The communications committee will debate and suggest, for approval by the board, the number and types of communications media the association should use to portray its message to its various constituencies. These may be regular newsletters, special technical bulletins, journals and/or magazines, and multimedia shows, including audio and video cassettes. Maybe most importantly in some instances, external press and media relations are also guided by these board members. It is imperative not only for the association to communicate with its membership constituency, but for the association to tell its story to the public at large.

In an association that derives a significant part of its annual revenue from trade shows and exhibits during the annual convention, the board **committee on conventions and meetings** is a vitally important activity. It is the policy direction formulated by this committee of voluntary members that guides the staff in the successful execution of an annual convention, while simultaneously contributing to the financial health of the association. This committee will set dates, participate in the choice of sites, designate headquarter hotels, and guide the staff in negotiations with facilities, show managers, exhibitors, and service contractors. Knowledge and experience in the conventions and meetings industry is important for effective participation on this committee.

The **education and human resources committee** has as its prime responsibility the formulation of educational and certification programs for membership. These volunteers also direct policy research and formulation designed to help association membership with recruiting, training, and retaining a highly qualified employee and membership pool.

The **government affairs and relations committee** will typically be a committee of the whole with all members of the board participating in the committee activities. Especially in a large national and politically active association, government affairs and relations take on a critical, central importance in the committee structure. This committee debates and approves policy and legislative program activity; it also directs the activities of other committees that might contribute to the health of the government affairs and relations program of the association. This committee works closely with professional staff members who are most familiar with and cognizant of the workings of government. With staff input, the government affairs committee decides the structure of the association's annual legislative agenda.

The **regional and/or states relations committee** works closely with regional and individual state-affiliated associations in the same industry or affiliated industries. Large associations will almost always have a parallel organization in each state and may also be divided into regions of the country. The American Bar Association (ABA), for instance, has parallel organizations in every state of the union, and it is important for the national organization to have close and harmonious relations with the organizations that exist to serve their membership at the state and regional levels. This committee is in contact with state and regional association directors and follows issues that are important to the state associations. They would typically invite state and regional officers and voluntary leadership to national meetings and board meetings for the purpose of gaining their insights and contributions on issues that may be of importance to all association members.

The **research, information, and technical services committee**, if an association has one, guides and directs the activities of staff involved in issues identification and research, information service, and library operations. They may also be involved in researching technical issues and reporting on them through the communications structure to the association membership.

The **ad hoc task force,** as designated here, are committees and/or groups assembled because they represent special expertise from the board or membership. They are charged with the obligation to look into, research, and formulate proposed policy relative to a specific issue or problem facing the association on a national, regional, or state level.

In concluding this overview of voluntary committee structures, it should be noted that this *typical association* committee structure may or may not reflect the activities of any specific association. Through their bylaws and rules and regulations, individual associations will provide for many of these sorts of committee activities, whether or not they are supported by a committee structure as detailed as shown here. The likelihood is extremely high that in most national associations these functions will be fulfilled by the voluntary leadership whether or not they are specifically separate as a committee function.

Staff Organization

The staff organization of the typical national association will reflect in most ways the functions and policy-making activities of the voluntary board membership committees. As seen in Exhibit 2.6, the typical national association staff organization chart outlines these parallels. Note that the government affairs section of this typical association is enlarged to reflect the intensity of activities of a large, politically active national association, and these activities parallel the importance and interest placed on them by the voluntary membership.

Because in many large national associations a significant portion of their annual revenues is generated by conventions, exhibits, trade shows, and funds generated by education and certification meetings, this staff organization depicts more detailed activities that reflect that importance. In practice, an association may employ only a part-time meeting planner or convention manager who may have other duties. This function, however, will grow parallel to the financial contributions made by the events.

The most critical relationship here is that which exists between the CSE and the chairman or president of the voluntary organization. These two individuals have a very intense symbiotic relationship, and it is important that the president of the voluntary organization clearly deliver to the chief staff executive the policy wants and needs of the board of directors through the committee structure. It is equally critical that the chief staff executive find the most

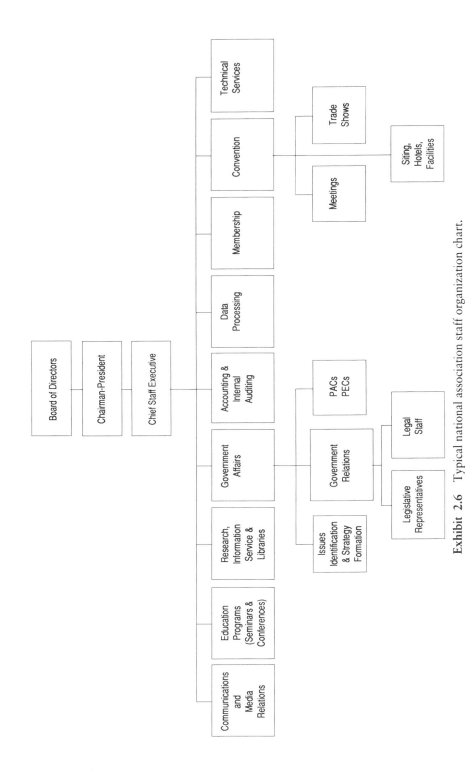

Exhibit 2.6 Typical national association staff organization chart.

effective ways to translate that policy direction into action on the part of his or her staff specialists and professionals.

The CSE is an individual whose importance cannot be overstated. The success of the association in many ways is measured through the actions of the CSE that result in board policy effectively carried out by the paid staff. Because it is the association staff who implement the policies of the board, it is through the actions of the CSE that the correct individuals are hired and trained to do the bidding of the voluntary association board.

The title of CSE distinguishes and identifies this person as separate from the elected CEO of the voluntary membership, and usually indicates a paid position. In the strongest and largest associations, this paid professional position can command salaries and fringe benefits in the US$100,000–$200,000 per year range. The Washington Association Research Foundation's (WARF) 1988 salary survey stated that the mean salary for a CSE in an association with a budget of US$2.5 million or more annually was US$112,070, which is up significantly from the previous year. Additionally, the foundation reported that the mean salary for an association's CSE for all

As seen by ASSOCIATION EXECUTIVES			As seen by VOLUNTARY LEADERS	
Percent	Rank	Quality	Rank	Percent
24.7	1	INTERPERSONAL RELATIONSHIPS, EMPATHY, RAPPORT	1	25.1
23.2	2	DEDICATION, COMMITMENT, ENERGY, HARD WORK	2	18.4
11.3	3	INTEGRITY	6	7.5
9.8	4	ORGANIZATIONAL/ADMINISTRATIVE ABILITIES	3	14.8
9.8	5	CREATIVITY	7	6.2
6.5	6	INTELLIGENCE, PLANNING	4	9.8
5.2	7	KNOWLEDGE OF INDUSTRY, OF PROFESSION, OF ASSOCIATION MANAGEMENT	5	9.2
4.7	8	PROFESSIONALISM, CONTINUING EDUCATION	9	3.1
2.6	9	COMMUNICATIONS SKILLS SPEAKING & WRITING	8	3.1
1.6	10	LEADERSHIP	10	2.2
0.6	11	SPOUSE	11	0.3

Exhibit 2.7 The most important qualities of a successful association executive. Adapted by permission of the publisher, from *Fundamentals of Association Management: Organization*. (Washington, D.C.: American Society of Association Executives, 1984), pp. 313–314.

responding to their survey was in excess of US$83,000, which was also an increase from the previous year (WARF 1988). The CSE must be able to manage all of the various association functions without alienating members, and this requires a special person.

In a study reported by the ASAE (1984a, 313–314), the most important qualities for a successful CSE were surveyed not only from association executives themselves, but also from voluntary leadership. These are set forth in Exhibit 2.7. Respondents were asked to rate how important the categories were for a successful association executive, and the CSEs and voluntary membership respondents agreed on the top two of *interpersonal relationships, empathy, and rapport* and *dedication, commitment, energy, and hard work*. However, the opinions of what is important start to diverge when you look at third- and fourth-ranked qualities. CSEs ranked *integrity* third on their list of importance, with *administrative and organizational skills* following. The association membership, in contrast, found that *organizational and administrative abilities* ranked number three, with *intelligence and planning ability* following as number four. These top four qualities on either list make up 69% of the respondents' most important qualities. Curiously, *knowledge of industry, profession, and association management* was ranked seventh of the 11 measures of successful qualities by the CSEs, and fifth by voluntary members.

It is possible to postulate that these qualities can be translated into a prescription offered by the ASAE in a white paper published in 1984:

> The chief staff executive of an association, then, provides an excellent complement to the activity of the board. The executive takes the raw theoretical material that is formulated by the board, and turns that material into specific action. It is the function of the executive to understand the goals of the board, to decide what the cost of effective action will be, to decide what staff will be needed to effectively implement the action, and then secure board approval for the overall administrative costs and for the plan of action. (ASAE 1984a, 320)

That is not to say, however, that CSEs merely have to implement board policy for the association to successfully achieve its goals. According to R. William Taylor, president and CSE of the American Society of Association Executives, CSEs of nonprofit organizations need to demonstrate the same "bottom-line discipline" as profit-making enterprises (Ballen, 1989, 170). This is especially important, for associations are subject to the same economic cycles as businesses. Taylor states that efforts of associations to be more businesslike (within the 506(C)(6) rules) will allow these organizations the financial flexibility and stability to ride out recessions and business downturns.

Because of the qualities sought in a CSE and the nature of the job, it can be suggested that it differs in many ways from that of a profit maker, but there are also many similarities. Understanding the difference, though, is the key to understanding the job and maybe becoming a success as a CSE, or at least successful in working with CSEs.

RELATIONSHIP AND IMPORTANCE OF ASSOCIATIONS TO THE CEMI

In many ways, the meetings and conventions held by associations represent economic activity in all facets of the conventions and meetings industry. If we consider Exhibit 1.1—the CEMI wheel in the previous chapter—we can postulate that not a single member of the CEMI is unaffected by a convention of a major national association. While board of director meetings, educational seminars, and miscellaneous smaller meetings may not require the expertise and services of all members of the CEMI, certainly large national conventions do, and it is through those activities that economic activity is sustained throughout the entire industry.

Among the most significant contributors to the CEMI from nonassociation meetings are those that are scheduled by businesses or corporations. It may be that a member of one business may attend a number of different types of meetings in any given year, all relative to his or her business, but falling under a different category of meetings. A member of the foodservice industry, for instance, may attend the National Restaurant Association Convention and Exposition held annually in May at Chicago's McCormick Place. He or she may also hold a position in a restaurant corporation such as McDonald's, which hosts a tremendous number of individual corporate meetings on an annual basis that make use of not only McDonald's corporate facilities, but hotel, conference, and convention facilities throughout the country. If that McDonald's executive has a further specialty, for instance, human resources or personnel management, he or she may also attend entirely separate meetings and conventions relative to that profession.

Associations hold a number of different types of meetings on an annual or other regular basis. Among the types are (Myers 1989, 36):

• Board of directors and executive committee meetings
• National conventions and expositions
• Regional and/or specialty meetings (especially health sciences and similar professions)
• Educational seminars and certification activities

These meetings of associations reported by ASAE members accounted for an extrapolated total of over 28 million room nights in hotels around the

TYPE OF MEETING	AVERAGE NO. PER YEAR*	AVERAGE TOTAL NO. OF DELEGATES PER YEAR*	AVERAGE TOTAL NO. OF ROOM NIGHTS USED PER YEAR*
Convention	1.13	9,512,792	11,342,488
Educational Seminar	11.9	20,039,600	14,974,960
Board and Executive Committee	6.4	1,796,187	1,699,840
TOTAL	**19.43**	**31,348,579**	**28,017,288**

* Based on 8,000 associations represented by ASAE members.

Exhibit 2.8 Association meetings: number, annual attendance, and annual room nights. Reprinted by permission of the publisher, from *Association Meeting Trends: 1989.* (Washington, D.C.: American Society of Association executives, 1989), p. 36.

country. As can be seen from Exhibit 2.8, these association activities also attracted over 30 million delegates on an annual basis. The amount of money spent by associations and their delegates to meetings and conventions such as this also lends significance to the economic importance of association meetings and conventions to the CEMI.

Meetings and Conventions Magazine (1988, 51) reports convention and meeting attendee expenditures in excess of US$20 billion for the year 1987, and association expenditures of approximately US$2 billion, for a total of nearly US$23 billion of economic activity accounted for by association meetings and conventions (Exhibit 2.9).

	MAJOR CONVENTIONS	ASSOCIATION MEETINGS	TOTAL EXPENDITURES
Total Expenditures on Association Meetings			
Total Expenditures in Past Years	$11,757,600,000	10,004,200,000	**$21,761,800,000** *
Association & Delegate Expenditures			
Association Expenditures in Past Year	$1,147,400,000	586,900,000	**$1,734,300,000**
Delegate/Attendee Expenditures in Past Year	$10,610,200,000	9,417,300,000	**$20,027,500,000**

* M&C Subscribers only.

Exhibit 2.9 Expenditures on association meetings. *Source:* Meetings and Conventions Magazine. 1988. *Meetings Market '87.* Reed Travel Group: Secaucus, NJ, p. 51. Used with permission.

AVERAGE DELEGATE EXPENDITURE*	ASSOCIATION PLANNERS
Under $400	18 %
$400 – 599	20
$600 – 999	20
$1,000 – 1,499	18
$1,500 or more	24
(Base = 404)	100%

Average delegate expenditure per convention: $988

* An estimate by planners of a delegate's average expenses at last major convention, whether paid for by his/her company or personally. Includes registration fee, hotel, transportation, meals, entertainment, shopping, etc.

Exhibit 2.10   Average delegate expenditure at major conventions. *Source:* Meetings and Conventions, 1988. *Meetings Market '87.* Reed Travel Group: Secaucus, NJ, p. 53. Used with permission.

Broken down into average-per-delegate expenditure, the meetings and conventions study reports a figure of about US$1000 per delegate at major association conventions (Exhibit 2.10).

These meetings are held in a number of different types of facilities, usually dictated by the size and type of meeting. Often, major conventions have to be held in a downtown hotel facility or convention center, and smaller education seminars or board meetings may be held in more appropriately scaled facilities. There is an increase toward using resort hotels for conventions and board meetings. Because of the nature of air travel, airport hotels have garnered a significant amount of educational seminar, board of directors, or executive meeting business, because in many instances attendees can fly in to an airport facility, hold a meeting, and fly out later that same day without having to spend a night at the meeting destination. This, in turn, has changed in many ways the way in which airport hotels do business. Increasingly, the transient lodging guests at airport hotels are not the groups and delegates who are using the meeting facilities at an airport hotel. In a downtown convention hotel, the guests and the meeting attendees are substantially the same people. Exhibit 2.11 illustrates types of meeting facilities that associations use for their meetings.

The factors that are considered very important in selecting a convention site illustrate the importance of association conventions to the CEMI. Exhibit 2.12 outlines those factors that were considered very important by those responding to an ASAE survey. In viewing each separate factor as a potential

TYPE OF FACILITY	CONVENTION	EDUCATIONAL SEMINAR	BOARD OR EXECUTIVE COMMITTEE MEETING
Downtown City Hotel	35%	23%	23%
Airport Hotel	6%	13%	12%
Suburban Hotel	10%	17%	12%
Resort Hotel	26%	12%	17%
Conference Center	8%	11%	6%
College/University Campus	2%	10%	3%
Association Headquarters	1%	7%	17%
Convention Center	10%	4%	2%
Other	.5%	3%	7%

Exhibit 2.11   Types of meeting facilities associations use for their meetings. Reprinted by permission of the publisher, from *Association Meeting Trends: 1989*. (Washington, D.C.: American Society of Association Executives, 1989), p. 37.

					ASSOCIATION BUDGET				
FACTOR	ALL	INT'L/ NAT'L ASSN.	REG./ STATE ASSN.	LOCAL ASSN.	UNDER $200,000	$200,000 TO $499,999	$500,000 TO $999,999	$1,000,000 TO $4,999,999	$5,000,000 OR MORE
Meeting Room Facilities	70%	75%	67%	62%	74%	70%	70%	73%	69%
Sleeping Room Facilities	47%	56%	42%	23%	53%	42%	43%	56%	56%
Air Transportation	36%	65%	15%	15%	26%	30%	32%	45%	69%
Membership Appeal (city image)	28%	33%	25%	15%	26%	30%	25%	22%	25%
Exhibit Facilities	36%	28%	41%	46%	42%	29%	39%	45%	13%
Overall Affordability	38%	40%	39%	15%	37%	41%	32%	33%	31%
Dining/Entertainment	21%	18%	23%	15%	16%	23%	14%	19%	25%
Accessibility by Highway System	27%	9%	39%	38%	37%	24%	21%	23%	19%
Recreational Facilities	15%	13%	16%	8%	21%	20%	5%	14%	13%
Geographic Rotation Policies	24%	29%	22%	8%	11%	20%	30%	23%	19%
Climate	19%	24%	14%	23%	16%	23%	16%	16%	25%
Overall Appeal	42%	43%	41%	38%	37%	48%	38%	38%	31%

Exhibit 2.12.   Scope and budget of responding association. Reprinted by permission of the publisher, from *Association Meeting Trends: 1989*. (Washington, D.C.: American Society of Association Executives, 1989), p. 38.

generator of economic activity among members of the CEMI (with the possible exception of climate), it is easy to see how many members of the CEMI can profit from participating in hosting or supplying services to the annual conventions and many meetings of associations.

One factor to note from among these is the quality of the exhibit facilities. This indicates the relative importance placed by associations on attracting exhibitors to expositions and trade shows. According to Meetings and Conventions Magazine (1988, 62–63), the average number of exhibitors per all conventions reported in 1987 was 106, renting in excess of 19,000 square feet of exhibit space each. The majority of this exhibit space (53%) was rented and constructed in one or more hotels used by the convention, with an additional 41% being housed in convention centers.

According to Myers (1989, 35):

> Associations exert significant influence over many spheres of American life, not the least of which is economic. But because associations are a diffuse community, it is difficult to measure the real economic impact. It is possible, however, to make some conservative projections about association spending patterns and the dollars that are influenced by the decisions of associations.

The foregoing statistics support the case for the vast importance of associations and their activities to the CEMI in particular, and the American economic climate in general. It is through activities such as association (and corporate) meetings that much of the economic activity of all industries in the American economy is debated, planned, and generated.

CONCLUSION

This analysis of what associations are, what their roles are, how they are organized and represent their memberships, and their importance to the CEMI was designed to demonstrate in sufficient breadth the pervasive nature of associations in the American society and economy. An in-depth discussion of elements of association activities was presented in order that other members of the CEMI and hospitality industries can have a more informed body of knowledge about associations as potential clients and guests. It is through greater understanding of the potential business from the association and meetings markets that CEMI and hospitality managers can better serve not only their guests and clients, but their own economic well-being.

REFERENCES

American Society of Association Executives (ASAE) and Chamber of Commerce of the United States. 1975. *Principles of Association Management.* Washington, D.C.: ASAE.

American Society of Association Executives (ASAE). November 1978. Qualities Needed for a Successful Chief Staff Executive. Leadership. In *Fundamentals of Association Management: Organization*, ed. Debbie L. Wolfe, pp. 313–314. Washington, D.C.: ASAE.

American Society of Association Executives (ASAE). May 1979. What Is an Association? Leadership. In *Fundamentals of Association Management: Organization*, ed. Debbie L. Wolfe, pp. 11–12. Washington, D.C.: ASAE.

American Society of Association Executives (ASAE). 1984a. Function of the Chief Staff Executive—An Informational White Paper. In *Fundamentals of Association Management: Organization*, ed. Debbie L. Wolfe, p. 320. Washington D.C.: ASAE.

American Society of Association Executives (ASAE). 1984b. Organization Charts—An Informational White Paper. In *Fundamentals of Association Management: Organization*, ed. Debbie L. Wolfe, pp. 298–302. Washington D.C.: ASAE.

Ballen, Anne. 1989. From the Desk of Bill Taylor. *Association Management* February:170–172.

Benjamin, Maynard H. 1988. Automated Systems. In *Principles of Association Management*, ed. Henry Ernstthal and Vivian Jefferson, pp. 96–106. Washington D.C.: American Society of Association Executives.

Ernstthal, Henry, and Vivian Jefferson, ed. 1988. *Principles of Association Management*. Washington, D.C.: American Society of Association Executives.

Hoyle, Leonard H., David C. Dorf, and Thomas J. A. Jones. 1989. *Managing Conventions and Group Business*. East Lansing, Michigan: Education Institute of the American Hotel and Motel Association.

Imming, Bernard J. 1988. Governance: Elected Leaders. In *Principles of Association Management*, ed. Henry Ernstthal and Vivian Jefferson, pp. 9–17. Washington, D.C.: American Society of Association Executives.

Jacobs, Jerald A. 1988. Legal Considerations. In *Principles of Association Management*, ed. Henry Ernstthal and Vivian Jefferson. Washington D.C.: American Society of Association Executives.

M&C/Meetings and Conventions Magazine. 1988. *Meetings Market '87*. Secaucus, New Jersey: Reed Travel Group.

Myers, Elissa Matulis. 1989. The Lion's Share of Meetings Business. *Association Management* February:34–38.

Washington Association Research Foundation (WARF). 1988. Association Executives Reap Higher Salaries in '88. *Meeting News* July:18.

Whittemore, Elsa. 1984. Associations Build Foundations. In *Fundamentals of Association Management: Organization,* ed. Debbie L. Wolfe, pp. 192–194. Washington, D.C.: American Society of Association Executives.

3.

Trade Shows
and Expositions

CHAPTER OBJECTIVES

1. To define what trade shows are
2. To identify the types of trade shows
3. To describe relationships of trade shows and the CEMI
4. To explain the economic impact of trade shows
5. To define and explain the complexities of trade show management
6. To introduce a partial inventory of issues facing trade shows and their management

INTRODUCTION

This chapter will investigate the function of the modern trade show or exposition as a major component of the CEMI. We will be looking at the relationships of the major players who are involved in trade shows, the growth of the trade show industry, and an in-depth analysis of the job of the trade show manager. Also examined will be issues pertinent to the management and execution of the modern trade show and its relationship to other elements of the CEMI.

Trade shows are an important, maybe even critical, element of the CEMI. For many associations and independent trade show entrepreneurs, the annual trade show contiguous to an association's convention is a primary revenue generator without which "many associations would not survive, and many entrepreneurs would be off into new ventures" (Dick Swandby, Exhibit Services, Inc., quoted in Mee 1988).

As the concept of what trade shows or expositions is developed throughout this chapter, their importance to the various segments of the CEMI will be documented.

TERMS AND DEFINITIONS

Trade shows, expositions, exhibitions, trade fairs, scientific/technical conferences are the names variously applied to activities generally associated with the term *trade show*. The names are often used interchangeably and that will be the case in this chapter, but predominantly we will use the traditional term, *trade show*.

While all of these have some differing aspects to them, the basic function of the activity remains the production of a major industry marketing event (Mee 1988). This marketing event is designed to bring together purveyors of products, equipment, and services in an environment in which they can demonstrate their products and services to a group of attendees at a convention, meeting, or trade show. These attendees, by virtue of their membership in an association or industry, constitute a self-selected market for the exhibitors.

According to Black (1986, 5), trade shows are events that gather together in a single location, usually in an exhibit hall, convention center, or exhibit space in a hotel, a group of suppliers or exhibitors who set up physical demonstrations and exhibits of their products and services designed to appeal to a given industry discipline or market segment.

A further definitional refinement, proposed by Tongren and Thompson (1981, 31), details three types of trade shows/events:

- **Industrial shows** are events used by manufacturers of equipment and products to exhibit their products to other manufacturers. These events may also include educational and demonstration sessions designed to describe and explore new industry techniques, tactics, and processes. At an industrial show, buyers are typically purchasing materials and inventory that they will either remanufacture into a processed product or resell either directly or in some adapted form.
- **Trade shows** are, in a sense, marketing events for *the trade*. These are a collection of exhibits that are specific to one or more closely allied or associated trades. In most instances, the buyers represent businesses that are shopping for services and products to use in the conduct of their business.
- **Professional or scientific exhibitions** are usually associated with meetings of professional groups, educators, scientists, and other people who could be

considered *end users*. At the annual convention of Hotel and Restaurant Administration (HRA) professors, known as the Council on Hotel, Restaurant and Institutional Education (CHRIE), there will be a group of technical exhibits sponsored by organizations wishing to sell their services to such professors and programs. Among those exhibits will be textbooks, academic and trade journals, computer programs, teaching aids, and representatives of companies who recruit and hire HRA program graduates. In a similar vein, the American College of Cardiac Surgeons' annual meeting will attract a broad range of companies offering products and services of special interest to heart surgeons.

It should be noted that trade shows as defined above are not public events. They are designed and executed for the members of specifically selected groups or attendees, but no discussion of trade shows in general would be complete without defining a fourth type of show that exhibits many of the same characteristics, the **public or consumer show.**

A consumer show usually has as a central theme, a particular type of merchandise; the most easily recognizable examples of these shows are flower and garden shows, home shows, and boat shows. Rather than appealing to a select group of people who have membership in an association or industry, these shows attract exhibitors from a broad range of manufacturers and purveyors who are related to the basic theme of the show. In most instances, a consumer show is the product of a private entrepreneur show manager who develops the concept, sells participation to appropriate types of exhibitors, rents space, and provides advertising to the general public. Because it is open to the general public, there is usually an admission charge and exhibitors are encouraged to contact consumers and sell their products and services on the floor of the show.

For our purposes, a working definition of a trade show has four elements:

- A group of product suppliers, assembled by a show manager
- Who set up physical exhibits
- In an exhibition hall of some type
- To appeal to a specific group or market

The size range of trade shows varies from fewer than a dozen tabletop exhibits for a small professional meeting such as an educational group, to those that use in excess of a million square feet of exhibit hall space in major convention centers around the country, attracting thousands of exhibitors and hosting more than 100,000 attendees or delegates.

A major explosion in terms of numbers and size of trade shows has occurred since World War II in the United States (Black 1986, 5). This growth has coincided with and can be attributed to in part to:

- Improvements in transportation
- Improvements in communication
- Improvements in data processing, information storage, and retrieval
- Sophisticated and statistical analysis of market segments
- The development of international markets
- Willingness of communities to build convention and exhibit facilities
- Growth in the numbers and memberships of associations

Given these developments, companies from around the world have chosen varying degrees of commitment to trade show participation as a part of their overall marketing strategy. According to Black (1986, 5), companies choose to participate in trade shows for a variety of reasons discussed below.

Attracting and identifying new prospects: Figures developed during Trade Show Bureau research (Mee 1988) indicate that it costs about US$230 to have a sales representative call on a new client. A new client contact at a trade show costs about US$107. The cost-effectiveness of developing new client contacts is substantial. Closing a sale with a new client costs about US$1500 by a field sales representative, and it should be pointed out that less than one-third of all sales calls produce new business. Closing a sale with a new trade show lead costs about US$290. The cost-effectiveness of a given contact can therefore be well argued.

Servicing current customers: Again, cost-effectiveness is the key issue in this sales context. It costs about US$290 to close an order with a current customer at a trade show versus US$1263 for a sales representative to close an order in the field from a current customer.

Introducing new products: Exhibiting companies offer customers the opportunity to test and try out new products under *customer conditions*. In many instances, the customer is encouraged to try out products or equipment on the trade show floor. The company then has an opportunity to judge the market response to a new product, and in some instances this may be more important than actual sales and lead generation.

Gathering competitive product information: What better place to find out what the competition is doing? At a trade show the exhibitor can see all of the company's competition vigorously demonstrating their products and services for the same *captive* market.

Enhancing corporate image and morale: This is an unquantifiable, fairly nebulous, but still important aspect to doing business in a competitive market arena. Absence from a major trade show inevitably starts questions circulating throughout the marketplace as to the financial health of a company. Responding negatively to a question such as, "Are you going to be at the big trade show?" or hearing, "I didn't see you at the big trade show," may give a company's competitors some insight into market vulnerability.

The future success of the trade show industry will be measured predominantly by the willingness of companies to continue to expand exhibiting at trade shows as a major marketing method. This in turn will hinge on an exhibiting company's analysis of the overall success of trade show participation. According to Thomas Bonoma (1983), some exhibiting companies felt used by their trade show experience, and that in turn could signal danger to the future of the trade show participation. Bonoma says that contrary to what many show managers would have potential exhibitors believe, there exists no objective measure of marketing return for dollars spent at a trade show.

He goes on to say that there is a difficulty of measuring efficiency compared to other marketing tools, and that high and rising costs of participation (including exhibit design, floor rental costs, transportation, personnel, entertainment, and travel, as examples) are inhibiting factors for many trade show participants and potential participants. Some companies, indeed, feel that trade shows are boondoggles and that they exist mainly as perks for managers

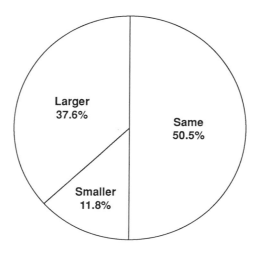

For every exhibitor whose budget will increase,
there's another whose budget will be capped at the 1988 level.

Exhibit 3.1   Exhibit budgets. *Source: Guide to MeetingPlace '89,* Meeting Planners International; copyright 1989 by Tradeshow Week, Inc., Los Angeles, California. Used with permission.

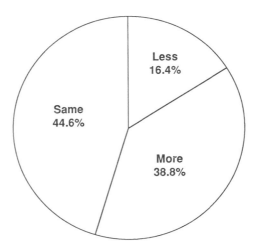

Less than one-third of the respondents will exhibit
in more trade shows in 1989.

Exhibit 3.2   Participation in trade shows. *Source: Guide to Meeting Place '89,* Meeting
Planners International, copyright 1989 by Tradeshow Week, Inc., Los
Angeles, California. Used with permission.

and current customers, and that there is not a cost-effective measure that can
be universally applied.

Contrasting views and data are supplied by Gisler (1989, 26, 29). Exhibit
3.1 suggests that 88.1% of companies that exhibit in trade shows will have
the same or larger budgets in the coming year, whereas only 11.8% of
exhibiting companies expect to spend less money on exhibit and trade show
participation. Although Gisler points out (1989, 25) that the initiation of new
trade shows peaked in 1984, 46 new shows were introduced in 1987 and 38
in 1988. He interprets this to suggest that the number of trade shows *in total* is
expected to increase because trade shows are still the most cost-effective way
to reach prospective customers. Statistics are also cited (see Exhibit 3.2) that
suggest that 83.4% of trade show participants will continue to participate or
expand their participation in trade shows in 1989.

Cited earlier as a contributing factor to the growth of trade shows since
World War II was the willingness of communities to build convention and
exhibition facilities. Exhibit 3.3 charts that growth through most of the
1980s, and it is easy to see that the growth in the number of facilities will
enhance not only competition among trade show and convention sites, but
also the opportunities for association and show managers to site their shows
at the most advantageous facilities. Exhibit 3.4 documents a concomitant
growth in available square feet of actual exhibit space.

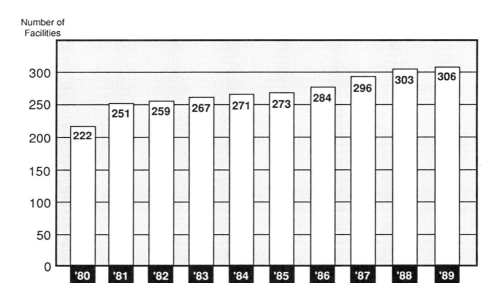

Exhibit 3.3 Growth in number of trade show facilities, 1980–1987. *Source: Guide to MeetingPlace '89,* Meeting Planners International; originally April 1988 *Tradeshow Week.* Used with permission.

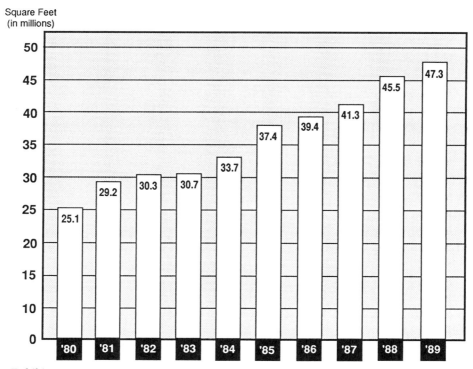

Exhibit 3.4 Growth in available exhibit space, 1980–1987. *Source: Guide to MeetingPlace '89,* Meeting Planners International; originally April 1988 *Tradeshow Week.* Used with permission.

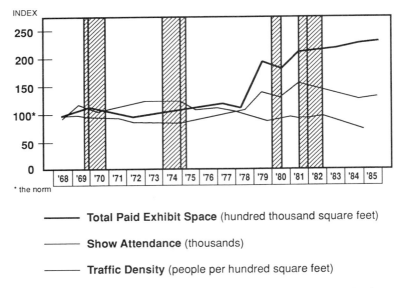

———— **Total Paid Exhibit Space** (hundred thousand square feet)

———— **Show Attendance** (thousands)

———— **Traffic Density** (people per hundred square feet)

Note: ▨ *areas indicate recession periods as designated by the National Bureau of Economic Research, Inc.*

Exhibit 3.5   Expansion in the trade show industry 1968–1985. *Source:* Mu, William W. 1988. "Trade Shows: This Marketing Medium Means Business." Association Management, June (reprint). Used with permission.

According to Mee (1988), new exhibitors have been expanding by more than 7% annually, and the only negative indicator that can be reported at this time is a flattening out of show attendance and traffic density from the growth of earlier periods prior to the 1980s (see Exhibit 3.5). The growth in numbers of facilities and available square footage may have contributed to this "flattening" by dispersing shows and attendees over more and larger facilities.

MAJOR PARTICIPANTS IN THE TRADE SHOW INDUSTRY

A number of different professionals contribute to the successful production of the modern trade show or exposition. Black (1986, 7) states there are four primary segments of the trade show industry:

- Trade show management
- Corporate exhibit management
- Trade show services
- Exhibit hall/convention center management

Each of these industry segments provides unique but closely interrelated services that coalesce in a successful trade show. Each of them in its own way performs discrete sets of tasks that have evolved into separate professions under the general umbrella of trade show/exposition activities.

Trade Show Management

The show manager or exposition manager is an employee of an association or a show management company, or is a private entrepreneur, who performs tasks such as conceptualization and development of shows, their sales, marketing, advertising, and promotion to qualified attendees. The show manager's job is concerned with the infinite details of selling the show, moving in the show, setting up the show, executing the show, and moving the show out of the convention or trade show facility.

The show manager may also participate in other activities relative to convention or meeting management and in some instances may be involved in housing and transportation. The show manager has, of course, overall fiscal responsibility for the show. The job of the show manager will be examined in more detail later in this chapter (Black 1986, 7–8).

Corporate Exhibit Management

The exhibit manager is an employee of the corporation that is exhibiting its products in a trade show. This individual is in charge of the exhibit and manages that aspect of the company's marketing media. The exhibit manager travels from trade show to trade show with the exhibit, and manages its setup, operation, and repacking for the duration of a show. The exhibit manager may also be in charge of a group of sales representatives who staff the exhibit during exposition hours.

Black (1986, 8) points out that the corporate exhibit manager may vary from a one-person operation that only exhibits at one major show a year, to a large staff of exhibit personnel who have multiple exhibits that travel to a number of different types of industrial, trade, and scientific shows throughout the country on a regular basis, and may visit as many as 200 shows a year.

The tasks and details attendant to the job of exhibit management will be examined in more depth in Chapter 8.

Trade Show Services

Trade show services generally come under the general rubric of *exposition service contractor* or what is commonly referred to as the *decorator*. Another name for these professionals is *general contractor*, a name that can be confusing since most think of the construction business when they hear the term. In the CEMI, this individual is most properly known as the exposition service contractor. As such, these professionals provide services for the trade show, exhibitors, and meeting planners that help the event take place. Among the services may be drayage, utilities, booth and exhibit setup and teardown, crating, pipe and drape erection, carpeting and other services called decorating. These may also include the rental of furniture and logistical help.

Chapter 10 will include a complete discussion of the duties and role of exhibition service contractors.

Exhibit Hall/Convention Center Management

A facility where trade shows are held—be it a freestanding exhibit hall, a comprehensive convention center, or ballroom or exhibit space in a hotel—plays the important role of providing the space for the execution of the modern trade show. Usually, one key member of facility management will be designated to be the interface between the event taking place in the building and the management of the center and facility. In a comprehensive convention center, this is most likely the event coordinator or someone from the staff of the event coordination manager.

In most facilities, once the event is in the building, the designated event coordinator effectively has control of the building on behalf of the client who is renting the building. This individual is familiar with the operation of the building and the details of the contract relative to the client and their event, and has the authority and responsibility for making sure that the building responds to the needs of the client within the framework of the contract that exists between the facility and the trade show. The role of convention facility management will be outlined in more depth in Chapter 4.

The compelling interest in producing expositions in convention facilities is, of course, the availability of large expanses of space dedicated to exhibits. Exhibit 3.4 tracks the growth in such space during the 1980s. This growth is paralleled by a corresponding growth in amount of exhibit space paid for by exhibiting companies, as seen in Exhibit 3.5. The increase in both the amount of available exhibition space and rental of that space seems to have contributed to a flattening of show attendance and a decline in traffic density.

If the trade show is being held in a hotel, functions similar to those of the facility event coordinator are performed by the hotel's convention services manager. It is the job of the convention services manager to make sure that everything the client has contracted for with the hotel is carried out by the staff and departments of the hotel. Hotels and their role in the production of convention or trade show events will be discussed in more detail in Chapter 6.

It is the relationship of these major actors in a trade show event that allows such events to be successful marketing tools for exhibiting companies and productive business ventures for trade show operators and associations.

While there are other professionals who influence to a greater or lesser degree the success of any given trade show, these are the major ones. It is their relationship and interrelationship that forms the economic model of a trade show.

RELATIONSHIPS OF MAJOR TRADE SHOW ELEMENTS

Exhibit 3.6 demonstrates the relationships between and among the major professional components of a trade show event by plotting how dollars are spent for services relative to the successful production of such an event.

The central player in this instance is the association or show manager, who originally conceives and provides for production of the event. Show managers, whether they work for an association, or a show management company or act as private entrepreneurs, face a dual marketing task. First, they must successfully entice exhibitors to make a decision to display their products and services at the trade show. Second, they must encourage attendance from association membership or interested industrial or trade memberships.

In addition to expenses associated with marketing, sales, and promotion before, during, and after the event, the show manager incurs various financial obligations for costs associated with the show's production. Building rent, decorator charges, arrangements for buses and overhead expenses associated

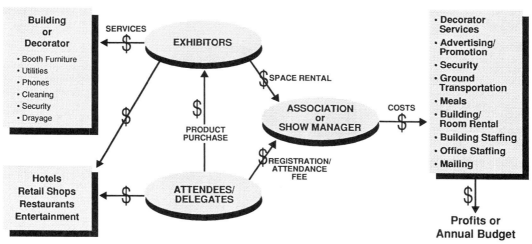

Exhibit 3.6 Economic structure and money flow for "typical" trade show/exposition. *Source:* Astor and Rutherford, (1989). Used with permission.

with staff, travel, and entertainment are significant costs to show management.

Exhibitors pay money to the show manager for space rental on the floor of the show. Attendees pay registration or attendance fees to the association or show manager. Exhibitors purchase services from either the facility or the decorator; among these are the aforementioned pipe and drape, booth furniture, utilities, and so forth. Exhibitors also spend money in the local community purchasing food, lodging, and entertainment services.

Similarly, attendees or delegates purchase food, lodging, and entertainment services and may also spend significant amounts of money on local retail shopping. But they also present a major marketing opportunity to the exhibitors who are displaying products and services on the floor of the convention, and depending upon the nature of the show or rules of the association, active financial transactions can take place between delegates and exhibitors on the show floor.

The show manager or association, in turn, spends money on promotion, decorators, ground transportation, and food and beverage service on the floor of the convention or trade show; purchases building or room rental from the facility; and may also budget money for facility staffing and office staff, along with other administrative and general expenses. After those costs are taken care of, the show manager will show either a profit or loss, and the association will hopefully have revenues in excess of expenses that contribute significantly to the association's annual budget. Again quoting Dick Swandby of Exhibit Surveys, Inc. (Mee 1988): "Expositions exist to generate revenue, either for the association or the independent entrepreneur. . . . Without this revenue, many associations would not survive . . ." This is reinforced by Nichols (1985, 201) where she indicates that, "An exhibition can be the largest non-dues revenue-producing activity for the sponsoring organization."

As a generator of economic activity, trade shows and expositions are significant components of both local and national economies, through the purchase of goods and services in the following catagories:

1. Air Transportation
2. Hotel Room Expenditures
3. Freight/Drayage
4. Show Contractors/Exhibitors Labor
5. Exposition Hall Rental
6. Plumbing/Electrical/Cleaning
7. Other Expenditures
8. Organizations Food and Beverage

9. Hall Food and Beverage
10. Car Rentals
11. Guard Service
12. Entertainment
13. Registration Service
14. Shuttle Operations
15. Audio/Visual
16. Hall Services
17. Paid Speakers
18. Other Hotel Expenditures
19. Florist
20. Insurance
21. Tour Operators
22. Photography
23. Telephone Translation Services and Meeting Tape Recording Service

(Exhibit Surveys, Inc. 1989, 5)

According to a recent survey (Exhibit Surveys, Inc. 1989) show managers spent significant sums of money on the above activities to produce their shows and expositions. Air transportation, hotels, freight/drayage, labor and hall rental (numbers 1 through 5) account for US$2.9 billion worth of spending authorized by show managers and their organizations.

The survey from which these data were compiled included respondents who managed 1,268 separate expositions and trade shows ranging in size from less than 1,500 to more than 150,000 square feet of exhibit space. When extrapolated to the entire membership of the National Association of Exposition Managers (NAEM), the economic impact on the nation's economy is on the order of US$4 billion (Exhibit Survey, Inc. 1989). The 25 different groups that provide services for the exposition field (telephone, translation and taping services are combined in dollar value) highlight not only the diversity of economic activity, but emphasize the complexity involved in planning and producing a trade show or exposition. Managing this complex series of tasks and challenges is the province of the trade show or exposition manager.

SHOW MANAGEMENT

The management of trade shows and expositions may be either through a sponsoring association, a private entrepreneurial trade show manager or a show management company who contracts with various groups for the production of trade shows and expositions.

Like all management, the show manager must exhibit highly refined managerial skills in the areas of planning, organization, coordination, leadership, and control. These classic managerial functions are no less important in the trade show industry than in the management of any for-profit or nonprofit organization.

An association that chooses to manage and produce its show "in-house" usually does so after determining that the details attendant to the production of an annual show or numerous shows may require the services of one or more full-time staff employees. If it is determined that less than one full-time association employee is required to produce the show, it may very well be that the show's production is contracted with an outside entrepreneur or show management firm (Hoyle, Dorf, and Jones 1989, 321). Such contractual obligations will generally spell out the duties and expectations of both the association or sponsoring organization and the show manager, and will also set forth in contractual form how the financial proceeds of the event are to be distributed.

Whether the show manager is an association employee, a private entrepreneur, or an employee of a show management firm, the duties and complexities of his or her job are similar, as outlined and discussed below (Hoyle, Dorf, and Jones 1989, 321–323; Black 1986, 7–8; and NAEM Introduction to Trade Show Marketing):

- Conceptualization and show development
- Marketing, sales, and promotion
- Working with exhibitors
- Working with facilities
- Working with labor unions
- Coordinating and hiring service contractors
- On-site show operations
- Postshow activities

Conceptualization involves activities on the part of the show manager that lead to a marketable product. The show manager must be familiar enough with the potential market to design and promote an attractive marketing event at which exhibitors will contact highly qualified potential buyers of their merchandise, equipment, products, or services. The show manager also selects a site if the site is not contingent upon an already scheduled convention.

Factors determining a successful trade show conceptualization are the interest on the part of the potential attendees and the products and services displayed by exhibitors, the setting for the exposition, and the "quality" of the potential attendees to the exhibitor as people able to make purchasing decisions. Other factors involved in successful conceptualization include the potential for everyone involved to have a financially successful event. Site selection is especially critical because it requires broad and in-depth knowledge of the requirements of the show and the expectations of the exhibitors and their potential markets.

Marketing, sales, and promotion involves a two-pronged marketing attack. On one hand, the show manager must be well aware of the psychographics, demographics, and professional characteristics of the potential attendees of the convention or trade show. At the same time, given these data, the show manager must be able to successfully entice the sorts of companies as exhibitors who have products that are appropriate to the attendee market. So, in effect, the show manager has to sell the show event to separate markets that are seeking to accomplish different tasks. The exhibitor wants to meet qualified sales contacts, and the attendees want to be able to peruse and judge the latest in products and services relative to their profession.

To do this, the manager must establish a marketing plan, set sales objectives, be able to define the benefits of coming to such an event, and embark on a number of sales and promotion activities. These include sales letters, advertisements in trade journals, personal selling calls to exhibitors, and various other appropriate and necessary promotional and public relations activities.

Promoting attendance among delegates presents a different set of challenges to the show manager. It requires in-depth knowledge of what the attendees at the conference, convention, or trade show wish to achieve by their attendance there, and then designing a program to make it as easy as possible for delegates and exhibitors to interact on the exhibit floor. These activities may include fliers mailed to conference registrants, information stuffed in registration packets, show directories designed to be easy to use for the attendee, information signs and video displays on the exhibit floor, and in some instances, show management participation in sponsoring social or entertainment events for convention or conference attendees.

Working with exhibitors involves activities of varying intensity, from the initial marketing and sales contact through the exhibitors' participation in the show itself. Sophisticated show management firms, entrepreneurs, and associations realize that the heart of the show in many ways is the exhibitor, and finding ways in which to ease the participation of the exhibitor pays off in positive exhibitor relations that can last for many years. It is the well-developed base of return exhibitors that contribute to the trade show's success year after year.

Positive relations with exhibitors start with communication. It is important that once an exhibitor has committed to space in a trade show, the exhibit manager and trade show manager have the means to communicate actively and easily with each other. This may mean that the show manager needs to provide a toll-free telephone service, have 24-hour facsimile (FAX) reception, and provide regular updates to exhibitors about activities relative to their participation in the show. This can be anything from a notification of various rules relative to the building facility, or advice on travel, shipping, and lodging, to on-site activities that help the exhibitor participate in the show with a minimum of difficulty. One show manager went so far as to notify all 1500 participants at its annual show that a major expressway in the vicinity of the convention facility was under construction and that the exhibitors should advise the companies transporting their exhibits that access to the convention facility would be restricted during certain periods of "commute hours," proposing alternative routes to and from staging areas and the convention facility. It is communications such as these that promote exhibitor loyalty and allow show managers to produce a marketing event at which exhibitors are happy to participate.

Show managers, working with exposition service contractors (ESCs), also communicate with exhibitors through some variety of official "exhibitor kit." This kit spells out rules and regulations; exhibit and general information; what show management is doing to promote the event; and a list of labor, utility, and other services that are available through the ESC. This may include information regarding booth furnishings, storage and security services, and the availability of parking, audiovisual, and foodservice.

Show management's experience in exhibitor communication is important to maintaining loyalty among exhibiting participants. Well-established national or international shows have often put together an advisory committee of exhibitors to help show management in formulating policy that is important to easing the participation of exhibitors.

One of the key components in the production of a successful trade show or exposition is the relationship that exists between the show management and the facility at which the show is produced. It was pointed out earlier that trade shows could be produced at freestanding exhibit halls, hotels with exhibit or ballroom space, and comprehensive convention facilities. In any of these venues, it is important that show management have a corps of key people who represent the facility with whom the manager works to see that the facility is best utilized on behalf of the trade show or exposition.

In an exhibit hall or convention facility, the key individuals are the event coordinator, who will effectively have charge of the building during the run of the event; the operations manager, who will oversee the physical transformation of building activities from one event to the next; and to a lesser degree, the foodservice manager, who, while probably not involved in banquet planning for show managers, plays an important role in the show manager's perspective by having concession stands staffed for exhibit personnel, service contractors, labor, and attendees. Increasingly, in facilities where it is part of policy, foodservice caterers are being asked to do foodservice directly in exhibit booths, and these activities have to be coordinated between the exhibit manager, the show manager, and the facility foodservice manager.

In a hotel, the central individual is the convention services manager, whose job is analogous to that of the event coordinator in a convention facility. The representative from the banquet/catering department will be in charge of foodservice. The building's chief engineer directs a staff that will configure spaces within the hotel to the show manager's stipulations. The chief engineer also understands the limitations of the hotel's potential exhibit space. Another hotel executive who may be a part of the core team in this instance is the director of housekeeping, who will provide cleaning services to the show manager as outlined in the facility contract.

Complexities of working with various labor unions and labor organizations vary significantly from city to city and region to region. In some cities, relations with labor unions represented in convention halls and facilities can be postively Byzantine, with as many as 35 separate unions and crafts being represented under one roof. It is situations like these that test the leadership abilities of the show manager to produce a smoothly run event. Oftentimes exhibitors will not understand local union rules and regulations, and sometimes major disagreements arise as a result of this lack of knowledge. It is important that the show manager, working closely with the ESC, have a firm grasp of the local union regulations and jurisdictions and be able to help the participants in the exposition interact in the most expeditious way.

Labor is also important because it can be extremely expensive for the show manager and exhibitors to hire and arrange for the various activities represented by crafts and trades on the exhibit hall floor. Exhibit 3.7 presents average labor rates for the various types of common crafts and trades utilized by exhibiting staff and show management personnel.

It should be pointed out that these rates are rates which are paid for the contracting agency; it may be that the building is providing labor at these costs, and the individual is paid somewhat less. The service contractors may also be providing labor at these "average" rates, and the individual laborer gets somewhat less. So these rates can be considered as contributing to the show manager's and exhibitor's costs, and at the same time considered profit centers for the building or service contractor.

The exposition service contractor's primary function is to convert the logistics of the show manager's concept into on-site reality. Typical service contractor functions will include warehousing, freight handling (drayage),

• Decorators $36.72	• Electricians...........................$41.69
• Draymen $29.17	• Plumbers $38.49
• Carpenters $42.09	• A-V Technicians $28.32
• Riggers................................$39.87	• Guards $10.89

• Forklift with operator (lowest weight range) $63.00

• Forklift with operator (higher weight range)..$79.02

• Drayage per CWT*, warehouse to booth, empty storage, booth to dock ...$27.54

• Drayage per CWT*, dock to booth, empty storage, booth to dock $22.75

• Uncrated van surcharge 41%

• Booth Cleaning per square foot per day ....$.12

* CWT — Hundredweight

Exhibit 3.7 Average labor rates for major trade show cities. *Source:* Annual Labor Survey; © 1989 by *Tradeshow Week, Inc.,* Los Angeles, California. Used with permission.

the provision of labor and supervision for services on the exhibit floor, the rental of equipment and providing for uncrating and crating exhibit materials, exhibit setup, furniture rental, floor plans and layouts, and direction of pipe and drape (Black 1986, 10).

From the foregoing inventory of exhibitor and trade show services, it is easy to see why the service contractor is such a critically important factor in the management of the modern exposition or trade show. Show management has a responsibility in many instances of choosing the service contractor and working with that firm to arrange the details of their participation in the show's layout, design, setup, and teardown. A typical service provided by exhibition service contractors is the rental of booth furniture, carpeting, signage and other accessories. Exhibit 3.8 displays national averages for various pieces of furniture and other typical booth accessories required by exhibitors at trade shows.

A survey indicated that rates for such items rose less than one percent over similar rates from the previous year's study. But when taken in total, it can be seen that if an exhibitor or show manager wished to rent a number of different pieces of furniture, carpeting, and audiovisual accessories, it could run into a significant sum over the course of a three-day trade show and can amount to a substantial expenditure of dollars when extrapolated to exhibitors at a major trade show with over 1,000 exhibits. Examples such as these highlight the importance of a good working relationship between the show manager and the ESC. It is through the show manager's relationship with the ESC that

ITEM	AVERAGE RATE NATIONWIDE
Chairs	
Upholstered Arm	$23.33
Upholstered Lounge	29.59
Fiberglass Side	17.36
Carpeting	
Increments of 9'x10'	$57.82
Cut & Lay per sq. yd.	11.47
Draped Display Tables	
4-Feet	$36.55
6-Feet	44.44
8-Feet	51.99
Telephone Service.	$136.25
Accessories	
Wastebaskets	$5.82
Easels	11.77
Smokers	11.03
Desks.	$113.48
Electrical/Audio-Visual	
One HP Motor Circuits	$69.12
35mm Slide Projectors (Daily Rates)	23.34
Lavaliers, includes PA System (Daily Rates)	48.17
1/2" VHS Video Setups (Daily Rates)	171.05
Flood Lights (300 watt)	49.61
Floral	
Boutonnieres	$3.10
4' Green Plants	37.60

Exhibit 3.8 Rental rates for furniture, floor coverings, and accessories survey. *Source:* National Association of Exposition Managers (NAEM) Inform-A-Gram #76-C. Survey by Darlene Gudea, copyright 1988 by Tradeshow Week, Inc. Los Angeles, California. Used with permission.

event participation is facilitated for all concerned, but particularly the exhibitors.

Perhaps the central function of the show manager's job coalesces in those activities that are related to on-site operations. This is the actual production of the event at which the foregoing planning, organizing, and coordination is realized in the activities and attendant details that are important to the success of the exposition. In this stage of the event's production, the majority of show management activities can be grouped into four major categories (NAEM, On-Site Operations):

1. Prior to move-in
2. During move-in
3. During show
4. During move-out.

If one phrase can describe the majority of show management activities during these four phases of the event, it is *attention to details*. These are details that are relevant to the realization of the planning, organizing, and coordination mentioned before, and this is where true leadership in management is practiced. The job of the successful show manager at this stage of a well-planned event is fine-tuning the production and making sure that key elements of the show represented by groups and people are managed toward a successful conclusion.

Upon arriving at a convention center or hotel, **prior to move-in,** the majority of activities and major details associated with the show manager's job involve reviewing, checking, analyzing, and evaluating the condition of the building and its components relative to the plan developed for the execution of the show (NAEM On-Site Operations). There are a number of special areas that deserve separate attention. A number of offices and areas that are set aside for special purposes of show management staff, association management, press, and so forth have to be double-checked to make sure that they are furnished and equipped to satisfy not only the elements of the management plan, but the practical realities of any group effectively running its home office in a remote location. The same holds true for press headquarters, the various meeting rooms, and registration areas. These have specialized functions, and it is important that the show manager determine that they are furnished, equipped, and located properly.

In the hall itself, the exhibit space and meeting rooms need to be checked for conformity to the floor plan developed by the show manager, exhibitors, and service contractor. It is also important that security be established prior to the move-in and that exhibitor products and materials be provided storage that is safe from theft or harm. The exposition service contractor must have a well-designed and well-located desk or series of booths from which the contractor's staff services the needs of the exhibitors regarding utilities, freight, drayage, and other services on behalf of show management. Other special service counters need to be properly located and designed, and signage needs to be arranged and erected. Special service counters offer such services to delegates and exhibitors as housing information, telephone messages, FAX transmissions, airline ticket desks, local activity planning, and general delegate information.

It is also important for the show manager to inspect the condition of the building. The contract between the building and show management will stipulate rights and responsibilities with both parties relative to the building's condition, and the show manager does not want to incur any financial responsibility for preexisting conditions. Items of importance to note include cleanliness, rain leakage, and damaged property that show management does not want to have to be responsible for upon leaving. Changes that may have been made in the building since the original contract was signed should also be noted. The show manager at this stage must also double-check any individual architectural or operational peculiarities that are unique to the building and decide how they may affect management of the event.

It is then necessary for the show manager to "customize" the building in order that the building's flexibility might be best utilized for the unique event about to occur. One of the services that can be contracted for by the show manager with the facility is the use of signage. These may be traditional or electronic, and can serve to control traffic flow, locate and highlight specific areas, or direct delegates to foodservice and restrooms, meeting areas, and social events.

Another service for the show manager to consider at this time concerns special security requirements. These may include personnel schedules, numbers of security staff, and electronic and visual security. Security arrangements are made using facility staff or through contractual arrangements with a service contractor or private security firm. Details such as these allow show management to configure the building in a way that will most appropriately serve a specific event.

Finally, prior to move-in, it is important for show management to conduct briefing and informational meetings with two major groups of professionals. One is the core team alluded to earlier, represented by the association meeting planner, the exposition service contractor, the facility event coordinator, the facility operations manager, and other people who may be particularly appropriate to this event. Other key personnel will vary from event to event, depending on the requirements of show management, and may range from the hotel sales manager to representatives of the convention and visitors bureau, to the telephone switchboard supervisor.

At these briefings, the show manager wants to accomplish two fundamental tasks to make it easy for these professionals to do their jobs and to establish lines of communication and understanding relative to the needs and requirements of the show, in order that the inevitable problems that arise in an event as complex as a trade show can be dealt with swiftly and effectively.It is a measure of the show manager's leadership that the correct people are chosen to be included in his or her communication network at this stage of the execution of the exposition event.

During the next phase of the show, **move-in** takes on a whole new meaning to show management. In one instance, it specifies the activities that are going on relative to the exhibitors, service contractors, labor unions, and so forth who are setting up the show. But the idea of motion extends in all practical ways the activities of the show manager. The show manager is constantly in motion. He or she is moving from place to place within the facility, checking and double-checking the activities relevant to the major elements of the move-in discussed below, (NAEM, On-Site Operations).

The flow of freight traffic needs to be managed, as does a concurrent commitment to floor security and safety. The decorator or exposition service contractor is a close ally of the show manager at this stage of the event, as are the representatives of the various labor groups and unions to make sure that the correct utility installations are available for appropriate exhibitors' booths. Continuing to play a major role at this stage of the production are the communication links between and among the designated core staff of show management and other key personnel in the facility, hotel, or exhibit hall.

Some show managers will say that the majority of activities **during the show** involve "putting out fires." By this, of course, they mean the need to respond, usually in an expeditious manner, to problems that arise during the time the show is hosting delegates and the exhibitors are demonstrating their wares. The major categories that these "fires" typically arise from are discussed below, with one of the most important being security. Because trade shows are nonpublic events, it is important that only qualified people be allowed on the show floors. Otherwise, the show manager finds that the show may be in a position of allowing people who are not qualified buyers to waste the time that exhibitors could have been using to conclude sales arrangements with qualified buyers. Perimeter security is therefore of critical importance to show management to maintain good relationships with exhibitors. (NAEM, On-Site Operations)

Cleanliness and environmental concerns can be ongoing problems, and it is important that aisles and walkways be kept clean. Exhibitors who have paid premium prices for special locations and have brought in large and expensively designed exhibits are understandably upset when they are confronted with an aisleway that is littered with food wrappers, cigar and cigarette butts, and other exhibitor's promotional literature. Similarly, overflowing garbage cans, wastebaskets, and ashtrays are likely to cause concern among exhibitors and fire marshals alike.

Sometimes show management finds itself in the position of having to deal with exhibitor problems. Some exhibitors have real or imagined contractual problems with the building or exposition service contractor. Show managers may have to involve themselves in arbitration or enforcement of rules and may have to arrange for refunds or rescheduling of charges depending on problems that may arise. These responsibilities may be delegated to assistants or "floor managers" who are always on the show floor.

During the show, the show manager double-checks and determines the amount of net square footage that was actually occupied to make sure that the show was charged according to the terms of the contract. Similar evaluations need to be made relative to services and products provided by the exposition service contractor.

A key element of leadership for the show manager to exhibit continues to be a commitment to communication, not only with core staff and other key personnel, but also with exhibitors. Mentioned earlier was the practice of providing updates and critical information to exhibitors that will allow them to better plan their participation in the show. Similarly, on the floor of the show during its run, it is important that show management provide exhibitors with bulletins or changes regarding exhibit hours, rules and regulations for exhibit personnel, direction information, and security stipulations. Finally, provisions for invoices, work orders for service, and billing information need to be effectively communicated to appropriate parties. (NAEM, On-Site Operations)

At the conclusion of the show, the show manager's tasks regarding **move-out** take on a different focus. In this instance, communication remains an important part of the manager's activities, as does an increasing emphasis on control.

Because the exhibit and meeting spaces of many hotels and convention facilities are booked years in advance with very little tolerance for overruns, it is important that the show manager, the facility, the exposition service contractor, and exhibitors agree on what time the show ends and what time formal move-out activities must commence. This is important because many facilities do not have a great deal of flexibility between the time one show is moving out and the next one booked is due to move in.

Security continues to be an important issue at this stage of the event's activities. It is at this time when a lot of valuable equipment and products may not be controlled or monitored as closely as during move-in or the show itself. The show manager must have established and continue to maintain strict security controls.

Communication is a continuing theme because the rules for move-out are in many ways as complex and specific as the rules for move-in. It is necessary that the exhibitors understand the regulations established by show management and the building.

Prior to move-in, the show manager has a responsibility to check the building for damage. At the conclusion of the show, there is a responsibility to double-check to make sure the show is not billed for any condition that predated move-in.

Finally, show managers have to review and approve for payment all billings, invoices, and other financial claims. In areas where it is appropriate and expected, a gratuity list needs to be formulated and gratuity checks distributed.

Show management's responsibilities do not end once the building is vacated and the move-out details are concluded. It is immediately after the show that planning for the next show commences. Provisions for event evaluation, either by show management staff or an outside firm, need to be made at this time. These reports include exhibition validation, attendance certification, booth visit analysis, and others that may be required by the various constituencies (See Below). These constituencies typically include exhibitors, association management, show management company, facilities, and hotels. These activities are the fundamental bases for planning for next year's event. It is through the continued contacts with the key players that future events will become easier to conceive, plan, execute, and manage.

Reports mentioned above can take a number of different forms depending upon size, type and management of the show. Briefly, they are defined as follows:

- exhibition validation—an independent report distributed to exhibitors that tracks current and historical data about the show. Includes data on exhibitors, attendance, audience profile, marketing data, admissions policies, and sample programs. This activity is often performed by the Exhibition Validation Council, an activity of the Trade Show Bureau.
- attendance certification—analyzes the trade show audience on the basis of attendee demographics. Other audience data can include net buying influences (NBI) which is the percentage of attendees who have either the final say, specify, or recommend purchase.
- booth visit analysis—these data count actual visits to an exhibitor's booth by show attendees and may include time spent in exhibit, tracking of exhibit personnel/attendee interactions.

Postshow activities such as these are the true measure of the ability of the show manager to demonstrate the practice of the management principle of control.

This brief overview of a "show in the life" of an exposition manager merely suggests the complexity, breadth and detail that are important to the successful execution of the modern marketing event we call a trade show. It is important to note that any given show manager's job description will include foregoing stipulations as fundamental activities. As shows become more sophisticated and complex, the show manager's job will take on additional and added dimensions. The old days when there was merely an empty building, row upon row of pipe and drape delineated booths, and little if any other considerations relative to the comfort, care, and feeding of the show or convention delegate are substantially over. The show manager's job is becoming one that demands individuals with well-refined management skills, vision, commitment, and ability to continue their education and acquisition of knowledge about not only the trade show industry, but the other facets of the meeting and convention business.

To be discussed in the following section on issues, the show manager's job is being complicated in many ways by activities and events that are, for the most part, out of his or her control. When trade show issues are discussed, challenges that will continue to test show management's ability to provide the services discussed herein will be highlighted.

ISSUES

Like the managers of most enterprises, trade show managers, management firms, and associations annually find that the challenges facing their ability to direct and execute their activities vary with social, economic, legal, and regulatory pressures. However, it is possible to suggest a list of issues that can be at least agreed upon by a varying number of commentators and researchers that encompass generic challenges to the trade show and exposition industry. In some cases, these represent perennial issues, and in other instances, they demonstrate that management needs to be ever-alert to emerging challenges that are either new or a combination of traditional challenges.

Abstracted here are a number of issues that have surfaced with varying intensity over the last few years and are recognized as being of major concern to trade show managers and the exposition industry in general.

Facility size has come to be considered an issue, although one that is perhaps difficult for any show manager to influence or control. It has been said (Liegler et al. 1986) that new convention and exposition facilities need to seriously consider building for larger trade shows and meetings. More than 200 trade shows need at least 200,000 gross square feet of exhibit space to comfortably produce the show. Many municipalities, however, will not find it economically feasible to build exhibit facilities of that magnitude, concentrating the marketing for large shows in a relatively small group of facilities in major market areas.

A related issue is that of **facility profit centers.** Ever-increasing numbers of convention and exhibit facilities are being encouraged by their political environments to become profit-makers or at least breakeven concerns, as opposed to the conventional wisdom of the past that viewed convention and exhibit facilities as "loss leaders" for other businesses in the community (Teibel 1988, 3). It has been pointed out (Crystal 1987, 50) that convention and exhibit facilities are easy targets for politicians to point to as money losers. They then demonstrate to their constituencies that they are being fiscally responsible by requiring centers to break even or turn a profit.

As a result, profit pressures on the managements of convention centers have led them to internalize a number of services that were, in the past, the province of exposition service contractors or independent specialty contractors. Convention centers are increasingly requiring that utilities, security, booth cleaning, and even pipe, drape, and decorating services be purchased in-house from the facility, rather than allowing the show manager to shop for the best price elsewhere. While this may, in fact, lower costs, the show manager may feel constrained by the building, which, in effect, serves as a prime contractor in space rental and, increasingly, as specialty contractor in other show services.

A related issue is that of **turnaround time.** Show managers are finding they and service contractors are suffering from a certain amount of time compression relative to move-in and move-out times. Pressure to cut down move-in and move-out times by convention facilities is, in some cases, intense. This pressure on turnaround times is compounded by the fact that for many trade shows, exhibitors are designing, producing, and displaying ever more complex and sophisticated exhibits in larger and larger formats. The increasing complexity and sophistication of exhibits, and the redundancy of such types of exhibits in any given show, put additional pressure on move-in and move-out times. This presents a critical challenge for show management to meet, particularly in the move-out arena because many facilities apply penalties for not moving out quickly enough.

The previous issue is closely related to the companion issue of **facility overselling.** With the aforementioned political pressures to break even or show a profit for the taxpayers, convention hall or convention bureau sales people want to maximize building and room usage and minimize the time the building is dark. In order to do that, sometimes there is the tremendous temptation to oversell the hall and try to book more events than the building and its staff can comfortably accommodate given the need for move-in and move-out days.

Douglas Ducate, past president of NAEM and association executive for the Society of Petroleum Engineers, which hosts several major trade shows each year, says, "It looks as if they griped about labor, security and prices sixty years ago, and they'll be griping about labor, security and prices when our grandkids are running the show in another sixty years." (Crystal 1988, 48). What Ducate is suggesting is that despite the configurations of some of the more recent challenges, the basic issues of **labor, security, and prices** will probably remain with the trade show industry much the same as they will remain with varying emphasis in any other industry. However, prices the show managers have to pay and prices they have to charge to their market are influenced by at least one other factor that looms as a major challenge to the management of trade shows and expositions: the availability and cost of insurance.

A survey by *Meetings & Conventions* magazine (Crystal 1987, 48) reported that the issue of liability insurance for show managers. ". . . is by far the most disturbing problem facing the trade show industry today. Some show managers are finding their coverage sharply reduced. Others are being socked with premium hikes of 300% or more."

Show managers say that this escalation of insurance rates and difficulty in purchasing coverage has not only cost them significantly more in overhead, but has also damaged their relationship with exhibitors because they have to pass along these insurance costs. A companion problem is that as exhibitors design ever more complex and technologically sophisticated exhibits that invite attendees into previously unheard of hands-on demonstrations and situations, the issue of safety engineering for those exhibits (Liegler et al. 1986) and insurance for those exhibit structures becomes even more complex.

Convention halls are also requiring as a part of their contractual agreements with hall users that certain types and amounts of stipulated insurance coverages be obtained and carried throughout the rental period. These stipulations may be legislatively mandated, or they may be policies that are issued by the center of hall's governing board. It should be pointed out, however, that a survey of trade show managers reported in the Crystal article (1988, 54) showed that over 84% of surveyed show managers seldom or never had trouble in obtaining liability insurance. But over 69% of those responding reported that costs of liability insurance have significantly increased in the previous two years (Crystal 1987, 54).

A final issue is that of the **relationships** between and among the major components of the CEMI from the perspective of the trade show management component. In a 1986 white paper, the NAEM suggested a number of guidelines for the exposition industry that encompassed the major issues and challenges that exist between exposition managements, facility managements, exhibitors, and service contractors. While these proposed guidelines should not at this time be considered a prescription, their merit and practical application among the components of the CEMI remain a topic of ongoing discussion and debate.

CONCLUSION

In the marketing mix associated with modern business activity, the trade show has significantly impacted the traditional methods of sales and promotion. It provides buyers and sellers with the unique opportunity to comingle in a specifically managed marketing event designed to optimize the buying and selling experience for both parties. That trade shows have thus become a significant economic factor in the CEMI is well demonstrated by the data and statistics associated with their production and management.

It also becomes obvious that the impact of a trade show in interacting with other major components of the CEMI is not only significant, but probably could be considered essential. Few, if any, modern conventions exist without some sort of trade show, exposition, or selection of exhibits. The marketing opportunity for sellers to contact highly qualified potential buyers is simply too important to ignore. The relationships between and among expositions and the other components of the CEMI discussed above are of enduring and mutual benefit.

REFERENCES

Astor, Kanellos J., and Denney G. Rutherford. 1989. Economic Structure and Money Flow for Typical Trade Show/Exposition. Internal working document, Group 2+ International, Inc., mimeo.

Black, Robert. November 19, 1986. *The Trade Show Industry: Management and Marketing Career Opportunities*. Lecture to Cornell University. East Orleans, Massachusetts: Trade Show Bureau.

Bonoma, Thomas V. 1983. Get More out of Your Trade Shows. *Harvard Business Review* January–February:75–83.

Chapman, Edward A., Jr. 1987. *Exhibit Marketing: A Survival Guide for Managers*. New York: McGraw-Hill.

Crystal, Susan. 1987. Trade Show Poll: The Issues, the Changes, the Challenge. *Meetings & Conventions* January:46+.

Exhibit Survey, Inc. 1989. 1988 NAEM Buying Power Survey. *National Association of Exposition Managers Newsletter*. July (4):5.

Gisler, David R. 1989. The Future of Trade Shows. *Meeting Manager* June:25–27, 29.

Gudea, Darlene. 1988a. Average Labor Rates for 44 Major Trade Show Cities. Reprinted from *Tradeshow Week*, Los Angeles, in *NAEM 1988 Inform-A-Gram* October (62D):1+.

Gudea, Darlene. 1988b. Rental Rates for Furniture, Floor Coverings and Accessories Survey. Reprinted from *Tradeshow Week*, Los Angeles, in *NAEM 1988 Inform-A-Gram #76C*.

Hoyle, Leonard H., David C. Dorf, and Thomas J. A. Jones. 1989. *Managing Convention and Group Business*. East Lansing, Michigan: Education Institute of the American Hotel and Motel Association.

Liegler, Tom, Doug Brado, Gary Huffaker, Howard Hamm, and M. A. Bell. 1986. Discussants at NAEM Open Forum on Strengthening the Exposition Industry's Operations, 27–30 August 1986, in Seattle, Washington.

Mee, William W. June 1988. Trade Shows: This Marketing Medium Means Business. *Association Management* (reprint—pages not cited).

National Association of Exposition Managers (NAEM). (No date.) Introduction to Trade Show Marketing. *Education Module*, mimeo. Indianapolis, Indiana: National Association of Exposition Managers.

National Association of Exposition Managers (NAEM) (No date.) On-Site Operations. *Education Module*, mimeo. Indianapolis, Indiana: National Association of Exposition Managers.

National Association of Exposition Managers (NAEM). 1986. Improving the Relationship Among Exposition Management, Exhibitors, Facilities Management and Suppliers to the Exposition Industry. *White Paper*, 9 pp. Aurora, Ohio: National Association of Exposition Managers.

Nichols, Barbara C., ed. 1985. *Professional Meeting Management*. Birmingham, Alabama: The Professional Convention Management Association.

Teibel, Amy. 1988. Show Managers Seek Extras, as Centers Dig in on Rates. *Meeting News* June 15:3+.

Tongren, Hale N., and James P. Thompson. 1981. The Trade Show in Marketing Education. In *Journal of Marketing Education* 3(2):28–35.

4

Convention Facilities

CHAPTER OBJECTIVES

1. To inventory and define public assembly facilities
2. To explain the concept of comprehensive convention centers
3. To introduce convention center siting, design, and financing
4. To describe convention center facility management and organization
5. To introduce convention center marketing
6. To present the concept of rate structures
7. To overview on-site event management
8. To describe facility profit centers
9. To develop an inventory of current critical issues

INTRODUCTION

At any given time in urban core hotels of major metropolitan areas, a substantial portion of rooms revenue is accounted for by delegates to conventions and meetings. The same may be said for other profit centers within the hotel and, to a lesser extent, other freestanding hospitality concerns. Various economic models also attribute significant retail, transportation, and entertainment sales to attendees and delegates at conventions, meetings, and trade shows.

As noted in Chapter 1, this vast, potentially positive economic impact has not gone unnoticed by states and, specifically, municipalities. The provision of venues and facilities designed to host convention delegates, trade show attendees, sports fans, and other "event-driven" markets has enjoyed steady

City	Date Opened	Space Added (Gross Sq. Ft.)	Existing Space (Gross Sq. Ft.)
Anaheim*	1982	100,000	250,000
Atlanta*	1984	300,000	350,000
Chicago*	1988	400,000	720,000
Dallas*	1984	100,000	420,000
Houston**	1987	600,000	—
Indianapolis*	1984	80,000	140,000
Las Vegas*	1983	120,000	620,000
Los Angeles*	1988	200,000	240,000
Miami*	1987	300,000	280,000
New Orleans**	1985	350,000	—
New York**	1986	680,000	—
Philadelphia**	1988	300,000	—
San Diego**	1988	250,000	—
Seattle**	1987	140,000	—
Washington, D.C.**	1982	320,000	—

* Expansion
** New facility

Exhibit 4.1 Growth in exhibition space, 1982–1988. *Source:* Graveline (1984, 4) Urban Land Institute (ULI) Washington, D.C. Used with permission.

growth since 1970, with over 100 convention centers finished or under construction (Listokin 1985, 43–44).

This building trend has carried forward robustly in the eighties with many new buildings or the expansion of existing facilities. Much of this construction activity is highlighted in Exhibit 4.1.

BENEFITS

Municipalities are finding convention facilities of economic benefit due to the expected large influx of dollars spent in the local economy by convention delegates and others associated with the event. The International Association of Convention and Visitor Bureaus (IACVB) sets average per delegate expenditures at US$477.49 in 1986. When monies spent by associations, exhibitors, and service contractors are added, the economic impact is equal to US$787.54 per delegate at an event that lasts an average of 3.8 days (Gartrell 1988, 26). Depending upon which economic multiplier is applied to these figures, this money stays in the local economy through three to seven rounds of spending before "leaking" out. (*Leaking* is an economic term that refers to money spent outside the local economy for goods, services, and raw materials.)

While this infusion of new dollars is probably the major economic benefit of convention facility construction and operation, a variety of secondary benefits are also cited to justify the large expenditure of tax dollars to pay for or leverage construction of such facilities.

Significant spending of new dollars in a local economy can directly or indirectly impact revenues derived from local and state tax structures. These include state and local sales taxes, hotel or occupancy taxes, food and liquor taxes, and cigarette and other tobacco taxes. Personal income tax revenues paid by employees in convention-related services are also enhanced, as may be "business and occupation" taxes, corporate income taxes, and commercial property taxes (Graveline 1984, 2).

Employer groups in the hospitality industry and labor unions are generally supportive of convention facility construction due to the perceived numbers of "new" jobs created attendant to convention operations. As pointed out by Graveline (1984,2), "hard" statistics are difficult to find, but generally accepted estimates attribute the creation of new jobs in the 1,100 to 1,900 range for each 100,000 convention visitors.

An equally difficult to quantify argument for convention facilities is that of the genesis of ancillary or service-specific private businesses designed to market to convention delegates, associations, and others involved in convention activity. Many of these are the expected hospitality-related developments such as hotels, restaurants, tour concessions, and so forth. Others include convention- or meeting-specific firms such as destination management companies (Chapter 11), exposition service contractors (Chapter 10), transportation companies (Chapter 9), and exhibit design firms (Chapter 8). Development of new or expanded convention facilities may also have a positive impact on such businesses as audiovisual specialists, florists, and a broad range of souvenir and memento purveyors.

The creation of new businesses spawned by a convention center seems to be limited only by the imaginations of the entrepreneurs themselves. In researching this topic relative to the new Washington State Convention and Trade Center in Seattle, Francisco (1987, 18+)found that " . . . businesses ranging from art promotion to human resources seminars have joined the ranks of more traditional convention support businesses like hotels, restaurants and exhibit design firms." Examples of such service-specific businesses found in that investigation were:

- A company that arranges tours, sporting events, and parties
- A firm that designs theme parties
- A company offering seminars on such topics as "peaceful parenting," "learning to love," and "making friends" to spouses and guests of delegates

• Purveyors of "investment art" to selected "high-caliber spenders" from convention delegates
• On-site child care to major conventions

From data displayed in Exhibit 4.2, we can postulate that expenditures for the above sorts of services and products are distributed between retail and other purhcases, and account for 29.1% of 1985 delegate expenditures. This represents an average of US$138.95 per delegate when applied to the US$477.49 figure cited above. In a convention market that attracts 100,000 delegates annually, this represents a potential market value of US$13,895,000 available to purveyors of retail goods and ancillary services.

It should be pointed out that simply building a convention center in most cities is not an automatic guarantee that all of the above benefits will immediately (or even eventually) accrue. This is especially true for cities that are not considered "primary" markets for conventions and meetings.

Primary market cities are those that have large, well-designed convention facilities; large inventories of first-class hotel rooms; an appealing and exciting city image; and good transportation and other infrastructure facilities. "Secondary" market cities that lack even one of the above criteria cannot hope to attract major national and international conventions and have to vigorously complete with all other secondary and tertiary market cities for smaller national, regional, and local conventions, trade shows, and meetings.

The IACVB has developed statistics that document the growth in the conventions market (see Exhibit 4.3). While figures such as these seem to

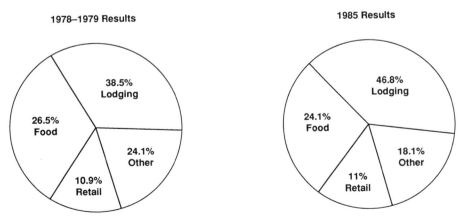

Exhibit 4.2   Distribution of delegate expenditures. *Source:* International Association of Convention & Visitor Bureaus, Gartrell (1988, 25). Copyright Kendall/Hunt Publishing Company. Used with permission.

Year	Number of Meetings (In Thousands)	Number of Delegates (In Millions)
1980	87.1	40.9
1981	n/a	43.3
1982	87.7	47.3
1983	94.2	48.0
1984*	100.1	52.7
1985	126.0	59.0
1986	135.0	65.0

* Estimated

Exhibit 4.3   United States convention activity, 1980–1986. *Source:* 1980–1984, International Association of Convention & Visitor Bureaus (IACVB) quoted by Listokin (1985, 43); 1985–1986, IACVB quoted by Gartrell (1988, 25). Copyright Kendall/Hunt Publishing Company. Used with permission.

reinforce all the positive aspects of convention center development, it must be realized that the largest, richest, and most attractive of these meetings will still gravitate to primary market cities, leaving secondary and tertiary cities to compete for the remainder. Add to this the fact that 77% of association conventions (see Exhibit 2.11) are still sited in hotels, and the marketing picture for new, smaller centers appears to constrict significantly.

According to Quinn (1987, 17), "Even the best-planned convention centers in secondary markets may suffer from the relentless construction of competitive structures nationwide." Another limiting factor in this market is that as the push to build centers develops in secondary markets, many of these new buildings are noncompetitive due to poor location, poor management, badly designed space, and/or lack of adequate high-quality hotel rooms. Facilities such as these "white elephants" (Quinn 1987, 17) become economic drains on the community rather than providing the benefits documented earlier.

Despite negative aspects of overbuilding or inadequate planning, convention centers will continue to be constructed as centerpieces of civic activity in seeking to attract the economic rewards generated by attendees and delegates to conventions, meetings, and trade shows.

PUBLIC ASSEMBLY FACILITIES—CLASSIFICATION

It is important to recognize that the comprehensive convention center is a relatively recent phenomenon. As pointed out in Chapter 1, it has only been in the last 20 years that municipalities have begun to construct buildings whose sole or primary purpose is housing conventions and trade shows. Many cities still rely on other types of public assembly facilities (PAFs) to house or augment hotel meeting facilities in hosting the city's convention attendees.

These other types of PAFs that contribute to a host city's convention space inventory are usually structures that have been erected for some other singular or multipurpose use. Typical of these are (abstracted from Peterson 1989, 6–7):

- Theaters
- Auditoriums
- Arenas
- Stadiums
- Special event facilities (tennis stadiums, horse-racing tracks, motor speedways, for example)
- Exhibition halls

While each of these types of PAF may play singular or multipurpose roles in hosting a convention, none of them accomplish the whole job, nor can they always be counted upon to be available for convention use.

A large domed stadium such as Houston's Astrodome may have sufficient space when configured as a trade show or exhibit facility, but may not be able to provide desirable or adequate meeting, office, banquet, and registration space. Houston's professional football and baseball teams also have contracted to have primary tenant consideration during their respective seasons. Of the 162-game schedule professional baseball schedule, the 81 home games are broken into 3- to 12-game series that require exclusive use of the facility between April and October. This overlaps with football's eight- to ten-game home stands, which commence in August and last through December. When playoff schedules, practice days, and conversion days are considered,the large open spaces offered by such stadiums are probably only marginally appropriate as regular convention venues.

The same arguments can be applied to the other PAFs listed above—their utility as convention sites is inversely proportional to their popular use by primary tenants. Theaters and auditoriums, for instance, are often close to fully booked for repertory groups, ballet companies, and symphonies, each of which has its own scheduling and configuration requirements.

For purposes of simplification, while other PAFs may play greater or lesser roles in a community's convention facility inventory, in this book, a convention center will be defined as follows:

A *comprehensive convention center* is a public assembly facility that is designed to host meetings and exhibits under one roof. It also has provision for banquet, food and beverage, and concession service. The building includes registration space, circulation areas, and other auditorium, theater, or special-purpose areas as required. It is designed and constructed with maximum flexibility in mind.

According to Dan Graveline, director of Georgia World Congress Center in Atlanta, Georgia:

> Today there's a demand for turn-key convention centers. The days are over when a meeting planner was handed a key to the exhibit hall and told to turn out the lights when he left. . . . (Hosansky 1986, 56)

Only a comprehensive center, creatively, responsibly, and professionally managed, can respond to these sorts of market demands.

CONVENTION CENTER SITE AND DESIGN CONSIDERATIONS

In the past, many convention centers were generally little more than large, featureless concrete boxes that added little if any positive aesthetic qualities to their neighborhoods. Additionally, these buildings were often awkwardly sited on the fringes of urban cores far from hotels and other facilities. What these designs and sites may have contributed in terms of flexibility, parking, and truck access, they gave up in terms of attractiveness to their markets. The issues of design and siting involve trade-offs among criteria that are of varying importance to owners, neighbors, operators, and users. As a result, the remote box is swiftly becoming an anachronism among comprehensive convention centers, and many older buildings are undergoing significant remodeling, enlarging, and upgrading.

Because so many site selection criteria will involve considerations necessitated by terrain, politics, land cost, marketability, and other modern facts of development life, it is unlikely that all potentially important criteria will be realized.

Of those trade-offs that exert the most influence on building sites, it is arguable that marketability is of foremost importance. According to Peterson (1989, 20):

> A convention center's occupancy and impact are most influenced by its proximity to support facilities: hotels, restaurants, retail shops, entertainment and local attractions.

Reinforcing Peterson, of the top 15 factors considered "very important" in facility selection by Association Meeting Planners, the following six are directly related to siting and design considerations (M & C 1988, 75):

- Number, size, and quality of meeting rooms
- Availability of meeting support services and equipment, such as audiovisual equipment
- Availability of exhibit space
- Convenience to other modes of transportation
- Proximity to airport
- Newness of facility

The marketing staff of the building and the convention and visitors bureau (CVB) must be able to describe advantages of the building in a market arena that is growing increasingly complex and competitive. Glaring site deficiencies must be balanced by other factors the market finds attractive.

It is becoming apparent that when a community has a choice of sites, the criteria for qualitative evaluation of the choices must consider marketability as a major influence. Exhibit 4.4 sets forth key site screening, marketing, and development criteria considered by "Big Eight" accounting and consulting firm Laventhol and Horwath in their feasibility models for evaluating convention center sites.

KEY SCREENING CRITERIA		MARKETABILITY CRITERIA		DEVELOPMENT CRITERIA	
Site Size and Expandability	(C)	Destination Appeal	(C)	Potential for Joint Operation	(I)
Adjacent Service Roads	(I)	Proximity to Headquarter Hotels	(C)	Impact on Surrounding Land Uses	(C)
Cost of Land	(I)	Proximity to Other Support Hotels	(I)	Economic Impact for Redevelopment	(C)
Capture of Tax Benefits	(C)	Proximity to Other Support Meeting Services	(I)	Stimulus for Additional Hotel Development	(I)
Possible Developer Relationship	(C)	Proximity to Airport	(I)		
Interest by Landholder	(C)	Proximity to Support Services	(C)		
		Access to Regional Highways	(I)		

Legend — (C) Critical (I) Important

Exhibit 4.4 Site analysis factors for convention center sites: qualitative evaluation. *Source:* Abstracted from Peterson (1989, 23) Urban Land Institute (ULI) Washington, D.C. Used with permission.

Of the nine factors considered critical analysis points on this list, three are related to the function of marketing, and all of the marketability factors are related to the concept of centrality of the facility's location. This strongly suggests that the decision criteria on facility selection by meeting planners and convention and show managers will continue to exert a major influence on municipalities' decision processes regarding facility site selection.

Because of the need for exhibition space, meeting rooms, banquet facilities, and public and circulation space, convention centers also have physical requirements that impact the siting decision process and can similarly influence design. The requirement that exhibit halls have up to one million square feet of (ideally) contiguous exhibit space, with 30-foot ceilings, can make a convention center highly visible. In most urban areas, the exterior dimensions and design will likely be required to conform to land-use and design regulations that may include aesthetic requirements. Political and regulatory requirements are varyingly complex, making the visibility of a center an issue that can significantly impact its site and, by implication, design.

Other physical requirements that may impact site selection include parking, truck access, interior and exterior pedestrian access/egress, and provisions for bus transportation of convention delegates and trade show attendees (Peterson 1989, 20–21). These considerations will have impacts that vary depending on the type of events(s) in the building at any given time. Local or regional corporate meetings may require proportionately more parking than a larger, national convention since most attendees at the latter will have arrived by air transport. Similarly, a local market consumer show may have different parking requirements than a national trade show. The national events, though, will have greater requirements for center areas to handle bus transportation for thousands of people.

Whereas convention facilities can be "stacked" on top of parking or parking can be built in adjacent structures, truck access to the exhibit hall level is generally deemed of critical importance. The ability of the center to conveniently and efficiently handle off-loading and loading of exhibit materials impacts marketability to conventions with exhibits, trade shows, and consumer shows. This in turn can significantly influence site selection because of the need for ease of access to trucks arriving from all directions.

Chapter 1 discussed the opening of Detroit's Cobo Hall in the late 1960s as a renaissance in convention center design. The provision of separate meeting rooms; enhanced circulation, registration, and function space; and trade show/exhibition floor space have become the givens of modern center design. Older centers seeking to expand markets and attract or produce new events have had to add to or enhance building designs that have become outmoded, too small, too ugly, or otherwise unmarketable. According to John Temple of

Touche Ross and Company (Quinn 1986, 36), "There are never enough meeting rooms. . .meeting rooms are a big item." As a result, a great deal of renovation in the areas of meeting rooms and exhibit space has been in progress since 1985, with some cities adding major components of exhibition space(Listokin 1985, 44).

Current design must take into account the physical requirements, displayed in Exhibit 4.5, of all comprehensive convention centers. The actual physical measurements of each of these requirements will vary with each project. They will probably be developed through an evolutionary process that combines input from the owner, operator, designer, and various users (Peterson 1989, 26).

An element of consideration that currently influences design is that of aesthetic qualities. Because of siting and development considerations discussed above, more and more communities are demanding a facility that is visually pleasing and/or unobtrusive.

The same philosophy carries inside to the lobbies, reception, registration, and circulation areas. While exhibit halls and meeting rooms need to be distinguished by their flexibility and therefore utilitarian design, the aforementioned public gathering areas are increasingly using glass, covered entrances, courtyards, sculpture, and artwork (Sowder 1988, 2) to aesthetically distinguish the facility.

An advantage of a visually pleasing and distinctive facility is its enhanced marketing image. Center and CVB marketing staff can cast the facility in the best light from the standpoint of the facility's public "face" and its internal

• Exhibition Space	• Service Kitchen(s)
• Ballroom	• Receiving
• Banquet Seating	• Storage
• Meeting Rooms (various sizes and combinations*)	• Mechanical & Service
• Special Rooms**	• Public Toilets
• Center Offices	• Circulation
• Full-Service Kitchen	• Miscellaneous

* Maximum flexibility ideal
** Theatres, arenas, dressing rooms

Exhibit 4.5 Architectural design requirements. *Source:* Abstracted from Peterson (1989, 29) Urban Land Institute (ULI) Washington, D. C. Used with permission.

public areas. To meeting planners and trade show managers who are considering siting their event at that particular facility, these can be influential if all other competitive factors are equal.

Another architectural/design phenomenon currently in vogue in many older cities is that of creatively siting and designing the center in urban core areas. Such designs may utilize parts of existing structures and are not inhibited by previously limiting considerations such as roads, highways, or railway tracks (Ballen 1989, 55). As part of the Pennsylvania Convention Center project in Philadelphia the designers and builders will renovate a train shed. The Jacksonville, Florida Convention Complex converted a historic landmark train station into an exhibit and convention hall. The Washington State Convention and Trade Center in Seattle located its facility in the heart of the urban core over ten lanes of the I-5 freeway, effectively reconnecting a major part of the city that had been bifurcated by the freeway's construction in the mid-1960s. Similarly, the Hyne Center in Boston, Massachusetts, was constructed over a complex of urban core arterials.

A final consideration in this context is the ability of the management of the center to effectively and efficiently operate the building. This is the reason that the evolutionary design process should include representatives of the operator or management as a key part of the design team. It is important that the management of the building be constrained as little as possible by architectural idiosyncrasies of building design.

It should be noted that one trade-off in this particular instance is that of cost. Because recent convention center construction costs have ranged from US$85 to US$300 per square foot (Peterson 1989, 26), ideal architectural design and siting considerations can be mitigated in any given project. In the final analysis, however, the management of the building should be able to operate the building smoothly and not be constrained by design flaws that, once constructed, are extraordinarily difficult to overcome or change.

LEGISLATIVE, FINANCIAL, AND LEGAL ISSUES

No project as complex as a modern comprehensive convention center is conceived, built, and operated these days with less than significant input by state legislatures. In most instances, lawmakers need to pass basic enabling legislation that grants the authorization to use the full faith and credit of the state to secure financing for projects of this scope. There are very few private businesses that are willing to take the risk of financing and constructing convention facilities on their own. This is borne out in a recent survey (Rutherford 1989) that showed 95% of a national sample of 108 primary and secondary market convention facilities were publicly owned.

The fundamental role that legislatures play in the development of the convention center is that of debating and passing legislation that authorizes some specified governmental agency within the state to build such a center. This legislation usually includes stipulations for how the center will be financed and how the center will be governed. Additionally, legislation may provide the center with a charter that stipulates design, construction, operation, marketing, and promotion policy.

While financing may be stipulated by enabling legislation, it may also be chosen by the operating authority from among a number of different options. The most common forms are some type of state or municipal bond issue that relies upon the "full faith and credit" of the issuing entity to generate the sorts of revenues that will retire the bonds and pay interest to the investors. Typical financing methods (Peterson 1989, 51) are:

- General obligation bonds
- Hotel tax bonds
- State grants
- Federal grants
- Hotel tax receipts
- Donated funds

Of these, the most currently popular is the use of hotel taxes to retire state- or municipal-issued bonds. Most state legislatures are increasingly unwilling to make direct grants to a single municipality in the state for the construction of convention facilities, but they are willing to issue bonds in the state's name that can be retired by hotel taxes on tourist, convention, trade show, and meeting attendees in the center's municipal area. This has proven to be a relatively painless method for legislatures to enable facility financing without proposing increases in general tax rates.

In the 1980s, there has been a steadily decreasing willingness of legislatures to commit general funds to these sorts of projects. As a financing option, general funds cannot regularly be considered a viable one. In practical terms, most convention centers are financed with some mix of the options in the above list.

In the modern era, large-scale projects that are publicly financed are increasingly subject to legal scrutiny in a wide variety of ways. Perhaps the first instance in which facility projects find themselves involved in litigation involve the environmental impacts of siting and constructing such a facility. Provisions of the National Environmental Policy Act and the various similar acts on a state-by-state basis usually require environmental impact statements and numerous supporting legal documents. Center policy-makers find that among the first things they need to pay attention to on any given project of this nature are what legal issues are presented.

The next legal relationships occur with contracts for architectural services and construction companies. Some communities impart legal obligations to provide for the construction of low-income housing when units of such housing are destroyed to make way for the convention project.

Cities may legally require a variety of landscaping, aesthetic, and public access considerations. States and municipalities may have affirmative action and minority and women business enterprise requirements for public developments. Similarly, provisions for handicapped access and public use of public developments may have legal impacts on the developing authority.

In the arena of facility operation, legal issues constantly evolve as a result of contracts with various suppliers and consultants. Financial arrangements and occupancy agreements with licensees (the users or renters of the building) have legal considerations. Labor contracts and other agreements the facility may have with various crafts and skilled labor organizations also play a major legal role in the ability of the center to manage its operations.

Overlying all of this is employment law and the recent widely documented problems with liability and insurance. Increasingly, as pointed out in Chapter 3, centers are requiring that licensees purchase insurance and hold the center harmless from any liabilities that arise as a result of the licensees' use of the building. They also require that users of the building provide their own substantial liability coverage while the event is on the premises.

The foregoing discussion only introduces the various contexts of legal issues that face convention facility policy-making boards and managements, but should be considered representative. Legal aspects of center management have mandated an increased reliance on contractual relationships with law firms to manage the legal aspects of the center's operation.

MANAGEMENT AND ORGANIZATION

It is difficult to address the topic of management and operations of a facility as complex as the modern comprehensive convention center without first paying at least passing attention to the concept of what the building is supposed to do. This is usually embodied in some sort of mission statement that not only guides the selection of the management team, but sets the agenda for management's activities on behalf of the owners of the facility. A typical mission statement could read:

> The purpose of the convention center is to provide economic stimulation to the community through creation of jobs, tax revenues and commercial activity. The center will also provide the community with a facility for community events such as

public meetings and local performing arts events. It should be a goal of the center to emphasize commercial activities to the extent that its operation will not require general fund subsidies. (Wallace 1989)

A clear statement of the goals of the owners of the building is necessary in order for management to plan, organize, and design management and control activities that will fulfill the criteria set forth in the mission statement.

Among the more critical aspects of management dimensions that need to be addressed in the operation of a successful facility are (Peterson 1989, 34–35):

- Rental policy and rate structure
- Scheduling and use
- Foodservice concessions and other service contracts
- Parking supply and rates
- Lease terms with tenants
- Staffing and training
- Maintenance levels and expenditures
- Utility costs

Add to these functions the topics of marketing and sales, event and client services, and control and administration, and the fundamentals of a functional organization for a typical convention center emerge as displayed in Exhibit 4.6. Note that this is a generic functional organization chart and, in some instances, lacks specifics that will be unique to individual convention center facilities. It should be noted, however, that each of the activities listed on this chart is fundamental to all convention centers.

The policy-making board or authority for most convention centers represents the ownership of the facility. On behalf of the ownership, the board sets policy and direction for management to follow. With very few exceptions, convention centers are usually owned by the public and operated by some designated board or authority on behalf of the taxpayers of the state, region, or municipality. Depending on the wording of the enabling legislation and, in many cases, political considerations, the policy-making board may be semi-autonomous from legislative activities, or it may be a direct function of the legislature. But, for the most part, as outlined in Exhibit 4.7, most facility operations are directed by either a board of directors or some designated city or county official. This policy-making authority will appoint (again, in various ways) an executive director who may also be called president, chief executive, managing director, or some other title that indicates the focal point between center operations and policy-making authority.

Active day-to-day management may be accomplished in a number of differ-

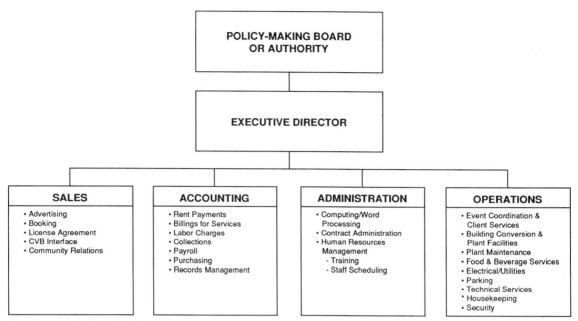

Source: Astor, Kanellos. 1989. Used with permission.

Exhibit 4.6   Functional organization chart for a comprehensive convention center. *Source:* Astor (1989). Used with permission.

ent ways through a number of different organizational structures. It may be a completely publicly-managed entity in which the management structure is staffed by public-sector employees. It may be a quasi-public or non-profit corporate management structure that includes government representation. In rare cases, the facility may be managed by a private company through a

Type	%*
• Board of Directors	37.5
• Municipal Authority or Commission	12.5
• City/County Council	6.3
• City/County Official**	25.1
• StateLegislature	3.8
• Other	15.0

* Percentage total exceeds 100.0 due to rounding.
** Mayor, County Executive, City Manager

Exhibit 4.7   Policy-making bodies for convention centers. *Source:* Rutherford (1989).

management contract arrangement. Each of these management schemes have their attendant advantages and disadvantages, outlined briefly in Exhibit 4.8 (Peterson 1989, 37).

Referring again to Exhibit 4.6, the primary function of the marketing and sales staff is to develop contacts, promote the building, and book events in line with marketing and sales policy of the policy-making authority. The thrust of marketing and sales activities will vary in specific terms from building to building, but fundamentally, it involves promoting and bringing business to the facility by selling the advantages of the building to meeting planners, trade show managers, convention managers for associations, and other potential building users.

Centers have a hierarchy of desirability built into their marketing policy that directs the activities of the marketing and sales staff to concentrate efforts on top priorities. Depending on the fundamental mission of the facility, the top priority for a convention center may be to book international, national, regional, or state conventions and trade shows that will use some predetermined number of hotel room nights during each day of the event. Under this

	Public Management	Authority or Nonprofit Corporation	Private Management
ADVANTAGES	• Owner Control • Financial Support • Coordination/Sharing of Staff	• Government Representation • Special Purpose Role • Increased Operating Autonomy • Independent Revenues • Less Contrained by Purchasing & Civil Service Requirements	• Greatest Operating Autonomy • Efficiency Incentives • Sensitivity to Tenants • Flexibility in Negotiations • More Experienced Staff • Greater Accountability • Less Financial Risk for Government
DISADVANTAGES	• Purchasing Procedures • Civil Service Constraints • Contract Approval Requirements • Changing Policies • Lack of Incentives • Less Responsive to Tenants • Limited Flexibility • Lack of Dedicated Source of Funding	• Subject to Political Influence • Lack of Incentives • Bureaucratic Inertia • Board Membership Loses Status	• Least Government Control • Profit Motive versus Impact Motive • Cost to Smaller Operations

Source: Peterson (1989, 37). Used with permission.

Exhibit 4.8   Advantages and disadvantages of alternative management structures. *Source:* Peterson (1989, 37) Urban Land Institute (ULI) Washington, D.C. Used with permission.

type of policy, space may be held for events of the highest priority as far in advance as required. If the center is marketing to a number of national associations who plan their annual conventions as far in advance as 10–15 years, this policy would allow marketing staff to commit building space as far in advance as the market requires.

Some policy priorities may carry stipulations relative to levels of room nights or number of days that the building would be in use. Others may refer to a certain maximum number of square feet, through, in descending order of desirability, to events that require a shorter sales horizon. Low-priority events, for instance, may be booked no further in advance than 18 or even 12 months. These lower-priority events, by their nature, are typically local events that may not use the entire facility and can be worked in around other major events or concurrently with other local events.

Other activities of the marketing and sales department can include advertising and interfacing with the convention and visitors bureau (CVB). In many cities, the convention facility and the CVB have entered into cooperative agreements whereby the CVB will handle most of the marketing activities for long-term high-priority contacts. This is consistent with the duties of CVBs regarding general promotion of the city and area to conventions, trade shows, and other major events (Chacko and Nebel 1988, 327).

Another potential major activity of the marketing and sales department is to execute what is called the license agreement or contract with representatives of the event being booked. The license agreement is a detailed legal document that outlines the rights, duties, and obligations of both parties relative to the rental of the space in the convention facility.

Once the event is booked and a license agreement is signed, for all practical purposes, the marketing and sales department "hands off" the event to the operations division—specifically to event coordination. An individual event coordinator will be assigned to be in charge of that event in interfacing between the event's sponsors and the building facilities.

The event coordinator works with the meeting planner or show manager to develop a plan of operation, to identify subcontractors who will be central to the success of the event, and to work out and schedule the various details of the event. The coordinator will arrange for building services, discuss and help design the room configurations, and determine the various space needs that the event will require. The job of an event coordinator is analogous to that of the convention services manager in a hotel. In essence, the event coordinator provides and arranges for all of the client services that the user of the building needs. At the same time, the event coordinator serves as a functional liaison between all of the other departments of the building and the client.

In this role, the event coordinator interacts with a number of other functional aspects of the building operation. The event coordinator will arrange for building conversion and other plant facility activities. He or she will work with foodservices and the meeting planner and will also arrange for housekeeping, security, and other technical services. Event coordination is often the most critical single relationship between the building and the planner's execution of a successful event.

Accounting and administration make up the remainder of the basic components of a facility organization and serve the same functions in this context as they do in any other organization. They provide the staff support for the components of the organization who are in active contact with the building's clients and users. Accounting is particularly important because of financial reporting stipulations that may have been made in the enabling legislation creating the center.

Among the most important aspects of the administrative services function are those activities related to the management of the center's human resources. While most modern centers can compete on a roughly equal basis relative to the facilities and amenities they offer their clientele, the area that is considered by many to be most critical is how well the staff of the building serves the needs and wishes of its clients. Increasingly, across the convention industry, more and more importance is being attributed to the hiring and training of high-quality staff. In a survey of convention center managers nationwide (Rutherford 1989), when asked to rate on a scale of one to five the importance of various issues facing convention center managers, respondents rated "staff quality" as the highest of 30 issues (with an average rating of 4.65). Other human resources activities also ranked in the top echelon of those rated (staff training, 4.38; staff recruiting, 3.82).

With the intense competitive environment discussed elsewhere in this book, the success of many convention facilities will be largely attributable in turn to their success at recruiting, hiring, and training high-quality staff with whom to serve the building's clients.

CONVENTION CENTER MANAGERS

Various trade publications explore topics relevant to the managements of all public assembly facilities, but outside of the annual International Convention Center Management Conference, specific managerial research and commentary on convention centers is sparse. While the architectural, finance, and land-use literature can be effectively mined for analysis and commentary of physical and political issues facing the modern comprehensive convention center (see Rogers 1988; Pierce 1988; and Peterson 1988, 1989, for instance), little recent commentary is available about the relatively new profession of convention facility management.

Although issues related to architecture, finance and land use can be documented, the specific managerial challenges facing center directors have yet to be explored in a systematic way. Rutherford (1989) sought to systematically gather, analyze, and present data about convention center managers, their backgrounds, their facilities, and the issues. For the purposes of this book, the data will focus on the background of center managers, the importance of various building services, and the development of an inventory of top convention center management-related issues. The questionnaire, with frequencies, percentages, and means, is reproduced in Appendix 1.

DEMOGRAPHICS

The convention facility managers that responded to this survey are overwhelmingly male (91.3%) and white (93.8%) and average slightly over 46 years of age, as displayed in Exhibit 4.9. Most of them are married and have children. Of the 80 respondents, 56 reported themselves to be college graduates, about a third of whose degrees are in some type of business administration, and two-thirds in a wide variety of disciplines. While the managers reported that they had been in the CEMI as long as 39 years, the average career has lasted about 16 years, with over half of those 16 years at the present facility. Most of the managers report that they have been employed in their present management position for slightly over six years.

Managerial salaries for this sample of center managers ranged from below US$40,000 to over US$100,000; 29% were below US$55,000; 40% were between US$55,000 and US$75,000; and the remaining 30% were above US$75,000. Only 10% reported salaries in excess of US$100,000.

In terms of career satisfaction, this group of managers was very positive, with the overwhelming majority of them reporting that their economic position had improved in the last five years compared not only to others in the CEMI, but to people in managerial positions outside the industry as well. Similarly, they considered themselves successful in the same two comparisons. These are managers whose talents are recognized due to the extent to which they are recruited by other facilities. Over 90% of them reported either an offer of another job or a serious inquiry within the last two years.

Given the public nature of convention center facilities, it is interesting that only 19% of the respondents reported that their current position was one of a civil service nature. Over 70% were either employed with a contract arrangement or employed at will (they can be dismissed at any time).

AGE

28-65 years, *mean = 46.2*

SEX

Male, 91.3%   Female, 7.0%

RACE

Black/Negro/Afro-American, 2.5%
Hispanic or Spanish surname, 1.3%
White/Caucasian, 93.8%
Native American, 2.5%

MARITAL STATUS

Never married, 2.5%
Married, living with spouse, 88.8%
Divorced, 8.8%

CHILDREN

Yes, 93.6%, *mean no. of children= 2.4*
No, 6.4%

EDUCATION

Business Administration Major, 33.9%   Other, 66.1%

EMPLOYMENT

Years in Conventions
& Meetings Industry, 2-39 years, *mean = 15.93*

Years at Present Facility, 1-25 years, *mean = 8.15*

Years in Present Position, 1-25 years, *mean = 6.17*

JOB / POSITION

Civil Service, 19.0%   Employed At Will, 50.6%
Contract Arrangement, 20.3%   Other, 10.1%

Average Number of Hours Worked Per Week
40-50 hours, 22.5%   71-80 hours, 3.8%
51-60 hours, 48.8%   81+ hours, 3.8%
61-70 hours, 21.3%

SALARIES

Range	Percentage
Below $40,000	2.5
$41,000 to $44,999	6.3
$45,000 to $49,999	7.6
$50,000 to $54,999	12.7
$55,000 to $59,999	7.6
$60,000 to $64,999	17.7
$65,000 to $69,999	6.3
$70,000 to $74,999	8.9
$75,000 to $79,999	11.4
$80,000 to $84,999	1.3
$85,000 to $89,999	2.5
$90,000 to $94,999	3.8
$95,000 to $99,999	1.3
Over $100,000	10.1

PERCEPTIONS

Economic Position, as compared to others *in/outside*
of the Conventions and Meetings Industry, has:

	In	Outside
Improved markedly	34.2%	15.4%
Improved moderately	47.4%	52.6%
Stayed the same	15.2%	10.3%
Worsened somewhat	1.3%	21.8%

Success in Career (as compared to other facility
professionals in terms of age and qualifications):
Very successful, 56.3%   Very unsuccessful, 1.3%
Fairly successful, 42.5%

Perceived Satisfaction with life *outside* of the
Conventions and Meetings Industry:
More satisfied, 7.5%   Less satisfied, 48.8%
Equally satisfied, 43.8%

OUTLOOKS

During the past two years:

Considered leaving Conventions Industry permanently
    Yes, 31.3%   Yes (but not seriously), 27.5%   No, 41.3%

Sought out or made serious inquiry about another position
    Yes, 31.3%   Have not sought, but made serious inquiry, 27.5%   Neither, 41.3%

Received job change offer or inquiry of availability
    Yes, have received offer, 47.5%   Not an offer, but a serious inquiry, 43.8%   Neither, 8.8%

Exhibit 4.9   Convention center managers' demographic and career data.

BUILDING SERVICES

One area in which centers emphasize commercial activities in order that operations not require additional tax fund subsidies is through the offering of services to clients as "revenue enhancers," "profit centers," or "deficit reducers." Increasingly, centers are internalizing the offering of these services, which in the past were sold mainly through exposition service contractors (decorators) or specialty service contractors. To measure the extent that these services are important as revenue sources to convention centers Rutherford (1989), provided a 21-item list of potential services and asked center managers to rate the importance of each service as a revenue source (if offered in-house). The top five are displayed in Exhibit 4.10, with the provision for electrical service to exhibitor booths being the revenue-generating winner with a mean rating of 4.32 from the 65% of centers who operated and offered this service to clients.

It should be pointed out that as a profit center, the most important activity offered by convention centers is that of food and beverage services, including both catering and concessions. For convention centers nationally, income from food and beverage operations "can constitute more than 25% of all income" (Peterson 1989, 34).

In the sample studied by Rutherford (1989), 80% of managers reported that a private contractor handled foodservice through some sort of exclusive catering contract that provides for specific levels of income to the center. This becomes all the more important when considered with the reported average of nearly 27 conventions with exhibits, 15 trade shows, and 66 non-convention-related food and beverage events annually. With the average convention or trade show lasting three days or more, the importance of food and beverage

Service (Importance rated from 1 to 5)	Mean Rating
1. Electrical Service	4.32
2. Telephone	3.25
3. Stage Construction/Lighting Service	3.18
4. Plumbing, Drain, Air	3.05
5. Sound Services	3.04

Note: These are the most valued services of those centers that offered them in-house, and are exclusive of foodservice

Exhibit 4.10   Top revenue sources. *Source:* Rutherford (1989).

services becomes all the more apparent to the revenue structure of the modern convention facility.

Increasingly, to avoid being deemed by legislatures and taxpayers as the economic "white elephant" alluded to earlier, centers have become very aggressive in the management and sale of services to their clientele.

MANAGEMENT CHALLENGES AND ACTIVITIES

Since there is a paucity of empirical management literature on details of professional challenges to convention center managers, those in this study were asked to consider a number of issues, challenges, and activities culled from trade literature, speeches, presentations, and interviews that suggest at least a possible universe of job-related issues. They were then asked to judge each of these in two contexts:

- How important this issue or activity was to them in their job on a scale from one (little or no importance) to five (of utmost importance)
- To provide an estimate of time spent on that activity on an annual basis judged on a scale from one (virtually no time) to five (a great deal of time)

The 80 respondents' ratings were then averaged, yielding a mean rating for each of these issues and activities. By rank-ordering the mean ratings for importance and time, one can gain a picture of those activities and issues that the managers find most important and time-consuming. The entire list is reproduced in Appendix 1. The top ten in terms of mean rating are presented in Exhibit 4.11.

IMPORTANCE	Mean Rating	TIME	Mean Rating
1. Staff Quality	4.65	1. Budgeting Responsibilities	4.05
2.5. Managing Facility Personnel	4.44	2. Managing Facility Personnel	4.03
2.5. Budgeting Responsibilities	4.44	3. Staff Quality	3.93
4. Creation/Generation of Revenue Sources	4.41	4. Dealing with Operations Manager	3.87
5. Staff Training	4.38	5. Creation/Generation of Revenue Sources	3.86
6. Public and Community Relations	4.29	6. Relations with CVBs	3.71
7. Dealing with Operations Manager	4.27	7. Dealing with Sales Managers	3.67
8. Relations with CVBs	4.05	8. Public and Community Relations	3.61
9. Strategic Marketing (18 mos. and beyond)	4.04	9. Working with Chief Accountant	3.55
		10. Working with Director of Event Coordination	3.53
Scale — 1 = of little or no importance; little or no time		5 = of critical importance; large amounts of time	

Exhibit 4.11   Management issues rated by importance and time consumption.

Of the issues and activities that fall into the top ten list rated as to their importance, those of staff quality, managing facility personnel and staff training, and dealing with the operations manager all have a strong personnel component associated with them. This suggests that center managers place a high priority on working with and through the facility's staff.

The twin issues of budgeting and creation or generation of revenue sources point up the importance of fiscal matters and revenue generation to the convention facility manager. Many convention facilities, because of the nature of their funding, are operating on budgets that are created for many years in advance. It becomes incumbent upon the facility manager to accurately predict what budget realities will be for the policy-making authority or legislative body. At the same time, because facilities are increasingly pressured to be something other than "loss leaders," finding and generating the sources of revenue assume a similar order of importance for the facility manager.

The remaining entries on this important list relate to tasks and activities the facility manager must accomplish in the external environment. Public and community relations are increasingly important aspects of doing business in a modern convention center. There are a number of publics that need to be served—governmental entities of the state, the county, and the municipality; the hotel community, which depends heavily on the convention center to generate room sales; and members of the general business community, who are increasingly placing a higher level of importance on retail sales to visitors from out of town or out of state.

Another public that must be served and, in many cases, worked with closely as outlined previously in this chapter, is the convention and visitors bureau. As stated earlier, many CVBs and convention centers have a cooperative marketing role and it is in that context that relations with the CVB and the concept of strategic marketing for the facility are closely linked.

It needs to be pointed out that the importance placed on public and community relations highlights the visibility that the convention center has in the community. Positive public and community acceptance appears critical to the management of the convention centers surveyed in this research.

Like all managers, the time to accomplish tasks is significantly different from the importance placed upon them, and such is the case with the convention facility managers. In all instances, the time managers reported spent on issues was statistically significantly lower than the importance they placed on each activity. That the majority of items they spend their time on and those ranked as high in importance were the same suggests that these managers have their priorities in order and are spending time, for the most part, on issues and activities that they feel to be most important.

The center managers reported that dealing with sales managers, chief accountants, and directors of event coordination took up significant amounts of their time. This demonstrates that time consumed on externally focused activities may be considered of greater strategic importance. In the near term, the managers reported more time on personnel- and operations-related activities. This suggests the immediacy that day-to-day operation issues take in the consumption of time devoted to managerial activities.

The job of convention center manager is emerging as a recognized profession. Among the issues that will gain more importance to such managers will be those related to professionalism, certification, and education of facility managers. These are issues that, according to the managers in this survey, assume average priority in terms of importance, but have less than average amounts of time devoted to them annually. At the International Convention Center Management Conference, issues of professionalism and certification and education are topics of general and specific discussion sessions. It is through the continued professionalization of center management positions that convention facilities will continue to improve and become closely identified with the prescription implicit in the following quote:

> The quality of management and marketing influences the occupancy and financial operating performance of a project more than any other factor. Professional and aggressive management can influence the supply of product (events) for the building, provide well-organized services to the tenant or event producer, and give the attendee an enjoyable and productive visit to the building.
>
> Strange as it may seem, many managers have been recruited and buildings have been operating long before the owner had defined the building's operating objectives. (Peterson 1989, 34)

Management, therefore, is among the most critical of all factors to the success of the modern convention facility. Professionalism, creativity, imagination, and experience brought to the chief executive function of a convention center will be the most sensitive measure of that center's success.

FOOD AND BEVERAGE

As mentioned in Chapter 1, the quality of foodservice at conventions and meetings was considered to be the most important factor by 80% of corporate planners responding to the survey done by *Meetings and Conventions Magazine* (1988). The importance to delegates, attendees, and their representatives is mirrored in the importance of foodservice in a number of different ways to the success of the modern convention center.

As centers and their managements continue to seek out ways to enhance revenues and identify profit centers among their operations, food and beverage service remains the predominant source of revenue and profit for most convention centers. Indeed, it is the most important source of revenue for some convention centers, even eclipsing the amount of revenue collected from the rental of exhibition and meeting room space. A recent study (Laventhol and Horwath 1988, 1) demonstrated that the revenue produced by food and beverage operations can vary from 10 to 50% of rental income.

The largest generator of food and beverage revenue at conventions and trade shows was fine dining catering, with average nationwide per capita revenues across all sizes of buildings of US$2.64, from a range of US$0.05 to US$7.15 (Laventhol and Horwath 1988, 2).

Food and beverage revenues will vary with the type of facility, type of event, size of facility and region of the country. It will also vary based on the mix of foodservice opportunities within the building. A typical breakdown of food and beverage service offerings in a convention center are (in order of importance as revenue sources):

- Food and beverage catering
- Concessions
- Restaurants
- Lounges
- Vending

Convention foodservices are organized in a number of different ways, but most typically they are either publicly manged in-house by a facility's staff or contracted to an outside foodservice company. If contracted, there are two different schemes by which the foodservice is handled: (1) an exclusive catering contact where the foodservice company has responsibility for all foodservice within the building; and (2) an "open" catering contract wherein there are a number of authorized caterers who have access to the building's equipment and spaces depending on the wants and needs of the client. Recent evidence suggests that 81% of foodservice is contracted to outside companies, and of those, 87.5% are on an exclusive catering contract basis (Rutherford 1989).

Convention centers, catering management companies, meeting planners, and show managers are now deeply involved in working together to use foodservice as a common selling point not only for the facility but for the event. It is in the best interest of show managers and convention mangers to promote high attendance, and one way to accomplish that is by holding the event at facilities that have an outstanding reputation for food and beverage service. In other words, if foodservice is driving people out of the facility, the event will be less than a success not only for the meeting planner, but also for the facility. Foodservice in all of its forms for the conventions and meetings industry will be discussed in more depth in Chapter 12.

RATES AND RATE POLICIES

Exhibit space is usually rented on the basis of net square feet (NSF) per show day. Net square feet usually means 50% of the gross square footage of the exhibit area because of the need to account for aisles and circulation space. Meeting rooms without exhibits have separate rate schedules. These rates are applied under most circumstances to three types of events:

- Convention with exhibits or trade show
- Commercial exhibit or paid-admission public show
- Meeting space, usually no exhibits

Obviously, some of the variables that apply to rental rate structures will not apply in every instance. The major variables for each type of event are highlighted and briefly discussed below:

- The competitive range of **cost per net square foot (NSF) per show day** varies around the country but in most instances is between US$0.10 and US$0.25 per NSF per show day. In an instance where a show manager is renting 10,000 square feet of an exhibit hall for three days at US$0.15 per net square foot per day, his or her total outlay to rent that hall would be US$4,500 (10,000 × 0.15 × 3).
- Another method by which convention centers charge for exhibit space is on the **net square foot basis for the run of the show,** in which there is a larger charge that includes move-in, move-out days as well as show days. For example, a center may charge US$0.50 per net square foot, which covers the total charge for the duration of the trade show and will include a specific number of move-in and move-out days. Move-in and move-out days are allowed either on a negotiated basis depending on the complexity of the show, or according to some ratio related to number of show days.
- In the event that the show runs over schedule, or the show manager or meeting planner has difficulty accomplishing move-out, most centers will usually levy an **extra day use** charge according to some specified and contracted formula that can range from one-quarter of the minimum rate per show day to one cent per gross square foot of space unavailable to the center per day.
- Most halls will require some **minimum charge** for the use of the facility to prevent the facility from being underutilized. For instance, a small ten-

booth show in one segment of a large exhibit hall effectively precludes that entire segment from being rented. Most centers will have a policy that there will be a minimum charge no matter how much of a particular hall a show takes up. These charges can range from US$0.02 per gross square foot of the hall per show day, to US$0.20 per gross square foot of the hall per show day.

- Most centers and convention/show managers will negotiate an **amount of free exhibit space** that the show manager can use for scientific, educational, nonpromotional use and display. For example, in large industrial trade shows, the show manager may allot a number of free 10′ × 10′ booths to professional societies and universities or trade schools to set up their displays and exhibits.
- Another negotiated item is **amount of free meeting room space** allowed to the tenant group. In most cases this is a subject of negotiations, but it ranges from all meeting rooms being free if all exhibit space is used to a ratio of meeting space per gross square footage of exhibit space.
- Increasingly, **items included in exhibit hall rental** are being limited by convention centers to a minimum of cleaning aisles and certain public areas; the remaining potential options in customizing the building by the show manager must be purchased from either the center or service contractors.

In the case of commercial exhibits in a gate-admission public show, the following variables apply: Building rental is usually some lump sum against a percentage of gross revenues and receipts for the show; move-in and move-out dates are negotiated and allowed on much the same basis as they are for a convention with exhibits and trade shows; extra day-use charges are negotiated, but can range from one-half the daily rate to some set lump-sum figure per day; and minimums are usually on a lump-sum basis or a percentage of gross receipts, much the same as the cost for building rent.

When a group wishes to rent meeting space only, with no exhibits, rates are usually applied on a lump-sum or per capita basis. These can be based on the number of rooms required or the number of attendees at the function. Equipment included with the rent almost always includes some basic setup of chairs and tables. Other options—microphones, sound systems, audiovisual systems, custom room setups—are usually subject to extra charges. Events using only meeting room spaces can incur extra charges for room changeover from, for instance, a meeting room to a meal function. These may be included in the price of the rent or may be charged for on the basis of the actual staff-hour rate required to do changeovers and special requests.

While most facilities have a policy against negotiating rental rates, there is a tremendous amount of room for compromise on other charges that the event can incur. Whereas rates per net square foot are usually established by the policy-making board on advice from the center management, other ancillary and additional charges may be negotiable between the center and the event planner.

Facilities may, however, offer rate discounts during off-season or nonpeak periods. Because of aggressive competition and the need to fill hotel rooms, convention centers and their representatives at CVBs are becoming more aggressive in negotiating and discounting. This is particularly true in those periods when hotel rooms need to be filled during slack seasons.

INTERACTIONS

It can safely be said that at any given time during the conception, marketing, planning, and execution of any particular event, the center will interact with varying intensity with virtually every member of the CEMI. However, the highest order of interactions can generally be categorized into two general headings: external interactions or internal interactions.

External interactions refer to work that the center staff accomplishes with and through other members of the CEMI on activities related to booking the event.

The other major external interactions, discussed earlier, are the activities undertaken by the executive of the center to discharge public and community relations responsibilities with neighbors, businesses, political entities, and other organizations that have an interest in the success of the convention center.

The majority of other interactions are internal and related specifically to the management of individual events. In this context, center staff and management will work closely with meeting and convention planners of associations, corporations, and other groups. Exposition managers will have regular contact with center staff members before, during, and after events. The center staff and management will also work closely with decorators and other service contractors who are associated with the physical production of events. These members of the CEMI, among others, are critical to the success of not only the events but, by extrapolation, the center itself.

ISSUES AND CONCLUSION

Specific issues and challenges that face the management of modern convention centers are many and varied. In addition to those discussed as part of the center manager's job earlier in this chapter, they generally fall into two categories related either to people or to the design and construction of the facilities themselves.

A number of facilities have been criticized for not allowing sufficient **size and scope of registration and circulation areas.** Additionally, convention facilities typically need **additional meeting rooms** as pointed out earlier. Along with the provision for additional meeting rooms, show managers and meeting planners would like to see better **loading facilities,** more **parking** and **storage areas,** and more **flexible meeting and breakout rooms** that can be divided into a number of different configurations.

Many show managers would also like to see facilities offer more and **larger expanses of exhibit space** that do not have columns and include higher ceilings and built-in provisions for utilities. Center managements would like to see centers **designed to be user-friendly** and management-friendly. Managers do not want to be locked into a design that is inflexible, difficult to configure, and therefore uncompetitive.

People-related issues range from the concept of professionalism for managers and staff throughout the entire industry to the various personnel **staffing and training** issues discussed above. Another people-related interaction issue is that attendant to the **relations between convention centers and hotels.** A specific problem that occurs in some markets relates to the center booking policy. Hotels in some cases are finding themselves in an ambivalent "love-hate" relationship with the center whereby they need desperately for the center to book events that fill up hotel rooms, but when the building is not used by a major convention, hotels are very wary of any commercial activity on the part of the center that might be seen as taking catering and meeting room business away from the hotel.

Political realities also present ongoing challenges and impacts to the ability of center staffs to manage their facilities competitively. In many instances, there is **legislative second-guessing** or tampering that significantly affects the activities of center management in effectively and efficiently marketing and operating the facility.

The modern convention center is critical to the success of primary, secondary, and, increasingly, tertiary cities' abilities to market themselves as convention and meeting destinations. While it is true that most corporate and association meetings are still held in hotels, the increasingly expanding market of major city-wide conventions and trade shows will mandate that such activities be sited in facilities that can comprehensively host large events under one roof.

The future of convention centers is therefore contingent on the marketing abilities of the host city, the ability of the CEMI members in that city to interact positively, and the political will of legislative bodies to establish and make provisions for the funding of modern, attractive, and efficient convention centers.

REFERENCES

Astor, Kanellos J. 1989. Convention Center Organization (Internal working document) Group 2+ International, Inc., Bellevue, WA.

Ballen, Anne. 1989. Form and Function. *Association Management* February: 53–56, 204.

Chacko, E. Harsha, and E. C. Nebel III. 1988. The Convention and Trade Show Business. In *Introduction to Hotel and Restaurant Management, A Book of Readings,* 5th ed., ed. Robert Brymer. Dubuque, Iowa: Kendall-Hunt.

Francisco, Lynn. 1987. Convention Center Is Spawning Many New Firms. *Puget Sound Business Journal* October 19:18+.

Gartrell, Richard B. 1988. *Destination Marketing for Convention and Visitor Bureaus.* Dubuque, Iowa: Kendall-Hunt.

Graveline, Dan. 1984. Convention Centers. *Urban Land* July:2–5.

Hosansky, Mel, et al. 1986. The Evolution of an Industry. *Meetings and Conventions Magazine* June: 48–67.

Laventhol and Horwath. 1988. Exhibition Hall Industry Annual Report. Tampa, Florida. Laventhol & Horwath Sports and Convention Facilities Service, mimeo, 7 pp.

Listokin, David, 1985. The Convention Trade: A Competitive Economic Prize. *Real Estate Issues* Fall/Winter: 43–46.

M&C/Meetings and Conventions Magazine. 1988. *Meetings Market '87.* Secaucus, New Jersey: Reed Travel Group.

Peterson, David C. 1988. Convention Centers: A Matter of Commercial Development *Urban Land* 47 (11):32–33.

Peterson, David C. 1989. *Convention Centers, Stadiums and Arenas.* Washington, D.C.: Urban Land Institute.

Pierce, Lawrence W. 1988. Tax-Exempt Financing for Convention Centers. *Government Finance Review* 4(6):40–43.

Quinn, Lawrence R. 1986. Growing Up in America. *Facility Manager* Winter 1(3):32–37.

Quinn, Lawrence R. 1987. For Convention Centers, an Uncertain Future Looms. *Facility Manager* 2(3):15–19.

Rogers, Michael C. 1988. Convention Centers: Analyzing Your City's Needs, Capacities. *Nation's Cities Weekly* 11(4):6.

Rutherford, Denney G. 1989. Convention Centers and Their Managers. Research in progress, Washington State University, mimeo.

Sowder, Robert R. 1988. Convention Center Planning: An Examination of the Critical Issues. *Trade Show Bureau Report* September: 7 pp.

Wallace Robert C. 1989. Bellevue, WA. Convention Center Task Force. (Internal Working Document).

5

Meeting Planners and Convention Managers

CHAPTER OBJECTIVES

1. To introduce the concept of modern meeting and convention management
2. To define the roles played by various meeting planners
3. To outline the types of meeting planners
4. To explain the interactions between meeting planners and other members of the CEMI
5. To provide a basic knowledge of the scope of meeting planning activities and responsibilities

INTRODUCTION

This chapter will introduce the reader to the theory and practice of modern meetings management. Specifically addressed will be meeting professionals and their roles in the management of a modern meeting or convention. This will include an overview of the details attendant to meeting planning activities, taking the meeting from its original concept through premeeting evaluations and decisions to executing the meeting and following up with activities designed to provide evaluation and control.

As pointed out in Chapter 1, over the last 20 years, the job of meeting planner has changed and evolved in a number of different ways. Most importantly, perhaps, it is becoming increasingly recognized as a separate profession within business environments. As such, meeting planning has become more complex and sophisticated. Meeting planners, therefore, have had to become true managers in the classic sense of the word *management*. They participate not only in **planning,** but **organization** and **leadership** activities; they **coordinate** and **communicate**; and maybe most importantly, they **control** the details that are attendant to the management of a meeting or convention.

If meetings and conventions are not executed with attention paid to the principles of management, they may be unsuccessful by a number of different criteria, probably the most important being financially. No company or association wants to be in the position of having its annual conventions or other types of meetings be effective fiscal drains on the entity's resources. Implicit here is a broad challenge to the professionals who plan meetings in the modern era to become more than *planners*. This chapter will develop ideas, practices, and data about planners that will focus on evaluating this professional challenge.

Meetings can range in size from a small five- or six-person event to a large and complex annual national convention for an association or trade group that may attract over 100,000 attendees. The small meeting may have a specific single goal and can be held on company premises or another location appropriate to the event, its goals, and attendees. The convention may fill every hotel room in an urban area and fully utilize the meeting and exhibit facilities at a number of hotels and/or a comprehensive convention center.

Between these two extremes lies the majority of events planned, managed, and executed by meeting planners. In many ways, the term *meeting planner* has become only a partially appropriate term for the activities that may be involved in executing an event as complex as a large national convention. Many associations now refer to their meeting planners as convention managers. For the purposes of this book, however, the two terms, *meeting planner* and *convention manager*, will be used interchangeably with emphasis on the use of the term *meeting planner*, because it is the term in most common use throughout the CEMI currently.

WHAT IS A MEETING PLANNER?

As pointed out earlier, 20 years ago the term *meeting planner* was virtually nonexistent in the lexicon of business activities. It is a measure of the growth of the CEMI that to corporations and associations *meeting planner* has become a common term for that individual in an organization whose duties consist in whole or in part of planning the details attendant to meetings of various types and sizes.

It is because of the variability of types and sizes of meetings and varieties of organizations that a precise definition of the term *meeting planner* is difficult to derive. Some meeting planners or convention managers spend 100% of their professional activities planning events for their organizations. This may be especially true in large national associations that count heavily on attendance and revenues from annual conventions and trade shows to financially support the activities of the association. According to Dotson (1988, 5), "Only two percent of corporate planners are full-time, while six percent of association planners are full-time meeting planners. An average of 28% of association managers spend from one-third to two-thirds of their time planning meetings, and 48% spend less than one-third of their on-the-job time on meeting planning. On the other hand, 78% of corporate planners spend less than one-third of their time on meeting activities."

These data suggest that while meeting planning has become more well recognized as a profession, only in a small number of cases is it something the corporate or association employee does on a full-time basis. The other segments of these people's jobs are distributed across other activities in their organizations. According to one study (M&C 1988, 47), the majority of corporate planner job titles fall in the general categories of corporate administration, sales, marketing, or advertising (73%). In this study, only 9% reported that their job title included reference to meeting or exhibit planning. The same study (page 85) reported a different breakdown of association job titles, with 48% of the meeting planners reporting that their job title included some reference to meetings, conferences, or conventions.

The meeting planner in these instances is an individual who does more than just plan a clearly defined linear activity called a *meeting*. Meeting planners manage all the details, activities, and interactions of meetings, from the meeting's conception through the categories of activities depicted in Exhibit 5.1, which conclude with evaluation and future planning.

Major activities (site selection, negotiation, program planning, for example) are arrayed around the outside of this circular diagram. On the interior of the diagram, in no particular hierarchy of importance, are displayed those members of the CEMI with whom the meeting planner will work as an intermediary on behalf of the meeting planner's client population. The meeting planner will interact with these CEMI members on an occasional, regular, or intensive basis that varies with the temporal proximity of the event or the timing of any individual stage of the event.

The central focus of meeting planning activities, therefore becomes the coordination of products and services from other professionals in order that the event can be executed.

Because the meeting planner serves as coordinator and manager of so many

Exhibit 5.1 Meeting planner activities, interactions.

diverse and varied activities relative to a meeting or convention event, perhaps a working definition, for the purpose of this analysis, might be along the lines of that proposed by Bitner and Booms (1989, 1–3):

> A meeting or convention planner is an intermediary in the travel distribution system who links business travelers with travel services, and coordinates the details of that linkage to produce a successful meeting or convention.

Key to understanding the central focus of a meeting planner's job is the phrase "details of linkage." In many cases, this is where the success or failure of any given event is decided. It presupposes that the planner has the professional knowledge to understand the universe of possibilities available and to choose from those possibilities which particular linkages and which members of the CEMI are best equipped to serve the purposes of the meeting or convention event.

TYPES OF MEETING PLANNERS

The diversity of organizations, nationally and internationally, has led to an amalgamation of "types" of meeting planners based on their primary organizational affiliation. Easily identifiable are the following generic types of meeting planners:

- Corporate meeting planners
- Association meeting planners
- Government meeting planners
- Independent or private meeting consultants

Emerging:
- Association management companies
- Travel agencies

Corporate meeting planners are employees of businesses who have as one of their responsibilities (but not necessarily their primary responsibility) the planning and execution of the details of meetings for the corporation's employees, management, and owners. This may or may not include activities related to the marketing function of exhibiting at trade shows, but the meeting- and convention-related activities within any given corporation can now be more easily identified and associated with a specific individual than in the most recent past.

With the number of corporate meetings reliably extrapolated at over 800,000 on an annual basis (M&C 1988, 1), this represents an increase of over 100,000 from the 1985 Meetings Market Study by *Meeting and Conventions* magazine. These corporate meetings were planned for an annual attendance in 1987 of over 47 million people, which represented a 19% increase from the 1985 study (M&C 1988, 3).

It can thus be comfortably stated that in most large companies, planning and executing the details of meetings at this volume level is no longer something the boss can simply foist off on a secretary. The importance and costs associated with such meetings make it imperative that they achieve their goals in the most expeditious and fiscally responsible manner. This calls for professional attention by someone whose training, qualifications, and experience qualify him or her as a professional meeting planner.

Association meeting planners are usually full-time paid employees of professional, trade, industry, scientific, and other types of associations. As we pointed out in Chapter 2, most of these types of associations have as part of their bylaws the provision for at least one national membership meeting and one or more regularly scheduled meetings of the association's board of directors. Depending on the size and financial resources of the association, it may employ a full-time professional as meeting and convention planner. *Meetings and Conventions Magazine* (1988, 11) reports that 97% of association planners are involved in planning a major convention, of which 68% plan one per year. The total number of conventions planned by association respondents to the 1987 survey had grown to nearly 13,000 for the year 1987, with an average delegate attendance of 848 (M&C 1988, 11).

Additionally, association meeting planners reported being involved in the execution of board meetings, educational seminars, professional and technical meetings, regional and local chapter meetings, and other meetings that may be required by the association executive board, staff, or membership.

Government meeting planners exist at all levels of government, from the smallest municipality to the huge bureaucracies of the federal government. Only recently have people who plan meetings for the various governmental organizations been recognized (at least informally) as a separate job category. Through their national association, the Society of Government Meeting Planners (SGMP), these planners have organized and worked to further professionalize these activities, which are no less common in government posts than they are in private industry or voluntary associations.

Government meeting planners face additional challenges from a budgetary standpoint. In most instances, government departments have extremely limited travel and lodging budgets, and government per diem (that amount of money allotted to anyone traveling on behalf of the government) is modest at best, and seldom if ever are exceptions made for high-cost areas. Government meeting planners, therefore, must plan meetings and gatherings around some fiscally limiting criteria that are more restrictive than those of other categories of meeting planners.

That should not diminish in any way the scope of the job, however, for it remains fundamentally the same whether in the public or private sector. The same sorts and kinds of details as depicted in Exhibit 5.1 exist for government planners as for the others. The government planners just have to be more creative with limited financial resources.

Independent or private meeting consultants are usually individuals or small firms who provide meeting planning services directly to corporations, associations, and other groups for a fee (Bitner and Booms 1989, 9). They function as intermediaries and arbiters of CEMI interactions. They do it, however, for a profit as opposed to a salary paid by any particular organization.

Association management companies perform tasks and services for associations similar to that of the paid association executive and staff, but act on behalf of associations that do not have their own full-time professional staff. As such, these management companies may provide management services on behalf of two or more associations through their individual boards of directors. As a part of this management package, they will provide meeting planning and convention management services to their clients (Bitner and Booms 1989, 9).

Travel agencies have only recently become involved in the CEMI as anything other than a supplier of travel services to meeting planners. Increasingly, travel agencies are offering various meeting planning services to clients. Many travel agents have begun handling the details of meetings for corporate business accounts in addition to planning travel itineraries. In this way, corporations that are already closely associated with an agency as a travel intermediary can take advantage of the agency's contacts with hotels, transportation, and foodservice firms to package meeting details along with travel details. This results in a trend toward centralization of corporate purchasing for travel-related services through the corporation's travel agency accounts (Leo 1986, 41).

It has been suggested that some of the larger corporate entities with major travel budgets will shift meeting planning activities toward travel agencies and disband or reassign their meeting planning personnel. These activities by travel agents have created controversy within the meeting planning profession, and it remains to be seen at this date how successful travel agencies will be in offering meeting planning activities. One drawback to a travel agent as a meeting planner is the requirement for intensive on-site presence to manage the details associated with major meetings. Only if travel agencies are willing to commit the personnel, time, and travel budgets to these meeting management tasks will they be able to effectively compete with professional in-house meeting planners.

One further distinction has been made among types of meeting planners within the last year. A study commissioned by the Educational Foundation of Meeting Planners International (MPI), and reported at MPI's annual convention in Seattle in 1988, categorized a *meeting manager* as a "principal planner" for an organization, and therefore responsible for "policy, budget, implementation, evaluation and all other aspects of key meetings" (Shure 1988, 32). This can be contrasted with the other category, *facilitator*, whose activities do not involve many of those key decisions, but whose authority extends to specific details of the meeting. The meeting manager, therefore, may be a direct representative of corporate or association policy-makers and has authority and responsibility for the meeting's overall execution; whereas a facilitator is one who carries out specific details of the meeting at the direction of the manager with limited authority and responsibility.

As meeting planning has emerged as a separate profession, these professionals have formed their own associations to promote professionalism, set standards, debate issues and ethics, and generally participate in all of those activities that associations perform on behalf of their membership as described in Chapter 2. Among the preeminent groups who represent meeting planners and convention managers specifically are:

- **Meeting Planners International (MPI)**, whose membership is open to all types of meeting planners—corporate, association, private, and others. Membership is open to affiliate members such as suppliers of services to meetings and conventions.
- **Professional Convention Management Association (PCMA)**, a professional organization for meeting planners who were originally specifically associated with the various health care and medical associations. Membership is now open to other professional meeting managers and suppliers. Additionally, a PCMA foundation administers educational programs for the profession, suppliers, and college and university students.
- **Society of Government Meeting Planners (SGMP)**, discussed earlier, is open to those who plan meetings, events and conventions on behalf of various government agencies. It is also open for membership by supplier groups.
- Additionally, **specialty meeting planner groups** can be found representing nationwide industries such as the insurance industry and religious conference planners.

TYPES OF MEETINGS

Meeting categories can generally be divided among those planned by corporate planners in the business environment and those for which association planners are responsible. Exhibit 5.2 outlines the major types of corporate and association meetings identified by a recent meetings industry survey (M&C 1988).

Corporate meetings from this study project a total of over 807,000 attendees, accounting for an average of 12 off-premises meetings executed by corporate planners for the period covered by the survey. Although management meetings accounted for only 19% of total meetings, planners were most intensely involved in the details attendant to management meetings. Over time, substantial changes have been identified in the new product introduction category, which reports a significant decrease in numbers since 1983, and incentive trips, which have nearly doubled since 1985 (M&C 1988, 9–10).

The data reported here for association meetings are in addition to planner activities related to the association's annual convention. The overwhelming majority (97%) of association planners, however, are involved in planning a major convention, and 19% of respondents reported scheduling two per year.

CORPORATE		ASSOCIATION	
Type	**Percentage of Total Meetings**	**Type**	**Percentage of Total Meetings**
Management Meetings	19	Board Meetings	21
Regional Sales Meetings	17	Educational Seminars	36
Training Seminars	26	Professional/Technical Meetings	19
National Sales Meetings	9	Regional/Local Chapter Meetings	17
New Product Introductions	6	Other Meetings	7
Professional/Technical Meetings	9		
Incentive Trips	8		100
Stockholder Meetings	3		
Other Meetings	3		
	100		

Exhibit 5.2   Major types of meetings. *Source:* Meetings and Conventions, 1988. Meetings Market '87. Reed Travel Group: Secaucus, NJ (9, 13). Used with permission.

Numbers of conventions have increased since 1979, from 10,300 per year to 12,700 in 1987. This represents an increase of 23% in the number of conventions planned and executed by association staffs (M&C 1988, 11–12).

Other than conventions, association planners accounted for a projected total of 181,700 meetings of the types outlined in Exhibit 5.2. Board of directors meetings and educational seminars combine here for a healthy 57% of all meetings. As noted in Chapter 2, many associations hold more than one board meeting each year, and some may hold as many as one per quarter. The projected number of total meetings in this study represents a small decrease (2%) over a similar study conducted in 1985. This may suggest that associations are combining some of the meetings from this list with annual conventions or dropping or rescheduling meeting activities that may have only marginal utility.

MEETING PLANNERS: QUALITIES, COMPETENCIES, AND COMPENSATION

No matter what sort of organization a planner works for and whether or not the planner can be considered a meeting manager or a meeting facilitator, planners must exhibit personal and professional qualities that prepare them for working within the diverse milieu that comprises the CEMI. This can mean that on any given day a planner will interact with a variety of hotel employees from top management to housekeeping and maintenance personnel. A typical day may also find the planner involved in negotiations with the sales staff of a convention facility and interacting with show managers, labor union representatives, and food and beverage directors. Therefore, of all the qualities that meeting planners may exhibit, perhaps the most critically important are highly developed **negotiation skills.**

Because so many corporate and association meetings and conventions span more than just the borders of one country, the meeting planner must additionally be **culturally adept.** It is important to realize that an increasingly varied number of people who represent different cultures and social fabrics may be attending any given event. As such, it is therefore important for planners to be sensitive to the sorts of challenges these situations can present. Planners may find themselves having to learn about elements of international protocol unheard of in planning meeting events in the most recent past.

Perhaps the quality that incorporates elements in the previous two is that if **diplomacy.** In any situation where multiple negotiations are going on, particularly involving culturally diverse clientele or audience, being able to accomplish objectives without offense may be of paramount consideration to the success of the event.

Finally, meeting planners increasingly need to be **creative.** Enough people have been to enough meetings and conventions that a certain sameness can creep into the structure. Planners are finding an increasing need to be continually looking for ways in which to accomplish the goals of the meeting that not only have practical validity, but concomitantly pay attention to the public's need for "something different."

Adding something different to planned events should not be viewed as merely a cosmetic change. It must be seen in today's competitive business environment as substantive and as furthering the goals of the corporate or association meeting; otherwise, it will be viewed as a waste of money. The opportunities, however, are virtually limitless for a planner to provide entertainment, logistics, speakers, and program events at meetings and conventions that are pertinent to the goals of the event and at the same time enjoyable and memorable to the attendees and delegates. Budget considerations, of course, are the major limiting influence.

Given these qualitative attributes, what sorts of quantitative or measurable factors are important to a meeting planner in his or her career? Part of that question can be answered by looking at the general categories of functions, the mastery of which is tested for in the Certified Meeting Professional (CMP) examination administered on a regular basis through the Convention Liaison

MEETING PLANNING FUNCTIONS

1. Establishing Meeting Design & Objectives

2. Selecting Site & Facilities

3. Negotiating with Facilities

4. Budgeting

5. Handling Reservations & Housing

6. Choosing from Transportation Options: Air & Ground

7. Planning Program

8. Planning Guidebook, Staging Guide, Documentation of Specifications

9. Establishing Registration Procedures

10. Arranging for and Using Support Services: Convention Bureau, Outside Services, Hospitality Committee

11. Coordinating with Convention Center or Hall

12. Planning with Convention Services Manager

13. Briefing Facilities Staff: Pre-Meeting

14. Shipping

15. Planning Function Rooms Setup

16. Managing Exhibits

17. Managing Food & Beverage

18. Determining Audiovisual Requirements

19. Selecting Speakers

20. Booking Entertainment

21. Scheduling Promotion & Publicity

22. Developing Guest & Family Programs

23. Producing & Printing Meeting Materials

24. Distributing Gratuities

25. Evaluating: Post-Meeting

Exhibit 5.3 Certified Meeting Professional (CMP) question categories. *Source:* Convention Liaison Council, quoted by Colby 1986, 10. Used with permission.

Council in Washington, D.C. (Colby 1986, 10). The meeting planning functions and knowledge tested for in this examination, with the approximate number of questions typically asked in an exam, are abstracted in Exhibit 5.3.

These functions and activities will be discussed in subsequent sections of this chapter. They are presented here to given an overview of what the meeting planning segment of the CEMI finds a quantifiable inclusion in its certification examination.

Meeting planners are generally found in mid-management positions in corporate organizations, either in corporate administration or associated with some function under the marketing umbrella. In associations, they are more likely to have a title that specifically includes meeting planning as part of their functions. In either event, corporate and association planners for the most part are also responsible for other duties in addition to planning meetings and conventions.

FUNCTION	SALARY (US$)	INCREASE/ DECREASE (%)
Corporate Meeting Planner	28,919	+8.1
Corporate Executive with Meeting Planner Duties	>50,000	+7.9
Association Meeting Planner	28,999	+8.1
Association Executive with Meeting Planner Duties	38,999	+7.0
Government Meeting Planner	41,659	+5.4
Educational Institute Meeting Planner	32,909	+6.7
All Planners	34,219	+7.6

Exhibit 5.4 Average meeting planner salaries by job function. *Source: Meeting News* November 1987:1. Used with permission.

Exhibit 5.4 lists typical salaries for meeting planners, with percentage increases over previous reporting periods. The average for all planners is slightly more than US$34,000, with association and corporate meeting planner salaries within US$1,000 of each other. The salary increases reported at all levels for all types of meeting planners are indicative of the importance that is attached to this function in corporate and association organizations. It also suggests that the complexities and sophistication required to execute the functions of modern event and convention planning are such that they will be compensated at attractive levels.

MEETING PLANNER FUNCTIONS AND ACTIVITIES

This section is intended to provide an overview and introduction to the central managerial functions and actual activities performed by a meeting planner creating and executing a meeting or convention event. As an overview, key elements will be presented. Should the reader desire more breadth and depth of detail, comprehensive presentations are available in *Professional Meeting Management* through the Professional Convention Management Association (PCMA) and the *Convention Liaison Council Manual* from the Convention Liaison Council (CLC). *Professional Meeting Management*, in particular, provides great depth and breath of meeting planner functions and activities, and includes pro forma organizing materials relevant to specific activities.

The inventory of a meeting planner's activities will, of course, vary from event to event and depend on the type of event, the size of event, the objectives of the event, and other variables that were discussed earlier in this chapter and elsewhere. But for purposes of overview organization, the meeting planner activities can be broken down roughly equivalent to the three time frames outlined in Exhibit 5.5 as stages of the event. For each stage, there are a number of primary management focuses that serve as an umbrella under which specific activities generally occur.

Pre-Event Functions and Activities

The central focus of managerial functions at this stage of the meeting revolve around planning, organizing, and staffing for the event. Meeting planners have varying amounts of time available to them for planning specific meetings, but generally speaking, the smaller and more focused the objectives of the meeting, the less lead time is required by meeting planners and managers. In the realm of corporate meetings, planning incentive award trips or national sales meetings require the longest lead time—an average of close to seven

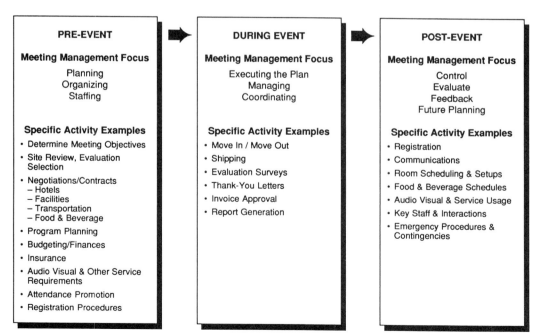

Exhibit 5.5 Array of meeting planner functions/activities.

months for both types of meetings. Other categories of corporate meetings require an average of about 3.7 months; association meetings other than conventions typically take five to five and a half months to plan and execute, with conventions requiring slightly over eight months of planning time (M&C 1988, 37, 73).

These time allotments, of course, will vary according to type of planner and type of meeting. As seen in Exhibit 5.6, corporate and association planners

MEETING PLANNING ACTIVITY	Reported spending "Great Deal" or "Moderate" amounts of time with designated meeting planning activity.	
	CORPORATE PLANNER	ASSOCIATION PLANNER
Selection of meeting hotel or other facilities	70%	89%
Selection of meeting location	66%	86%
Decision to hold off-premises meetings	62%	74%
Planning entertainment, social functions, sports tournaments	65%	78%
Planning of meeting agenda	77%	77%
Establishing meeting expenditures/budget	70%	85%
Establishing meeting objectives	75%	67%
Rental/Purchase of audio-visual equipment	46%	53%
Planning for air travel arrangements	62%	52%
Planning for car rentals	49%	38%
Planning for ground transportation (not including car rentals	47%	41%
Trade show planning or exhibit planning	65%	**
BASE	(787)	(488)

* Those with decision-making authority/responsibility over policy, budget, etc. (Shure 1988, 32).

** Trade shows only associated with annual convention, not generally applicable to other association meetings, but may be at corporate gatherings.

Exhibit 5.6   Principle Planner* time allotments. *Source:* Meetings and Conventions Magazine, 1988. *Meetings Market '87.* Reed Travel Group: Secaucus, NJ (44, 81). Used with permission.

differ significantly in the amounts of time reported on the activities of selecting meeting facilities and locations, dining, entertainment, and social functions and developing budgets for these and other activities.

While determining meeting objectives may be part of the decision process of others within the organization, association meeting planners are deeply involved in the site review, evaluation, and selection of not only the locale for the meeting, but the facilities within that locality. Exhibit 5.7 depicts factors considered important in the selection of a destination site by corporate and association planners. Note that association planners' importance considerations are divided between conventions and other association meetings.

Because corporate meetings may take place on a one-day basis in a local or regional locale, they may not require overnight facilities, although they do. But conventions obviously have a high requirement for hotel rooms, and their suitability and importance are brought out by the fact that 84% of association

FACTORS CONSIDERED "VERY IMPORTANT"	CORPORATE PLANNERS	ASSOCIATION PLANNERS	
	All Types of Meetings	Conventions	Association Meetings
Availability of hotels or other facilities suitable for meetings	68%	84%	65%
Ease of transporting attendees to/from location	57%	53%	50%
Transportation costs	46%	35%	37%
Distance from individual attendees	44%	28%	44%
Climate	28%	32%	14%
Avalability of recreational facilities, such as golf, swimming, tennis, etc.	26%	26%	15%
Glamorous or popular image of location	12%	16%	8%
Sightseeing, cultural, other extracurricular attractions	11%	21%	9%
Mandated by by-laws	n/a	15%	8%
BASE	(724-735)	(389-431)	(355-387)

Exhibit 5.7   Factors considered important in selecting a destination. *Source:* Meetings and Conventions Magazine. 1988 *Meetings Market '87.* Reed Travel Group: Secaucus, NJ (38, 74). Used with permission.

planners considered the availability of hotels very important in this particular study.

The other factors considered important do not vary greatly between corporate planners and the association meeting planners, although there are some differences in the factors that relate to transportation. The distance from individual attendees, for instance, may be less important in consideration of a convention site because as a national event, some members of the association are going to be coming from far corners of the country. No matter where the event is held, this may hold more importance to associations whose membership is unevenly distributed geographically than to those whose members come from a wide variety of regions and locales.

Sightseeing, cultural, and other extracurricular activities, by the same token, may be slightly more important in the convention realm than to other meetings because of provisions for pre- and post-event vacations, spouse programs, and on-site recreational activities.

It should be pointed out that not only are physical aspects of the destination site considered important by planners in the decision-making process, but people also influence these decisions. A study by Heidi Bloom (1981, 47) demonstrated that meeting planners also paid considerable attention to recommendations from other planners, others in the organization, and hotel sales representatives, suggesting that "grapevine" activities and personal contacts also have a significant bearing on the decision-making process. However, brand loyalty is apparently not a large factor among planners, many of whom say that under most circumstances, it is very difficult to differentiate among the rooms, facilities, and amenities offered by the major hotel chains (Lowe 1984). It may be, therefore, that all other things being equal, planners with decision-making responsibility may rely heavily upon their own personal experience and the recommendations of others in their profession.

The site selection process may find the meeting planner, along with corporate and association executives, traveling on "familiarization and sales trips" to a number of potential sites for major meetings. In the case of smaller, more specialized meetings, the planner may rely on personal experience relative to the type of meeting and its objectives. Other site selection variables that will help determine the appropriateness of any individual site include:

• Who will attend
• Size of the group
• Meeting program
• Physical requirements for the program
• Length of total meeting and individual sessions

- Quality and quantity of hotel room requirements
- Quality and quantity of food and beverage requirements
- Recreation and entertainment
- Prestige or image desired
- Group history data
- Budget

These decision criteria are consistent with what is considered important by meeting planners in the development of the CMP certification program. They are also widely discussed on an annual basis in the meeting planning literature (Shure 1987 & 1988).

Once the site has been reviewed and evaluated and the selection process is completed, the meeting planner, perhaps with the participation of association or corporate executives, enters into negotiations and the signing of contracts with suppliers of meeting services. These can include hotels, convention facilities, transportation companies, food and beverage caterers, destination management companies, and other members of the CEMI. Their common function is the provision of goods and services to the planner during the execution of the convention or meeting.

A number of variables exist relative to services, products, and facilities negotiated for by planners on behalf of any meeting or convention. Because they are variables, they are subject to change under any given set of circumstances. What is important to understand from the types of variables listed here is the realm in which planners have to actively participate on behalf of elements that can significantly contribute to the success of the event. A list of pre-event activities that is neither exclusive nor exhaustive can include:

- How to calculate attendance
- Arrival and departure dates and patterns
- Ratio of complimentary rooms
- Coordination with housing bureaus for city-wide conventions
- Room rate considerations
- Occupancy determinations
- Hospitality suites
- Reservation forms
- VIP reservations and suite allocations
- Tax structures—sales and occupancy taxes
- Rates for meeting rooms
- Rates of exhibit space
- Rates for buses and their schedules
- Release of facility—time and dates

As can be seen from this list, the elements of any particular meeting or convention event can be varied and complex. The skill with which the planner negotiates these and other requirements with suppliers contributes substantially to the success of the meeting or convention event.

One supplier that assumes a central focus of negotiations is the facility at which the event is to be held. Facility negotiations and subsequent contracts are dependent upon the type and size of the meeting. Exhibit 5.8 outlines the types of facilities that corporate and association planners have used for conventions and meetings.

From this data, midtown and resort hotels still garner the lion's share of the conventions and meetings business from both corporate and association planners. Convention centers are not listed in Exhibit 5.8, but it should be noted that in those major conventions planned by association planners that included exhibits and displays, 41% of those events were planned in convention centers; the remainder were held in hotels or other facilities.

TYPES OF FACILITIES AT WHICH MEETINGS WERE HELD IN THE PAST YEAR	CORPORATE PLANNERS	ASSOCIATION PLANNERS	
	All Types of Meetings	Conventions	Association Meetings
Midtown hotel	57%	49%	70%
Resort hotel	47%	30%	36%
Suburban hotel	44%	16%	34%
Airport hotel	28%	5%	29%
Suite hotel	13%	5%	7%
Condominium resort	7%	3%	3%
University owned conference center	7%	2%	10%
Privately owned conference center	19%	1%	11%
Cruise ship	4%	*	*
Did not use overnight accommodations	n/a	2%	n/a
(Multiple Types of Facilities Mentioned)			

* Less than .5%
n/a = Not available

Exhibit 5.8   Types of facilities used in the past year. *Source:* Meetings and Conventions Magazine. 1988. *Meetings Market '87.* Reed Travel Group: Secaucus, NJ (40, 76). Used with permission.

From these types of facilities available to the planner, the decision process incorporates evaluation factors regarding the facility or hotel that are important to the success of the particular meeting or convention. Exhibit 5.9 outlines the factors considered very important by planners in the choice of facility or hotel.

Note that while quality of food service is a vehicle of importance to corporate planners and associations planning conventions, it does not assume quite as high a priority for association meeting planners. Similar to differences found between conventions and other meetings relative to site selection are the differences reported here in a selection of the facility or hotel. Because of

FACTORS CONSIDERED "VERY IMPORTANT"	CORPORATE PLANNERS	ASSOCIATION PLANNERS	
	All Types of Meetings	Conventions	Association Meetings
Quality of food service	80%	80%	63%
Number, size and quality of meeting rooms	68%	85%	59%
Efficiency of billing procedures	57%	n/a	n/a
Meeting support services and equipment	57%	54%	32%
Number, size and quality of sleeping rooms	56%	74%	40%
Efficiency of check-in/check-out procedures	51%	60%	42%
Assignment of one staff person to handle all aspects of meeting	47%	51%	33%
Previous experience in dealing with facility and its staff	43%	47%	37%
On-site recreational facilities; i.e., golf, swimming, tennis	28%	24%	8%
Proximity to airport	25%	20%	24%
Special meeting services such as pre-registration, special equipment, etc.	22%	22%	8%
Convenience to other modes of transportation	21%	23%	21%
Availability of exhibit space	21%	43%	7%
Number, size and quality of suites	15%	25%	9%
Proximity to shopping, restaurants, off-site entertainment	14%	27%	11%
Newness of facility	8%	4%	3%
BASE = Those answering for each item, ranging from	735-749	440-447	370-387

n/a = Not asked this question.

Exhibit 5.9   Factors considered important in the selection of a facility/hotel. *Source:* Meetings and Conventions Magazine. 1988. *Meetings Market '87.* Reed Travel Group: Secaucus, NJ (39, 75). Used with permission.

the different requirements for a convention, the number, size, and quality of meeting rooms, particularly the number of meeting rooms, will have a higher order of importance to the planner.

Also of greater importance to the association convention planner are those facility measures linked to meeting support services, sleeping rooms, and the efficiency of check-in and check-out procedures. Check-in and check-out procedures and the ease by which meeting planners can move their people in and out of a facility are particularly important to convention planners because of the details that coalesce at a meeting's commencement and the variety of travel arrangements that need to be catered to at the meeting's conclusion.

Finally, the availability of exhibit space will be more important to convention planning than to the execution of other meetings.

A recent study (Renaghan and Kay, 1987, 76) underlines the importance of the number, size, and quality of meeting rooms through research that suggests the provision of the greatest ratio of space to participants as a major point in a meeting planner's selection criteria. Another recommendation of this study was to allow meeting room users to have more control over the inside environment of the meeting rooms relative to sound, light, and climate controls. While they gathered no empirical data on the issue of personnel in the facilities and the competence of the facility's staff, this issue was the most frequently mentioned problem between meeting planners, hotels, and convention facilities.

Attention given to all of the above details is critical, but usually not enough to assure a meeting's success. Meetings must also be substantive (not perceived to be a waste of time) and they should be memorable for all of the right reasons. This highlights the quality of creativity discussed earlier in this chapter. First and foremost, however, the meeting's purpose and the activities designed to achieve the organization's meeting objectives must be provided for. The rooms must be reserved, speakers must be contracted for and scheduled, general and breakout sessions must be planned and timed, and meal breaks and social functions must be interspersed at the proper times in order for the entire program to be possible to execute and manage in an expeditious fashion. To be substantive, speakers and meeting sessions must each bear elements relative to the successful achievement of the meeting's objectives. From that point, the planner has only the restrictions of his or her budget to intersperse other activities and event elements that can make the meeting fun, memorable, and creative.

In many ways, the budget is an appropriate metaphor through which to present the remaining details associated with pre-event planning functions. Exhibit 5.10 displays a sample pro forma functional expense budget for a

EXPENSES	AMOUNT (US$)		PERCENTAGE
Program Development and Production			
Program committee expense	$ 1,200		
Abstract printing, distribution, selection	3,120		
Speaker honoraria, travel, lodging	2,600		
Program production	9,500	$ 16,420	6.00
Board and Committees			
Travel, lodging	10,100		
Meeting expenses	1,500	11,600	4.24
Promotion		4,700	1.71
Exhibits			
Promotion, prospectus	2,700		
Decorator, drayage	84,00		
Posterboards	2,000		
Security	5,300		
Exhibit space rental	9,200	27,600	10.00
Registration			
Badges, forms	1,900		
Personnel	2,100		
Computer analysis	3,500	7,500	2.74
Audio-visual		10,200	3.73
Social Functions			
Tickets	450		
Opening reception	20,000		
Banquet	35,000		
Awards Luncheon	19,000		
Coffee breaks	3,000	77,450	28.30
Operations and Overhead			
Staffing and overhead	75,000		
Telephone	8,500		
Duplication	5,300		
General postage	9,800		
Insurance	2,400		
Staff travel, lodging	1,700		
Meeting room rental, setups	9,300		
Extra microphones	1,100	113,100	41.34
Contingency		5,000	1.83
TOTAL EXPENSE		$ 273,570	99.89
*			

* Does not equal 100.00% due to rounding.

Exhibit 5.10   Sample functional expense budget for meeting *Source:* Professional Convention Management Association (1985, 85). Used with permission.

fictitious meeting. Included are dollar amounts and category percentages of total expenses budgeted for the meeting. Note that nearly 70% of a planner's budget is devoted to personnel staffing, administrative overhead expenses, and production expenses related to social, food and beverage, and coffee break functions.

Other expense categories outlined here suggest the relative importance of

INCOME	AMOUNT (US$)	PERCENTAGE
Registration fees		
Member (400 members x US$75 fee)	$ 30,000	10.88
Non-member (600 non-members x US$90 fee)	54,000	19.58
One-Day (125 people x US$25 fee)	3,125	1.13
Exhibit space rental		
(125 booths x US$800 average booth rental)	100,000	36.25
Social functions		
Opening reception	25,000	9.06
Banquet	38,000	13.78
Awards luncheon	20,000	7.25
Investment income	5,700	2.07
TOTAL INCOME	**$ 275,825**	**100.00**

Exhibit 5.11   Sample functional income budget for meeting. *Source:* Professional Convention Management Association (1985, 87). Used with permission.

these functions and are roughly analogous to the importance placed by planners on the other categories of planning functions discussed earlier.

Perspective on the expenses detailed in this budget may be gained by addressing the pro forma functional income statement in Exhibit 5.11. Whereas budget expenses for promotion of exhibits only account for 10% of the expense budget, the exhibit space rental provides more than 36% of the planner's total income for the event. Also, while expenses for the social functions take up over 28% of the expense budget, they only account for 30% of meeting income. In dollar figures, social functions bring in US$83,000, but cost US$77,450 to produce. It should therefore be obvious why planners and associations place a high value on the provision of trade shows and exhibits at their annual conventions.

Investment income, as reported here, is usually associated with long-term planning for conventions and is derived from preregistration monies that are either banked or invested on behalf of the association. Any interest income that accrues from those sorts of investments are typically applied to the income statement for the event.

Other activities suggested by the expense budget outline and listed in Exhibit 5.5 as part of the pre-event planning process deal with audiovisual and other service requirements that may be provided by exposition service contractors, the hotel, or specialty suppliers in the conventions field. Insurance, discussed in Chapters 3 and 4, is also becoming a more significant aspect of a meeting planner's managerial challenge. For any given event, it may represent significant expense and negotiating time.

Finally, the meeting will not be a success unless a certain critical mass of attendees are encouraged to participate. Strategies and tactics to encourage participation in meetings and conventions at which attendance is not compulsory is an important element of pre-event planning and organizing activities. This may be more critical to convention management than it is to meeting planning because participation in the various corporate and association meetings other than conventions is often mandated by organizational authority or, in some cases, self-interest.

Functions and Activities During an Event

The central functional focus of this time frame involves, for the most part, setting the plan in motion. The meeting planner will arrive at the site and facilities several days in advance of the first attendees and double-check all of the arrangements negotiated, contracted, and planned for in the previous time frame. Perhaps the key management function involved at this stage is the planner's ability to coordinate the activities of a wide variety of professionals operating in a number of different, physically remote areas. At any given time (depending on the size of the event), a meeting planner may have activities going on at more than one hotel, a convention and trade show facility, and entertainment or recreational sites around the meeting's facility. Similarly, VIPs, speakers, and guests are coming and going according to their own schedules and requirements.

At the same time, the planner must make sure that speakers are in the right rooms, meeting materials are distributed, coffee breaks and social functions are set up for proper service, head counts at banquet and cocktail parties are accurate, and the audiovisual equipment is setup and working at the time and place required. If this sounds hard to do, it is.

Increasingly, shortwave radio-based communications are a fundamental requirement for a planner and his or her staff to monitor, coordinate, and execute the details of meetings and functions at multiple sites or in multiple rooms at the same site (Hoyle, Dorf, and Jones 1989, 311–312).

Key people with whom the planner interacts during the execution of the meeting are the event coordinator at a convention center or the convention services manager in a hotel. The facility sales manager, the trade show or exposition manager (if appropriate), and the manager of destination services, if utilized, will be responsible to the planner for key parts of the meeting's plan. The decorator or exposition service contractor and a representative of the food and beverage caterer round out the major CEMI actors who play roles in most event productions.

An emerging trend in convention facilities and hotels is for there to be one key interactive contact person between the facility's organization and the client using the building. Whether that individual is a facility's event coordinator or a hotel's director of convention services, his or her primary task is to serve as the focal point, interfacing all hotel or facility departments on behalf of the client meeting planner.

Some facility organizations have formalized this arrangement to the point of using it in their advertising. These advertisements suggest that the convention services manager (CSM) assumes operational control of the hotel on behalf of the planner. One such ad is that of the Palmer House in Chicago, displayed in Exhibit 5.12, where the hotel underscores the value of a planner's meeting business by altering its organization chart to reflect the importance of the CSM interface. Chapter 6 will develop additional aspects of the CSM's tasks and importance to not only meeting planners, but also the hotel.

Some meeting planners have described their activities during the execution of their event as basically "putting out fires." In most instances, that is meant *figuratively*, meaning they have had, on frequent occasions, to deal with contingencies that are outside the scope of the planning that had taken place up to that point. One measure of success for a meeting manager is how well he or she is able to anticipate potential contingencies and have in place the resources and knowledge with which to deal with them. These can range from speakers not showing up, through problems with audiovisual equipment and foodservice, to true emergencies of a medical or safety nature. Strategies for such contingencies should be part of all meeting planners' calculus. Other emergencies can include demonstrations, confrontations, and weather emergencies such as snowstorms, hurricanes, or earthquakes.

Labor strikes or labor shortages are also part of emergency planning that most meeting planners need to at least consider. It is wise for meeting planners to ask hotel, facility, and transportation managers what sorts of labor arrangements they are involved in, at what stage contracts are, and if labor unrest might be anticipated during the time of the scheduled meeting or event. Fire represents another potential emergency for which hotels and facilities will have contingency plans. It is important for the meeting planner to be familiar with each facility's emergency plans in order to participate in dealing with any fire emergency that might arise.

Post-Event Functions and Activities

Wrapping up the meeting or convention event is not simply a matter of turning out the lights, closing the doors, and turning the key over to the hotel or convention center. Central managerial functions at this stage involve activities that represent control, both in terms of financial and physical assets;

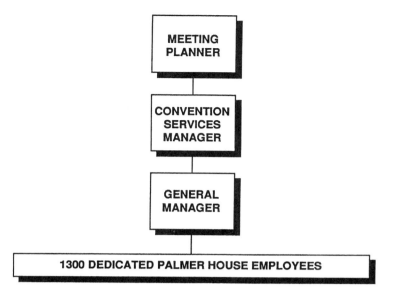

When you meet at The Palmer House we do more than rearrange the rooms.

We rearrange our organization. So that meeting planners have instant access to the hotel's top management.

Before, during, and even after an event, our staff of 1,300 dedicated employees provide outstanding service to meet your needs. Our entire organization is here to help chart your course to success.

In addition to our reputation for excellent service, The Palmer House offers: 38 meeting rooms in Chicago's most complete meeting facility, Conference Center 7; 36,000 square feet of exhibition space, and more.

Seventeen hundred guest rooms and suites are just an elevator ride away, as are five luxurious ballrooms, and one of the top hotel fitness centers in the country.

So give our Director of Sales a call and see just how well you'll fit in at The Palmer House.

The Palmer House.

A Hilton Hotel

A Pleasure to do Business With.

The Palmer House · 17 East Monroe Street · Chicago, IL 60603 · (312) 726-7500

Exhibit 5.12   Copyright 1989 The Palmer House. Used with permission.

evaluation; feedback; and implications for future planning. Increasingly, at this stage, meeting planners demonstrate their true managerial acumen, for it is here that the relative success of any event is evaluated. This evaluation, in turn, provides planners the information they need to modify plans for future meetings of the same type and provide essential feedback to association or corporate officers. Exhibitors, show managers, and other members of the CEMI who were linked to the execution of the event also depend on evaluation data to track the success of their participation.

Move-out activities will generally be mandated by the various contracts that the planner has signed on behalf of his or her organization. Among the stipulations in a convention facility, for instance, may be that the event must be physically out by a certain time. Signage might be required to be changed back to some preestablished form; and decorations, balloons, and other evidence of building customization for an individual event will probably have to be removed. Rental equipment needs to be returned, and charges, fees, and invoices need to be settled. The planning staff is also responsible for shipping office supplies, association or corporate equipment, and capital back to the home office.

Evaluation typically consists of some tabulation of judgments by the various categories of participants so that the planner and association or corporate officials have data upon which to judge the success of the event. This evaluation procedure may be informal, or it may be a formal, scientifically designed survey performed by a professional meeting evaluation company.

In either event, the results will assist planners and their organizations in evaluating the current event and planning for future events. Attendees may be asked to rate meal, social, and entertainment functions. Most importantly, however, business sessions, general sessions, breakout group activities, and speakers are the focal point of planner post-event inquiries. It is through this feedback that the company or association can accurately tabulate its success at achieving the meeting or convention goals.

Exhibitors at trade shows and expositions are surveyed about aspects of their participation in the event. Questions may ask about booth traffic, quality of attendees as sales leads, exhibitor goal realization, and details of show mechanics.

A related activity is the generation of statistics and reports that serve to enhance the results of evaluation surveys. Typically, statistics will be gathered about registration, ticket sales, and income from social events. Public relations activities, as measured by press notices and numbers of press members in attendance, may also be of importance, especially to large trade organizations. Data need to be generated for various suppliers in order that they might judge the relative success of their contribution to the event (McGee 1985, 90–91).

Other data that may be important to meeting planners, not only in evaluating an event but in positioning for future event negotiations, can be gathered about the following (Letwin 1984, 105–106):

- **Rooms used by attendees:** Accurate counts of singles, doubles, suites.
- **No shows:** What percentage of room reservations not used and not canceled; compare to historical data.
- **Restaurant/bar use:** Did attendees significantly impact hotel's food and beverage services?
- **Room service:** How was hotel impacted?
- **Audiovisual equipment:** Level and types of usage.

In some locales, planners will have agreed to accumulate data and generate a list of suppliers and hotel and facility employees who are traditionally the recipients of meeting-related gratuities. Planners will then disburse funds based on some previously arranged formula.

Other financial arrangements a meeting planner needs to manage are invoice and disbursement approvals, auditing of hotel and facility master accounts, verification of food and beverage attendance, and determination of staff hours, salaries, and benefits.

Finally, most meeting planners will have accumulated a list of people whose contributions to the event helped make it a success. These people will be the recipients of acknowledgment and thank-you letters complimenting them on their help, service, and professionalism. Planners who are meticulous about proper acknowledgment of services rendered gain positive reputations as people who represent events that are desirable to host in a city, hotel, or convention facility.

CONCLUSION

In this chapter the concept, scope, and functions of modern meeting and convention management in the person of the meeting planner have been overviewed, discussed, and exemplified. Various types of meeting planners have been identified, and their roles have been abstracted. As these planners go about discharging their responsibilities, they interact with and generate business for a diverse population of CEMI members. In so doing, they play significant roles in the generation of economic activity within the CEMI.

Meeting planners function as true managers in that they practice the functions of management in carrying out the activities outlined here to produce a given event. It should be pointed out that the activities discussed throughout this chapter are only representative of the myriad of details that face the modern meeting planner. The reader should be aware that the universe of possibilities overviewed in this chapter merely suggest the complexity of the tasks involved in these sorts of events. Attention again is drawn to selected works and references that provide additional breadth and depth of detail relative to the job of the modern meeting planner.

REFERENCES

———. 1987. Meeting Planner Salary Survey. *Meeting News* November: 1.

Bitner, Mary J., and Bernard H. Booms. 1989. *Channels of Distribution in the Tourism Industry*. Seattle: Washington State University, work in progress.

Bloom, Heidi. 1981. Marketing to Meeting Planners: What Works? *Cornell Hotel and Restaurant Quarterly* 22(2):45–50.

Colby, Lincoln H. 1986. The Certified Meeting Professional (CMP) Program: Who Really Benefits. *The Meeting Manager* October: 8–12.

Dotson, Penny C. 1988. *Introduction to Meeting Management*. Birmingham. Alabama: The Education Foundation of the Professional Convention Management Association.

Englander, Todd. 1986. How to Negotiate with Convention Centers. *Meetings and Conventions* July: 55–62.

Hoyle, Leonard C., David C. Dorf, and Thomas J. A. Jones. 1989. *Managing Conventions and Group Business*. East Lansing, Michigan: The Educational Institute of the American Hotel and Motel Association.

Leo, Darrell. 1986. The Travel Agent . . . Wolf at the Door? *Meetings and Conventions* February: 39–43, 113.

Letwin, Robert. 1984. Convention Management: It's Not Over When It's Over. *Successful Meetings* June: 105–108.

Lowe, James. 1984. A Study of the Meeting Planner Market. Unpublished Master of Professional Studies Thesis, Cornell University.

M&C/Meetings and Conventions Magazine. 1988. *Meetings Market '87* Secaucus, New Jersey: Reed Travel Group.

McGee, Regina, ed. 1985. *The Convention Liaison Council Manual*, 4th ed. Washington, D.C.: The Convention Liaison Council.

Nichols, Barbara C., ed. 1985. *The Professional Meeting Manager*. Birmingham, Alabama: Professional Convention Management Association.

Renaghan, Leo M., and Michael Z. Kay. 1987. What Meeting Planners Want: The Conjoint Analysis Approach. *Cornell Hotel and Restaurant Administration Quarterly* 28(1):67–76.

Shure, Peter. 1987 & 1988. The Best of the Meeting Manager's Work Book (annual editions). *Meeting News* December.

Shure, Peter. 1988. New MPI Study Draws Line Between Manager, Facilitator. *Meeting News* July: 32.

6

Hotels and Other Meeting Facilities

CHAPTER OBJECTIVES

1. To provide an introduction to the specific roles hotels and other facilities play in the CEMI
2. To develop the importance of the CEMI market to hotels
3. To inventory the types of hotels and facilities available for CEMI events
4. To provide basic knowledge about hotel organization.
5. To describe the roles and activities of key hotel departments and personnel in hosting CEMI events.

INTRODUCTION

At first glance, most observers would say that the role hotels play in the CEMI is that of rooms provider. Upon reflection, many would also mention that hotels derive food, beverage, and banquet revenues from conventions and meetings. But their role goes much deeper than that. According to sources quoted by Hosansky and others (1986, 54), as recently as 1966, group business was a relatively small percentage of hotel, motel, and resort sales activity. In recent years, the picture has changed dramatically and, for many hotels, ". . . group business may account for as much as 80 or 90% of bookings."

When 90% of the rooms in any given hotel are rented to members of a group or a collection of group meetings and conventions, the effects of these figures ripple throughout every department in the hotel.

These effects apply neither exclusively nor specifically to high-rise, urban mega-hotel properties. According to Dave Dorf, director of education and training for the Hotel Sales and Marketing Association International (HSMAI), smaller hotels also vigorously market to group business (Hosansky et al. 1986, 55). These properties may not qualify in terms of size and scope of facilities for the big conventions, but as has been demonstrated in foregoing chapters, significant numbers of nonconvention meetings are held on hotel premises and the size of the meeting may in many ways dictate the size and location of the hotel chosen as host property.

Large hotels, however, are also recognizing the value of small group meetings. Whereas there is a limited or finite number of the types of conventions that are city-wide or would fill up totally on a regular basis a 1000- to 2000-room hotel, the opportunities to fill hotels with numbers of small groups appear to be close to infinite. This recognizes that the corporate market can play a major role in filling rooms. Hotel marketing and operational activities are therefore significantly and broadly impacted by the CEMI across all sizes and types of lodging facilities.

The ways in which hotel food and beverage departments have traditionally organized and operated themselves have also been significantly impacted by the demands of the diverse CEMI market. Separate facilities, staff, and policies dedicated to group events are becoming the norm. CEMI requirements for food events that are unique, memorable, refined, and sophisticated have focused increased attention on the management of all aspects of banquet and catering functions.

Hotels' meeting facilities have undergone a significant renaissance in response to demands from the CEMI market. Not only have the physical aspects of meeting rooms been changed and upgraded to be more flexible, but ballrooms and, in some instances, separate exhibit halls have emerged as a requirement of the CEMI market.

CATEGORIES OF CEMI-RELATED HOTELS

Downtown high-rise mega-hotels or the urban hotels specializing in catering to the small or corporate meetings market are not the only lodging facilities significantly involved in activities relevant to the CEMI. Other types of hotels and meeting facilities that have traditionally been unidimensional have recognized the value of the CEMI market and have become active in capturing portions of that market.

The **resort hotels** of the past that were designed, constructed, organized, and operated to cater to the individual or family market have undergone significant change in the last 20 years. There are a number of reasons for this, not the least of which being the cost of land and construction activities and the significant expense involved in purchasing furniture, fixtures, and equipment for a resort hotel. Operational activities that are centered around recreational environments also require increased investments in human resources.

One of the most important influences, however, has been the expansion of the conventions and meetings market. Because resort facilities are usually designed around some sort of recreational activity such as golf, tennis, or skiing, or take advantage of natural phenomena such as seashores, mountains, or deserts, they provide a relaxing environment in which, according to Nichols (1985, 8), ". . . the registrant feels removed from day-to-day pressures." Because of this, resorts may be particularly attractive to meeting planners whose meeting objectives can be enhanced in such environments. In many instances, it is possible for planners to market the attractiveness or desirability of a particular site and garner significantly higher attendance than would be the case with a traditional urban core hotel.

An additional advantage that resorts can offer to groups is that a large group (for instance, a regional or national convention) may very well take over the entire resort and have no competition from nongroup guests for the resort's amenities. Because of the lack of pressure to get on the golf course, business programs are better attended than at a resort-based meeting where attendees came for the meeting *and* the golf, but found that due to competition for tee times, the meeting plans and schedules were disrupted or poorly attended.

Whereas resorts have their roots in the early-day "spas" that centered around improving one's health either through soaking in hot springs, lying in the sun, or breathing clean dry desert air, the fact remains that the surroundings were almost always rural, remote, and fairly inaccessible to large numbers of people. Among the effects of this remoteness were, on the positive side, a feeling of tension relief and relaxation on the part of the hotel guest; and on the negative side, a difficult challenge for the hotel to fill rooms during other than peak seasons and times (Vare 1986). Many resort hotels, in fact, only stayed open during certain seasons and were inactive for the rest of the year (Edwards 1988, 74–75).

Increasingly, for the reasons outlined above, meetings and conventions business now represents a substantial part of the business at many resorts. Many more resorts are spending significant sums building facilities that allow them to stay open year-round, even if it means significant capital expenditures to install, for instance, golf or tennis facilities either nearby or on the premises of what is nominally a winter ski resort (Barbati 1985, 87–88).

Similarly, sunbelt resorts that have traditionally suffered very low revenues during summer seasons have targeted meetings, conventions, and other group business as a mechanism to attract clientele even during the least attractive times of the year from a temperature standpoint. In these instances, resorts may be more willing to significantly discount room rates or other services in order to sell the resort to meeting and convention planners.

The importance of the conventions and meetings market to resorts has grown substantially in the past few years and is specifically demonstrated by the interest that major chains have placed on the resort market. When Westin, Marriott, Hyatt, Sheraton, Hilton, and other large hotel operations specifically designed large resorts with ample meeting facilities, it became clear that resorts would play a major role in the future of the meetings and conventions market (Bergen 1988, 78). Indeed, it has become fairly common for any large-scale land development in a physically attractive or desirable area to include resorts with meeting facilities as major functional components.

These resorts are attractive not only for their obvious surface amenities and activities, but also for the psychological aspect of the role that relaxation and recreation can play in enhancing performance (Griffin 1985, 20–21): "Play, in this context, becomes a rationale for meetings at resorts and most meeting planners will include in their programs elements of recreational activities that are either structured or unstructured that are designed to enhance the performances of people in achieving the objectives of the meetings."

Since airline deregulation of 1978, travel patterns have changed considerably. Because many airlines now predominate at certain "hub" airports, a significant amount of hotel construction activity has taken place around these hub airports, offering meeting planners an opportunity to execute short-duration regional or national meetings at **hotel facilities adjacent to hub airports** that involve a minimum of logistics problems. Planners recognize that "Airport facilities offer excellent space for brief committee meetings or one-day sessions. Complimentary shuttle bus service often is available to airport area hotels on a frequent basis" (Nichols 1985, 8).

Other attractions for planners are that for smaller regional or national meetings with uncomplicated agendas, planners may book meeting space and rooms (as needed), fly in the attendees, execute the meeting, and fly attendees out in a relatively expeditious fashion. The downside is that restaurant and food and beverage options may be limited (Nichols 1985, 8), and activities, amenities, and area ambiance are usually significantly less desirable than in urban cores or resort areas.

Conference centers can offer opportunities for meeting planners to site their events in facilities that may be specifically designed and managed for meeting purposes. A conference center is a facility the primary purpose of which is to accommodate small to medium-sized meetings and offers a total meeting environment. This environment includes conference facilities and services, and may often include the very latest in audiovisual and meeting room design that may be impossible or extremely expensive to achieve in a large hotel or convention center. They also offer lodging, food and beverage, and, increasingly, recreational activities.

Conference centers are generally of three basic types: A public-access center is one that operates and competes in the meetings environment and whose lodging, food, and beverage facilities may also be accessed by free independent or vacation travelers. These are primarily operated and marketed, though, as for-profit meeting and lodging facilities.

Nonprofit centers are often operated by churches, universities, or other governmental entities, and if they are not totally utilized by the primary tenant or operator, they may be available to planners as alternative meeting facilities.

Corporate proprietary facilities are owned and operated by large nationwide or regional firms and probably do not present anything other than minor opportunities for meeting planners outside of the sponsoring corporate realm. They are designed and operated for the primary purposes of providing meeting, education, and training facilities for in-house corporate activities. Examples are McDonald's Hamburger University, Holiday Inn University, and corporate meeting centers for IBM, Kodak, and American Telephone and Telegraph (Green and Lazarus 1987, 60).

The advantages of a conference center that is designed specifically for small meeting activity is that everything in the facility ". . . is built to enhance the success of a meeting. Developers have consulted not only architects and interior designers, but also behavioral scientists, industrial psychologists, professional trainers and meeting planners" (Hughes 1984a, 32). These sorts of physical amenities go a long way toward making the conference center environment extraordinarily attractive to planners who are putting together small to modest-sized corporate and association meetings.

Among the positive aspects of siting executive-type meetings at conference facilities is that privacy and confidentiality of proceedings may be of utmost importance to successful execution of the event (Hughes 1984a, 33), and being able to provide meeting rooms that are booked for the group's purpose for their entire stay enhances requirements for not only privacy but flexibility.

Another major reason that conference centers are proving popular among planners is the increasing professionalism exhibited by management and employees that places the meetings market as their number-one priority

(Waldrop 1986, 94). Because of this specialization, conference centers in many instances are able to offer customized services for planners that, due to their highly visible public nature, hotels may find impossible to provide.

Other facilities that play varying roles in the CEMI market can include college and university campuses, which are a very viable option for planners who have extremely limited budgets. Universities typically make meals available through university foodservice and lodging in dormitory rooms during the summer. These facilities play a significant role in hosting meetings sponsored by religious, fraternal, and educational groups whose resources do not allow them to compete with corporate and large association events for mainstream meeting facilities.

Other emerging types of meeting facilities are only limited by the creativity of those making the facilities available and the imaginations of planners in their site selections. One trend has been meetings planned and executed on

TYPE OF FACILITY	CORPORATE PLANNERS*	ASSOCIATION PLANNERS*	
	All Types of Meetings	Conventions	Association Meetings
Midtown	57%	49%	70%
Resort	47%	30%	36%
Suburban	44%	16%	34%
Airport	28%	5%	29%
Private conference center	19%	1%	11%
Suite hotel	13%	5%	7%
Condominium resort	7%	3%	3%
University conference center	7%	2%	10%
Cruise ship	4%	**	**
BASE	*(765)*	*(n/r)*	*(n/r)*

  * Multiple responses
 ** Less than .5%
n/r = Not reported.

Exhibit 6.1 Types of facilities used by planners. *Source:* Meetings and Conventions. 1988. *Meetings Market '87.* Reed Travel Group: Secaucus, NJ (40, 76). Used with permission.

cruise ships which, in effect, represents a blend of hotel and resort facilities that have the added capability of moving from place to place.

From the range of choices that planners have in deciding where to hold their meetings, they still opt for midtown, resort, or suburban locations, as evidenced by the data displayed in Exhibit 6.1. The other choices enjoy some popularity given specific meeting agendas or objectives, but for the most part, traditional choices remain from the top three.

The choice of resort hotels for association conventions has not declined since 1983 (M&C 1988, 18), but the use of resort properties for association meetings other than conventions has declined steadily since 1981. This decrease is most likely a result of associations planning fewer meetings and therefore reducing the opportunities to site those meetings at a wider variety of facilities.

Site popularity for corporate meetings over the last few years has remained fairly stable, and as mentioned in previous chapters, once site selection has been established, other factors such as food and beverage, quality of meeting room configuration/design, and other factors become important to planners.

It can be seen from the foregoing data and discussion that meeting planners and convention managers have available to them a wide variety of choices in types of hotels in vastly varying settings. Hotels that actively find ways in which to design, organize, staff, and manage their properties with the meetings market in mind will be well positioned to compete for significant portions of the CEMI market.

HOTEL ORGANIZATION

In order to fully understand the range of effects that competition for the CEMI market has had upon hotels and other lodging facilities, it is important to look at the way a modern hotel's organization has evolved. Departments that are specific to the important interactions between the hotel, its staff, and elements of the CEMI have been created in response to this evolutionary pressure.

Exhibit 6.2 depicts how the evolution of hotel functional organizations demonstrates effects of the CEMI market. Simplified chart A is a traditional classic hotel organization where rooms and food and beverage are the preeminent generators of revenue and are also the dominant forces in the hotel organization. The other departments essentially provide staff support to the activities of these two main departments.

Chart B shows a step in the evolution of hotel organizational thought that pays attention to the role that markets and marketing lay in a hotel's organization. This can be interpreted to suggest that another "line" department can

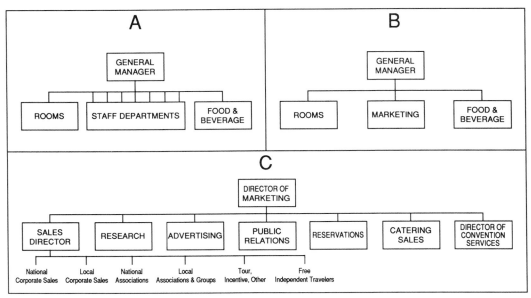

Exhibit 6.2 Evolution of hotel functional organizations demonstrating effects of CEMI market.

be created around the general rubric of marketing. This is known as a *market-driven* organization.

Looking more carefully at a market-driven organization, specifically at how the responsibilities for identifying markets, selling to those markets, and delivering the hotel's services to those markets might be seen in the idealized chart depicted in chart C, note that each significant market segment has associated with it a functional division of the sales director's department. In any given hotel, some of these functions may be combined; a small property, in fact, may have only one sales director whose duties involve bringing the hotel's marketing message to the entire spectrum of potential clientele, whether it be free independent travelers (FITs) or groups of various types. For the purposes of this discussion, these functions are depicted and titled separately.

In a large, sophisticated hotel marketing operation, there may be separate individuals who direct their efforts toward market research, advertising, and public and, increasingly, community relations.

Regarding public and community relations, a case can be made for the major role that a hotel's community involvement can play in helping garner significant association business. Richmond (1988, 263) describes a strategy whereby hotels, through their donations and support of charitable and cultural events, place themselves in favorable proximity with community leaders who comprise the policy-making boards of sponsoring organizations. These volunteer leaders also serve in the memberships and on the boards of national trade, cultural, and professional organizations. Close working relationships between hotels and these organizations can be positively manifested in marketing advantages during times of site and facility selection for meetings, conventions, and trade shows.

Perhaps the most striking change in the organization of a market-driven hotel is demonstrated on the right of chart C. Traditionally, reservations have been a front office function, directed and coordinated through the front office manager and the director of the rooms division. Increasingly, market-driven hotels are transferring reservations to the department of marketing because it is this direct linkage between sales efforts and reservations that represents a critical interaction between hotel functional units and the clientele.

Similarly, the planning of catered events for groups would, in the past, have been a function of the food and beverage department. Increasingly, because of the need for a total coordinated sales and planning effort, the function of catering sales in the marketing department has become more and more common.

A relatively recent phenomenon has been the rise in importance of the function of convention services. In hotels that cater to group business, this managerial function takes on an ever-expanding set of responsibilities to the point, in some organizations, where a convention services manager (CSM) will be assigned specific responsibility for each event in the hotel. Depending on the size of the event, the CSM may have effective operational control over every department in the hotel that services the event. As discussed in previous chapters, CSM functions are similar to those of the director or manager of event services in a convention center, and these professionals provide the interactive focal point between the hotel and event sponsors and managers.

The function of convention services is found in the marketing department because the focus of this department's job is to carry out the contractual details decided upon in the sale and booking of the meeting or convention event. It is this attention to the contracted and promised details that makes the difference between a successful and an unsuccessful event. The job of a convention services department is therefore one that is critically important to the success of the event by virtue of its responsibility to assist the event's managers in realizing the contracted obligations of the hotel's marketing activities.

The organization of the modern hotel that counts CEMI events as a major portion of its business can therefore be shown to have evolved both structurally and functionally to demonstrate the importance of the CEMI market.

KEY HOTEL STAFF AND CEMI INTERACTIONS

The key people on a hotel's staff who carry the majority of responsibility for interaction with meeting planners and convention managers are:

- The specific sales manager who initiates, contacts, and sells the hotel to the group planning the event
- The catering manager who works with the meeting planner or convention manager on establishing a program of food and beverage events for the meeting
- The convention services manager (CSM) who has effective responsibility for carrying out the hotel's obligations once a convention or meeting has been booked and contracts signed

To be sure, at one time or another, and in varying degrees and intensity, virtually every other department within the hotel will have occasion to interact with the meeting planner, his or her representatives, and delegates to the convention, meeting, or event. However, the sales manager, the catering manager, and the convention services manager are the individuals whose activities focus the capabilities of the hotel on the requirements of the meeting planner.

It is the job of the **sales manager** to generate both new and repeat business prospects on a regular basis. This individual uses a variety of techniques to accomplish this fundamental goal of the sales job, and as the chart in Exhibit 6.2 suggests, there may be one or more persons whose primary function is to focus their sales activities and techniques on aspects of the conventions and meetings market.

Having a specifically designated sales manager working exclusively with the conventions and meetings market is generally seen as a positive organizational step in hotels by the CEMI. This person should be knowledgeable about the CEMI and the unique requirements that various blocks of group business can bring to a hotel. Caution, however, is suggested by various CEMI observers because hotel managements place a great deal of pressure on the sales staff to generate bookings and potential profit for the hotel (Nichols 1985, 131).

Hotel management sets goals for sales staff, usually stated in job descriptions as a specific number of room nights sold for certain periods of time. A sample job description (Astroff and Abbey 1988, 122) suggests quotas of 1200 room nights per month, 45 telephone sales calls per week, 10 personal calls per week, and the generation of 10 new accounts per week.

Ambitious goals such as these generate stress on the part of sales staffs, as documented by Whitney (1986, 200). Because many of these sales managers are young, well-educated, and very much oriented toward upward mobility (Troy 1984, 8), there is a lot of job movement among sales staffs in hotels nationwide. It is therefore critical for meeting planners, when working with hotel sales managers, to be very detail-oriented in negotiations and see to it that specific promises are written into whatever booking or contractual document may be agreed to by both parties. It is extremely likely that the hotel sales manager who sells and books a given meeting or convention will be long gone by the time the event takes place.

Outstanding hotel sales people are those who are well informed as to their potential markets, particularly in the conventions and meetings industry. They know what associations are, how an association works, and what associations do for their members, and with that knowledge they are able to help associations plan meetings that best utilize the facilities of the hotel to meet the objectives of the association and its membership. A similar knowledge is imperative for the hotel sales staff to service the corporate market, and sales staffs who are able to exhibit a depth and breadth of knowledge about their markets are typically the ones who succeed most regularly in the CEMI market arena.

Sales executives have a concomitant responsibility to have broad and deep knowledge about the hotel and its departments; the roles, missions, and personnel of those departments; and how those people and functions are best utilized to serve the needs of any given client.

Another staff member who is critically important to the planning and execution of a meeting or convention event is the **catering manager.** Catering is a modern appellation that covers the delivery of food and beverage services in all areas of the hotel other than permanent sit-down restaurant facilities. As the organization chart in Exhibit 6.2 suggests, the role of catering sales and management is moving from purely a food and beverage-related activity to one that is more closely aligned with the marketing function. This change reinforces the importance of the role that food and beverage plays in marketing a hotel as a convention and meeting destination center. It should be noted that catering sales staffs are also given goals to meet, much the same as the sales managers are, and these goals "are frequently based on the number of food and beverage events that catering personnel book directly, independent of the convention sales staff" (Nichols 1985, 131).

For catering sales staffs, challenges in planning group food and beverage events several years into the future are similar to those of hotel sales managers. Because the time span between planning an event and its execution can be a number of years, the facility may also undergo changes other than sales staff turnover. Chefs come and go; facilities and kitchens are upgraded, changed, and remodeled; and entire staffs can be reorganized.

The commitments and promises made by a catering sales manager in 1985 may be difficult or impossible for a new kitchen staff to execute in 1999. The challenge for both convention planners and hotel catering staffs, in this instance, is to plan meeting and convention details that recognize the capabilities and expectations of both organizations.

In a sense, once the details of the meeting and convention are hammered out between hotel sales, catering sales, and the meeting and convention planner, the whole package is then "handed off" to the convention services manager.

The **convention services manager** (CSM) is a relatively modern phenomenon, and it is with the staff of the convention services manager that the final responsibility for the success of the meeting rests. According to Nichols (1985, 132), the hallmarks of a CSM are "long hours and the need to adapt to varying personalities and degrees of competence."

The CSM, therefore, becomes the intermediary between the promises the hotel contracted to deliver and the execution of the event by the meeting or convention planner at the time the event begins. The immediate conclusion that can be drawn about the CSM is that he or she is an individual who must be very detail-oriented and tolerant of a high degree of organizational stress over long periods of time during an event.

Dorf, of HSMAI, says, ". . . service is better because convention service departments have improved. Once convention managers were either catering people or housemen who really were responsible only for setting up. Now you're starting to see convention services develop as a profession" (Hosansky et al. 1986, 55). As the profession of convention services management evolves, it is, indeed, becoming more than the unidimensional task that Dorf suggests it started out as.

Today, virtually every major convention hotel and, increasingly, smaller hotels, resorts, and other lodging venues have at least one individual who is designated as a CSM. As hotels get larger and their reliance on the CEMI market becomes more extensive, they will have entire staffs of people probably reporting to a director of convention services, as depicted in Exhibit 6.2.

Typically, CSMs will have the authority and responsibility for strategic and tactical details of the meeting and convention while it is in the hotel. Once the group is in-house, the CSM has authority equal to that of the general manager as far as that group is concerned.

Specific duties of the CSM begin when the files and contracts compiled by the sales and catering departments come to the CSM's desk. Even though the event may be several years on the horizon, at this stage, most convention services managers view it as essential that they become familiar with the contract and specific needs of the group in order that mistakes or imperfections of predictions of the hotel's capabilities might be caught at the earliest possible stage. Typically, a convention services manager will write a letter to the meeting or convention planner introducing himself or herself, stating how he or she might be contacted, and letting the planner know how the details are proceeding. Basically, this works as a "transfer of trust" from the sales staff to the convention services department (Windom 1987, 2).

At this time, it is important that the planner be apprised of any potential problems that may have been built in during negotiations with the sales staff, perhaps reopening negotiations on certain terms of the contract. Because of the CSM's familiarity with the hotel's facilities and how those facilities can be best configured and used to execute group events, the CSM may be deeply involved in planning the final details of catered events that have been sold by the catering sales staff.

Once the event begins, the CSM must be available to oversee the entire process. He or she will work very closely with the meeting planner and other key event figures, including show managers, service contractors, and, of course, every hotel department that plays a role in the hotel's hosting of the event.

The function of communication among key staff mentioned in earlier chapters is critical in this particular interaction between CEMI professionals and the hotel CSM. Because of the need for the convention services staff to pay careful attention to all of the details attendant to any given event, communication by VHF radio, cellular phones, and/or personal communication "beepers" are the most often used media in which communications are organized for such events.

Because a CSM needs in-depth knowledge of multiple-market segments; a good grasp of convention- and meeting-related services available in the local market area, and broad and deep knowledge of the management, organization, and staff involved in every hotel department, the CSM is today a position that is swiftly becoming professionalized in the hotel management structure.

In a typical large convention-oriented hotel, there is a director of convention services on whose staff serve multiple convention service managers. That the job of CSM has become organizationally formalized in hotels and recognized broadly across the entire CEMI further serves to point out the importance of this new professional manager in the hotel organization. A sample job description for a convention services manager is included in Appendix 3.

It should be noted that in this sample job description, the typical convention services manager discharges his or her duties under four general categories: administrative responsibilities involving group business, working relationships with the sales and marketing department, the various interdepartmental relations within the hotel organization structure, and specific responsibilities to servicing the clientele.

Holly Hughes (1984b) reports how these responsibilities play out in the typical day by following a CSM at the Chicago Marriott Downtown during the course of hosting a major convention and juggling details for other upcoming and current events in the hotel. This overview provides an insider's look at the sorts of details and interactions that the modern convention services manager must handle in order to discharge the hotel's responsibilities to convention and meeting events.

Perhaps typifying the esteem with which high-quality, modern CSMs are held by their hotel organizations is the recent report that the director of convention services at the Waldorf Astoria Hotel in New York is a member of the hotel's executive committee and reports directly to the hotel's general manager. There are indications that most of the major hotel chains are standardizing the position of convention services director on a chain-wide basis, and in many of them, the director of convention services will have a seat on the hotel's executive committee (Ghitelman 1989, 109–110).

Perhaps no other measure of a manager's professionalism is more indicative of its importance than the fact that an international association has been formed to advance the goals of that profession. Currently with close to 500 members, the Association for Convention Operations Management (ACOM) has been operating as a resource and voice for CSMs on an international basis for the last two years. According to William Just (1989), the association has identified 4000 hotels in the United States and Canada that have an identifiable convention services management function. Furthermore, Hilton, Hyatt, Marriott, and Sheraton have all established corporate directors of convention services. Marriott Hotels, in fact, now actively recruits and has established a management training "track" for people to become convention services managers and directors at that firm's hotels.

Two-thirds of ACOM's membership is currently made up of convention services managers from hotels, with one-third being event and client services managers from convention centers and convention and visitors bureaus. The broad emergence of the CSM position across the many types and categories of hotels underscores the importance with which this function is being viewed by hotel managements as their organizations evolve to meet the challenges of the CEMI market (Myers 1989, 77–78).

CONCLUSION

In this chapter, we have seen that the role of hotels and other lodging facilities is more than just the provision of rooms. In fact, the challenges and requirements implicit in the CEMI market have permanently altered the way in which many hotel companies do business. Because so many hotels across the entire lodging spectrum count the CEMI as a major focus of their marketing efforts, their facilities, organizational structures, personnel, and training have had to change to reflect this. This process of change is one that will continue as the various CEMI markets continue to be developed and identified.

REFERENCES

Astroff, Milton T., and James R. Abbey. 1988. *Convention Sales and Services,* 2nd ed. Cranbury, New Jersey: Waterbury Press.

Barbati, Carl. 1985. Meetings at Mountain Resorts. *Meetings and Conventions* February: 87–94, 175.

Bergen, Mona. 1988. Resorts Ride High, but Face Challenges on the Way. *Successful Meetings* January: 77–84.

Edwards, Mauri. 1988. What the Devil Is a Resort? *Successful Meetings* January: 73–75.

Ghitelman, David. 1989. Convention Services Managers Get Respect. *Meetings and Conventions* May: 109–117.

Green, Walter A., and Harold Lazarus. 1987. Corporate Education Centers: A Growing Hospitality Segment. *The Cornell Hotel and Restaurant Administration Quarterly* May: 58–65.

Griffin, Marie. 1985. The Importance of Play at Meetings. *Successful Meetings* January: 19–30.

Hosansky, Mel, et al. 1986. The Evolution of an Industry. *Meetings and Conventions Magazine* June: 48–67.

Hughes, Holly. 1984a. Maximizing the Meeting Environment. *Successful Meetings* September: 31–34, 38.

Hughes, Holly. 1984b. A Day in the Life of a Convention Services Manager. *Successful Meetings* August: 21–31.

Just, William H. 1989. Private communication. Atlanta, Georgia: Association for Convention Operations Management.

Koeth, Barbara. 1985. Renaissance of Hotels Downtown. *Meetings and Conventions Magazine* June: 82+.

M&C/Meetings and Conventions Magazine. 1988. Meetings Market '87. Secaucus, New Jersey: Reed Travel Group.

Myers, Elissa Matulis. 1989. Making Meetings Happen. *Association Management* September: 77+.

Nichols, Barbara, ed. 1985. *Professional Meeting Management.* Birmingham, Alabama: The Professional Convention Management Association.

Richmond, Louis B. 1988. Putting the Public in Public Relations. In *Hotel Management and Operations,* ed. D. G. Rutherford. New York: Van Nostrand Reinhold.

Troy, David A. 1984. Unleashing the Hotel Sales Tigers. *The Cornell Hotel and Restaurant Administration Quarterly* November: 7–10.

Vare, EthlieAnn. 1986. Mountain Resorts. *Meetings and Conventions* April: 94–101.

Waldrop, Heidi. 1986. Conference Centers Are Made for Meetings. *Successful Meetings* November: 93+.

Whitney, David L. 1986. Attentional Styles and Stress Factors of Hotel Sales/Marketing Managers. *International Journal of Hospitality Management* 5(4):197–200.

Windom, Deborah A. 1987. Convention Service Managers: Where Hotels Make the Meetings Work. Monograph, Washington State University mimeo, 9 pp.

7

Convention and Visitors Bureaus

CHAPTER OBJECTIVES

1. To define the role and functions of convention and visitors bureaus (CVBs)
2. To explain how CVBs can be organized and funded
3. To review the activities of CVBs relative to convention marketing and sales
4. To overview and define other CVB services

INTRODUCTION

Although there is some disagreement over the formulation of the first true CVB, there is general consensus that it came about sometime around 1895 when a group of Detroit hotel operators dispatched the *Detroit Journals*'s hotel reporter, Milton Carmichael, on a trip designed to promote and sell the city as a convention site. Because of his success, the next year a "convention secretary" was hired to facilitate travel to Detroit as a convention host city. Other cities that were railroad transportation hubs created similar positions, and these "convention secretaries," of course, formed an association in 1915 (Markarian 1989, 7).

As business, population and transportation grew and changed, so did the concept of marketing cities as convention and visitor destinations to the point where today, all major cities, most secondary markets, and even some small, very specialized destination communities have a CVB (Gartrell 1988, 4). There are currently bureaus in cities across North America ". . . from Valdez, Alaska . . . to Kissimmee, Florida" (Hosansky 1986, 57). The majority of this CVB growth activity has taken place in the past decade as cities have recognized the economic and political value attached to being considered a good convention destination. The actual number of CVBs has more than doubled since 1980, from 100 to more than 250, and is still growing (Hoyle, Dorf, and Jones 1989, 10).

This recognition has, in turn, created a need for organizations staffed by professional marketing and sales people who understand the convention and tourism markets. Cities can no longer afford bureaus that are run by political fiat through an "old-boy" network. The competitive nature of the convention market requires an organized staff of people who, in the words of one observe,

> . . . serve like a cooperative, representing all components of the visitor industry, including hotels, motels, restaurants, convention facilities, tour operators, attractions, transportation carriers, as well as the retailer and commercial resources that are important to visitors" (Charles Gillett, quoted in Gartrell 1988, 5)

One way to visualize these relationships between CVBs, other CEMI members, and the retail and commercial segment would be to refer back to Exhibit 1.1 and put the CVB at the center of the hub, with retail taking its place as a spoke.

CVBs, therefore, are usually established in communities as ". . . not-for-profit 'umbrella' marketing organizations . . . [that represent] . . . a community in the solicitation and servicing of all types of visitors to that destination" (Nichols 1985, 19). It is under this umbrella that CVBs organize to, in the words of one bureau's principals:

> . . . extract valuable information from all of the professionals in the hospitality industry from our community, and focus those ideas, goals and objectives into a solid marketing services plan to bring conventions and tourists into the community. (Beckelman and Marks 1984, 22)

In a phrase, bureaus exist to sell cities as convention and tourism sites. How they do this and how they are structured to accomplish their goals will vary according to the city itself, the political and membership structure of the bureau, the desirability of the area as a tourist and convention destination site, and the professionalism of the bureau itself. The key to the successful use of umbrella organizations like CVBs is the ability of the management and staff of the bureau to:

- Carry out their coordination functions in representing the city and the area
- Provide services to membership and clients
- Help with meeting and convention execution
- Serve as an interface between visitors and governmental entities and a central clearinghouse for information about the city's capabilities as a destination site

ORGANIZATION OF CONVENTION AND VISITORS BUREAUS

To accomplish the foregoing management activities, bureaus are generally organized around a framework that reflects the range of services and activities available in the bureau's destination area. Exhibit 7.1 depicts a typical organization chart developed along the functional lines according to which a CVB may be organized.

The chief executive of the bureau serves a key coordinative role because it is this manager who not only has to provide the leadership and knowledge to direct the activities of the bureau, but must be politically astute to balance the interests of the numerous forms membership may take and the municipal, county, or state governmental entities that may provide tax revenues to the bureau. This individual must direct the activities of the bureau so that all members and political constituencies feel well served by bureau activities.

The chief executive must also be sensitive to the convention and tourism market forces and work well with not only staff people, but members of the community at large. In most circumstances, it is no longer enough for the bureau executive to be well thought of by only the hotel sales community. The leader of the CVB has to market the bureau's value to all segments of bureau membership and be continually alert for opportunities to enlarge membership, particularly from the nonhospitality segments of the business community.

It is important that the bureau chief executive direct the bureau activities in such a way that the benefits of those activities are not seen by parts of the membership as being inequitably distributed. In this context, it may be that many of the members of the CVB are in competition with each other, and any seeming inequities or favoritism will erode membership confidence in the activities of the bureau and therefore erode membership's financial support of the bureau.

Finance and administration, as in most organizations, involves accounting,

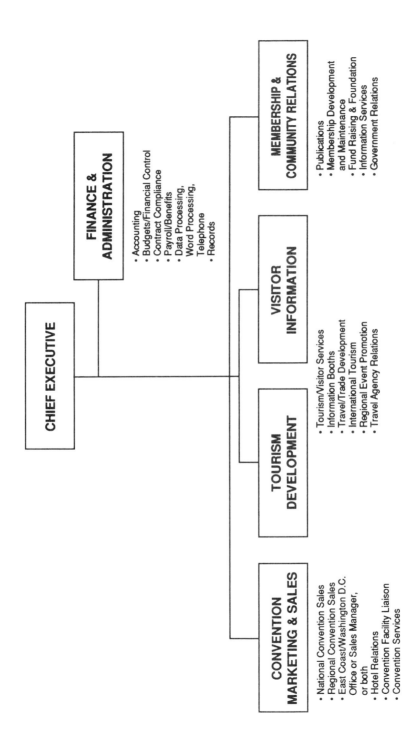

CHIEF EXECUTIVE

CONVENTION MARKETING & SALES
- National Convention Sales
- Regional Convention Sales
- East Coast/Washington D.C. Office or Sales Manager, or both
- Hotel Relations
- Convention Facility Liaison
- Convention Services
- Research
- Incentive Corporate Sales

TOURISM DEVELOPMENT
- Tourism/Visitor Services
- Information Booths
- Travel/Trade Development
- International Tourism
- Regional Event Promotion
- Travel Agency Relations

VISITOR INFORMATION

FINANCE & ADMINISTRATION
- Accounting
- Budgets/Financial Control
- Contract Compliance
- Payroll/Benefits
- Data Processing, Word Processing, Telephone
- Records

MEMBERSHIP & COMMUNITY RELATIONS
- Publications
- Membership Development and Maintenance
- Fund Raising & Foundation
- Information Services
- Government Relations

Exhibit 7.1   Convention and visitors bureau functional organization.

the preparation and overseeing of budgets, and financial control. In the case of CVBs that are actively growing and developing large staffs and a broad range of activities, an increasing requirement for data processing, word processing, and sophisticated telecommunications systems is also administered by this functional aspect of the CVB's organization. Additionally, payroll and benefits administration and other miscellaneous recordkeeping will be accomplished by this department.

Membership and community relations include activities on behalf of the bureau and its membership that are as diverse as overseeing and producing bureau- and destination-related publications to fund-raising and other developmental activities that link the bureau to the community through its membership. This segment of typical CVB organizations will also keep membership records, administer membership development and recruitment programs, and serve as an information point. This department may participate in government relations, including, in some circumstances, active professional lobbying and informational activities to legislatures on behalf of the CVB membership community.

The range and scope of these activities, of course, will vary from community to community, but it should be recognized that under the general rubric of membership and community relations, a vast array of activities can take place on behalf of the bureau, its membership, and other affiliated parties.

Tourism development and visitor information are depicted in Exhibit 7.1 in separate functional segments, but often they are administrated together. The primary thrust of activities under this organizational group is the promotion, development, and maintenance of the free independent traveler (FIT) market. These include vacationers and other visitors not associated with organized groups, meetings, or conventions. As such, this bureau department will interact closely with travel agencies, state and regional tourism development offices, bureaus in other nearby destinations, and tour operators who work with international travelers. This function may also participate in the design, promotion, and execution of regional or cultural entertainment events that attract vacationers and individual visitors.

Another important routine generally managed through this office is the organization and staffing of information booths at airports, harbors, borders, and other points at which tourists enter the bureau's market area. In these booths the CVB personnel will have available for visitors and vacationers brochures, literature, information, and inventories of attractions and visitor services to help travelers enjoy their visit to the bureau's community.

The **convention marketing and sales** department is responsible for all the services and functions the bureau performs that relate to the CEMI. Typically headed by a vice president or director of marketing, this segment of the CVB organization is divided along the functional lines of national convention sales, regional convention sales, or corporate or incentive sales and may include the provision for a specific sales presence in the form of a sales manager or a "satellite-type" office located in another city; a Washington, D.C., sales office is one example. This recognizes the importance of Washington, D.C. as the home base of the vast majority of the nation's associations (see Chapter 2). Many bureaus now maintain a year-round presence in the nation's capital to serve as a visible representative of the community, the bureau, and its membership in this concentration of potential business.

The other divisions of the convention marketing and sales department depend on the CVB, its size, and what particular groups the bureau is targeting as its primary market focus. Most, however, will have a national sales manager and a regional sales manager.

The provision of a corporate or incentive sales management function recognizes the potential contribution the corporate market can make to the destination's CEMI economy (Tritsch 1988, 121, 123). Because meeting planners acting on behalf of corporate events generally have shorter lead times and do not necessarily need to meet during the most desirable seasons, this segment of the market has been attracting increasing attention from CVBs nationwide (Englander 1985, 68).

The responsibility of CVBs to market destinations have mandated close working relationships with not only hotels, but also such convention and meeting facilities as may be available within the community. Whereas most bureaus' marketing activities on behalf of hotels stop short of actual booking of hotel space and rely mainly on activities that generate sales leads for the hotels, the relationships with freestanding convention and exposition facilities may be significantly different.

Under some community circumstances, the bureau serves as the strategic marketing arm for the facility and, in cooperation with facility management, may in fact be responsible for booking conventions past, for instance, an 18-month horizon. In such an arrangement, booking the association market for a convention that makes site decisions ten years in advance would be the responsibility of the bureau marketing staff; booking local events in the convention center facilities that require a lead time of less than 18 months would fall to the marketing and sales staff of the facility itself. While many bureaus have such marketing arrangements with the city's convention facilities, under most circumstances, the bureaus do not have any line authority or operational control (Nichols 1985, 21).

Other services offered by the convention marketing and sales department on behalf of bureau clientele are convention services activities. These services can include meeting planning and management activities for groups or associations that do not have their own meeting planner. In a way, this function can serve as a sort of destination management company (see Chapter 10) that researches and promotes to the client the various CEMI and hospitality services offered within the bureau's destination area.

The convention services department may also assist associations and groups with registration activities with personnel, equipment, or materials. Some CVBs run a housing service, particularly under circumstances of city-wide conventions where they serve as a central clearinghouse for hotel reservations. If all of the attendees of a given event are staying in one hotel, they usually make individual arrangements with the individual hotel, but if every hotel in the city is involved, or multiple properties are involved, some bureaus have the resources to perform the task of serving as a central reservations and housing service.

Bureaus whose services have expanded to include wide ranges of convention services are now charging for the provision of these services because they take up significant amounts of bureau resources in the form of personnel and materials. As revenue generators, these services have also been responsible for creating some controversy because of the increasingly important need for high-quality statistics and reports relative to housing activities. Show managers and meeting planners negotiate future conventions and expositions based on the number of room nights they have delivered at past events. So, if a bureau, through its housing activities, does not generate precise and accurate statistical reports, this deficiency negatively affects the ability of convention and exposition managers to negotiate favorable rates for their events in the future (Blair 1988, 1, 21).

While CVBs have traditionally offered housing services free of charge, the problems that can arise from these activities have given rise to active competition to the bureaus by private travel agencies and travel companies who offer housing services to planners and managers for a fee, and guarantee accurate statistics (Levin 1988, 26, 28). A direct effect of travel company/CVB housing competition has been to force bureaus to tighten and professionalize their procedures and statistical reporting, and in some instances, start charging fees for housing services.

The organization of CVBs has grown from the days of a "convention secretary" to the modern era that reflects the complexity and sophistication of the markets which bureaus pursue. As the number of communities establishing CVBs increases, so will competition. CVB staffs and organizations will reflect that competition in their evolving structures and activities.

FUNDING OF CONVENTION AND VISITORS BUREAUS

Most bureaus that are not part of a governmental entity are usually organized as a 501(C)(6) organization to promote the general business interest of its constituencies (see Chapter 2). As such, it cannot engage in regular business activities that are normally conducted on a for-profit basis, and the revenues generated by bureau activities must be primarily expended on bureau programs that constitute the basis for its tax-exempt status under the rules and regulations of the Internal Revenue Service (Gartrell 1988, 38).

Even though they may not have a direct line relationship with governmental bodies, most bureaus are "quasi-governmental" in nature in that substantial portions of their funding come through some special taxation provision. Taxation, of course, is enabled only through legislative activity, therefore providing the linkage between CVBs and governmental agencies. Governmental agencies may, in fact, also participate in bureau activities as dues-paying members. Governmental agencies and legislatures may also contribute to CVB funding bases through the provision of matching funds to enhance bureau programs or outright grants from general revenues in aid of either specific projects or general bureau activities.

The largest revenue source for most bureaus, however, is some form of the **hotel room tax.** Variously known as bed taxes or pillow taxes, these are taxes that are added to a visitor's hotel bill on a percentage basis of room rate. This tax is in addition to any other state, city, or county taxes that may already be levied on hotel rooms that are destined to finance local, city, or state governmental activity. The average **hotel tax** nationwide is 5.15%; and the average total tax on a hotel room, including the other taxes mentioned above, amounts to 8.8% nationwide (Gartrell 1988, 44). These hotel taxes are used for a number of different activities that vary from community to community, but nationally account for 60.7% of the total annual budgets of CVBs.

These taxes can generate a certain amount of controversy because, in some circumstances, the proceeds of hotel taxes are not used to enhance the community's ability to attract or host convention and visitor activity. Hotel taxes have been known to be diverted to fund school arts programs, professional athletic facilities, and other community, cultural, and entertainment projects that do not necessarily enhance the ability of the community to market itself as a convention, group meeting, and vacation destination.

Many bureaus, meeting planners, and show managers are generally in favor of room taxes if the proceeds are used for augmenting bureau marketing programs, enhancing a community's convention facilities, and enabling the local CEMI community to compete for conventions and meetings business.

Escalation of the room tax to double-digit figures, in addition to other taxes, may serve, however, to drive meetings and conventions into suburban areas (Siskin 1988, 20), and may generate active opposition to the community as a destination site.

The National Association of Exposition Managers (NAEM), for instance, has voted not to go into a city where less than 50% of the room tax is designated for convention facilities, public safety, or the CVB. The American Society of Association Executives (ASAE), representing the cream of the association convention market, has also expressed displeasure over what they deem misappropriation of hotel room taxes.

Room taxes will probably continue to be a vital funding source for bureaus and other convention- and group business-related activities in a community. How well the taxation process is managed will dictate how important a source of bureau funding the hotel room tax remains in the future. Because 85% of bureaus responding to an International Association of Convention & Visitors Bureau (IACVB) study indicated they get room tax support to enhance their revenue stream (McGee 1986, 42), and because most bureaus are quasi-governmental agencies, this puts them in a difficult spot from a political standpoint. It remains to be seen in this era of taxpayer resistance to general taxes whether purpose-specific taxes can be designed to please all constituencies.

The second major source of most bureaus' funding is membership dues. In the past, as much as 90% of membership dues were accounted for by hotels and other CEMI businesses. There is now evidence that CVBs are finding a broader spectrum of potential membership from among the retail and commercial businesses in their communities. This emerging diversity of membership serves to broaden the base and disseminate the importance of CEMI-related economic activity to a wider spectrum of the local economy. In the words of Charles Gillett of the New York City Convention & Visitors Bureau, "You're got to go out and convince the banks, department stores, newspapers, etc., that is's worth their while to be members" (Englander 1985, 77).

This recognizes the reality that hotels and other CEMI businesses most closely associated with bureau activities are, in most markets, a fairly finite number of potential memberships. Although in most major markets, hotels, and other visitor-related businesses are experiencing growth, it is generally slow or measured. It is in the larger sphere of a community's economic activity that bureaus will find the majority of new memberships.

Other funding sources that can provide revenues for CVB budgets include miscellaneous and general city, county, or state taxes that are appropriated as part of legislative processes. Governmental agencies may also provide the aforementioned matching funds or block grants to support specific programs or services.

Due to the competitive nature of the CEMI market, CVBs and their executive leadership find themselves in what amounts to a constant search for additional funds. In other to remain competitive with other convention, meeting, and group business destinations, the modern bureau, through its activities, needs to generate revenues that allow it to offer the kinds of services, hire the sorts of professionals, and travel to the industry functions it must to maintain competitive stature.

Many bureaus are seeking out nontraditional sources of income which may include engaging in cooperative programs with members, putting on special revenue-generating events, charging for bureau services, and offering educational programs (Gartrell 1988, 46).

The charging of fees for such services as registration, housing and convention management, and event assistance is a relatively new concept, but as pointed by one CVB executive, the bureaus had to become more entrepreneurial. Twenty years ago, his payroll for registration services amounted to about US$15,000 a year, and in 1985, it had risen to US$550,000. It becomes impossible for any nonprofit CVB organization to maintain budget integrity by offering those kinds of services at that level for free (Hosansky 1986, 59).

It is anticipated that funding sources will become one of greatest ongoing challenges facing CVB executives and their governing boards. To remain competitive in the modern CEMI market and serve their membership according to their charters, CVBs need to seek out and implement programs that allow them to be fiscally solvent.

CONVENTION AND VISITORS BUREAU RESOURCES

Like all other segments of the CEMI, the CVBs have organized to form a professional organization that is designed to promote professionalism, ethics, and information exchange in the solicitation, booking, and servicing of meetings, conventions, trade shows, and other group business on behalf of a community.

Founded in 1915, the International Association of Convention & Visitors Bureaus now has over 300 members in 22 countries around the world. It serves as a central location for the exchange of information between and among its members, provides research data, administers educational programs, and provides systemwide information on conventions booked and hosted by members through a computerized database network called INET.

```
IACVB CONFIDENTIAL CONVENTION REPORT                        File #NA890000-09

Organiz'n    NATL ASSN OF COLL & UNIVERSITY CEMI PROGRAMS
Mtg Name     ANNUAL JUNE/JULY NATL CONV
Street 1     ONE DIVINE CIRCLE                 Phone (202) 555-1990
Street 2     STE 500
City         WASHINGTON                        Market Segment         --
State        DC    Zip/Country  20036          Offshore               N

Chief Exec   MR ROBERT L CARR                  Title EXEC VP
Mtg Exec     MR DONALD H COLE                  Title VP
Mtg Region   US    States  ___/___/___/___/___/___/___/___/___/___/___/___/___/
```

MEETING HISTORY

City	LAS VEGAS	SAN JUAN	ATLANTA	CHICAGO
Mtg Start Date	07/13/86	07/14/85	06/11/83	06/23/82
Mtg End	07/16/86	07/17/85	06/16/83	06/26/82
Mtg Start Day	SU	SU	--	--

==DELEGATES==

Registered Attendance	01100	01000	00600	00863
Total Attendance	02000	01490	00600	00863
Rooms Used	00755	00800	00500	00526
Suites Used	0009	0017	0000	0016
Peak Arr Day	SU	SU	--	SA
Peak Dep Day	WE	WE	--	WE
Name of HQ Hotel	WESTIN	DUPONT	HYATT REG	FAIRMONT
Room in HQ Hotel	0735	0700	0500	0526

==SERVICES BY BUREAU===

Housing	N	N	N	N
Registration	Y	Y	Y	N

==FACILITIES===

Lgst Meeting (Seat)	01200	01000	00600	00800
Simultaneous Mtg Rms	05	15	02	03
Lgst Meal (Seats)	1200	1400	0600	0500
Net SqFt (000) Exhibits	000	005	000	000
Move-in (Days)	00	08	00	00
Exhibit Start Day	--	SU	--	--
Exhibit End Day	--	TU	--	--
Move-out (Days)	00	01	00	00
Hotel or Convention Cntr	N	H	--	--

===

Advise Call Bureau	N	N	--	--
Call Bureau for Arr/Dep	N	N	--	--
Date Last Updated	09/02/86	10/23/85	07/08/83	08/09/82

FUTURE MEETING SITES

City	SAN FRAN	TIJUANA	BOSTON	VANC, BC	HOUSTON
Mtg Mth/Yr	07/87	00/88	00/88	07/88	00/89
City	PORTLAND	HONOLULU	--	--	--
Mtg Mth/Yr	00/90	06/97	___/___	___/___	___/___

```
Last Updated By:  LAS VEGAS      Date:  09/02/86

REPORT RUN BY:    COLFAX
```

Exhibit 7.2 Mock-up of CINET confidential convention report. *Source:* IACVB (1989). Used with permission.

A mock-up of an INET report is presented in Exhibit 7.2. This report on conventions hosted by member CVBs provides others in the network with an opportunity to track the requirements and monitor key activities of conventions as they are hosted by other communities that subscribe to the INET service (Gartrell 1988, 11–13).

Note that the major categories of information involve the following:

- The name and address of the association or group
- Basic membership information
- Key contacts within the group
- A four-year review of the meeting's history
- Data about delegates
- Data about room nights used
- Typical peak arrival and departure days
- Services provided by the bureau
- Convention and meeting facilities used

In addition, subscribers have an opportunity to track future bookings of this convention, and if the reader of the report is among the future meeting sites, that CVB will have an opportunity to track quality data about the group and its convention activity.

These data are useful in bringing strategic focus to CVB efforts. With the meeting history, current activities, and future activities of a highly desirable convention or meeting, a CVB marketing staff can map out a series of sales and promotional activities designed to match the destination's strengths and facilities with the requirements of the group.

Among bureau sales activities are probably an annual travel schedule that includes a presence or trade show exhibit at key CEMI conventions and meetings around the country. Typical of these would be the annual meetings held by the Professional Convention Managers Association (PCMA), the National Association of Exposition Managers (NAEM), Meeting Planners International (MPI), the American Society of Association Executives (ASAE), the Greater Washington Society of Association Executives (WSAE) and other meetings and conventions that concentrate convention and meeting market decision makers in one place. Individual sales calls and travel relative to specific sales targets are also a regular part of CVB activities.

Additionally, bureaus will host familiarization trips called "FAM" trips and "fly-ins" within their community with the help of their hospitality and CEMI membership. These are designed to host meeting planners and executives of associations and groups who are in the process of making site selections for future conventions.

CONCLUSION

This chapter has focused on the convention- and meeting-related activities of a typical community's CVB. As outlined in the discussion of bureau organization, most major market CVBs will also have functional components that perform specific activities at various levels to promote other aspects of the visitor market (for instance, the free independent traveler). CVBs, in the modern era, are a critical and fundamental member of the CEMI and serve as conduits of marketing information among the purchasers of a region's CEMI services and the providers of those services.

REFERENCES

Beckelman, Jeff, and John Marks. 1984. Working Effectively with Convention Bureaus. *Convention World* May/June: 22–25.

Blair, Adam. 1988. Show Managers Are Mad as Hell: Hotels, C&VBs "Low Ball" Room Counts. *Meeting News* June: 1, 21, 103.

Englander, Todd. 1985. CVBs on the March. *Meetings and Conventions* May: 65–72, 77–78.

Gartrell, Richard B. 1988. *Destination Marketing for Convention and Visitor Bureaus.* Dubuque, Iowa: Kendall/Hunt, 309 pp.

Hosansky, Mel, et al. 1986. The Evolution of an Industry. *Meetings and Conventions Magazine* June: 48–67.

Hoyle, Leonard H., David C. Dorf, and Thomas J. A. Jones. 1989. *Managing Conventions and Group Business.* East Lansing, Michigan: The Education Institute of the American Hotel and Motel Association.

Levin, Jay. 1988. The House Vise: CVBs vs. Travel Companies. *Meetings and Conventions* December: 26–37.

Markarian, Margie. 1989. Turning Back the Clock: The History of CVBs. *Meeting News* 13(11):7–53.

McGee, Regina M., ed. 1985. *The Convention Liaison Council Manual.* Washington, D.C.: The Convention Liaison Council.

McGee, Regina M. 1986. Who's Getting the Room Taxes You're Paying? *Successful Meetings* September: 40–43.

Nichols, Barbara, ed. 1985. *Professional Meeting Management.* Birmingham, Alabama: The Professional Convention Management Association.

Siskin, Jonathan. 1988. Tracking Hotel Taxes and Their Impact on Meetings. *Corporate and Incentive Travel* February: 18–21.

Tritsch, Catherine. 1988. C&VBs Discover Corporate Meetings. *Successful Meetings* January: 119–125.

8

Exhibitors and Exhibit Design

CHAPTER OBJECTIVES

1. To delineate the place of exhibitors in the CEMI
2. To provide knowledge of the decision criteria corporations use to choose exhibiting at trade shows as a marketing medium
3. To overview the professional activities of the exhibit manager
4. To introduce the concept of evaluating exhibit effectiveness
5. To overview the process and personnel involved in the design and production of trade show and exposition exhibits

INTRODUCTION

In order to put the importance of exhibitors and exhibit designers in perspective to the overall context of the CEMI, one has only to refer to Exhibit 1.1 showing the CEMI wheel to see the number of CEMI components that would be affected if large numbers of companies decided overnight to cease using exhibits at trade shows to carry a significant portion of their marketing message.

Without exhibitors renting space from show managers, show managers would have diminished reasons to rent large spaces in convention centers and hotel exhibit facilities. At the same time, without the income produced by trade shows and expositions, many association meeting planners would not be able to afford to hold the lavish annual conventions they do now. Also, the funding bases for other association activities would be significantly diminished.

A decision to cease exhibiting would ripple through virtually every member of the CEMI, from the immediate effects felt by show managers, to buildings and meeting planners. So, in a major way, exhibitors, by making the decision to utilize trade shows as an avenue to further their marketing efforts, are financially intertwined with all segments of the CEMI.

Description of Costs	Three-Year Average 1975-1977,%	Three-Year Average 1977-1979,%	Three-Year Average 1979-1981,%	Three-Year Average 1981-1983,%	Three-Year Average 1983-1985,%	Three-Year Average 1985-1987,%
Exhibit Space Rental	25	22	21	21	21	24
Exhibit Construction	31	30	27	24	21	23
Refurbishing	12	9	11	12	12	10
Show Services	16	17	17	19	21	22
Transportation	7	9	12	12	13	13
Special Personnel*	3	2	3	4	5	2
Specialty Advertising	2	3	2	2	2	2
Miscellaneous	4	8	7	6	5	4
	100%	100%	100%	100%	100%	100%
Exhibit Personnel Expenses as a Percentage of Total Direct Costs	37%	41%	41%	37%	34%	33%

* Presenters, models, other live talent.

Note: Exhibit construction costs used in calculating the allocation percentages are amortized costs, i.e., new or original construction costs divided by the number of times the exhibit was to be used.

Exhibit 8.1 Average allocation of direct exhibit and personnel costs. *Source:* Exhibit Surveys, Inc., for the Trade Show Bureau (1988, 7). Used with permission.

Exhibit 8.1 displays the distribution of these financial relationships as percentages of total cost for the exhibiting company. These percentages represent three-year averages going back to the 1975–1977 period, and are current through 1987.

Note that space rental for exhibits has risen recently after stabilizing for several years dating back to the 1977–1979 period. There also seems to be a steady rise in the cost of various show services reported by exhibit managers, along with a similar increase in transportation costs. Most of the other major categories of cost remain constant, with the exception of a decline over the reporting period in budgeted costs for exhibit construction and design.

Note also that exhibit personnel expenses, displayed on the bottom line, are in addition to the costs reported in the table and are expressed as a percentage of those total direct costs. If, for instance, exhibiting costs were US$100,000 for the 1979–1981 period, personnel costs would total an additional US$41,000. Exhibit personnel costs seem to have declined from the 1977–1979 period. This decrease is probably attributable to using fewer personnel in staffing exhibits since personnel costs have certainly risen over the past 10–12 years. These personnel costs include salaries, travel, hotels, meals, and other corporate obligations incurred by employees on behalf of the exhibiting effort.

The importance of exhibiting and exhibitors as a corporate marketing medium is further evidenced by the organization that advances the cause of professionalism for exhibitors internationally, the International Exhibitors Association (IEA). Incorporated in 1968 as the National Trade Show Exhibitors Association (NTSEA), it changed its name in 1983 to IEA to reflect the international composition of its membership and the increase in the scope of its professional activities.

As an educational, technical, and professional organization, it also sponsors an annual conference at which the membership of IEA attends what is known as the "TS^2," which is a trade show about trade shows. It is at this trade show for exhibitors that IEA members learn about the latest in exhibit technology from corporations that display exhibits designed to market directly to exhibitors whose professional activities can be enhanced by the products seen at TS^2 (Ball 1986, 4).

If that sounds confusing, it must considered in the overall context of how the CEMI works: There are companies producing products that are designed, either exclusively or in part, to be utilized by other companies as a vehicle through which to further *their* marketing efforts. This underscores the intricate financial and professional relationships that exist among and between members of the CEMI.

EXHIBITING AS A MARKETING MEDIUM

Companies choose to participate in exhibiting and trade show/expositions for a variety of reasons, but those most often cited focus on advantages that exposition participation has over other forms of marketing and sales (Walter 1989, 36, 39):

- "You can target the market you want to reach based on the type of attendance and/or the function of the attendee. This enables you to pinpoint the market and eliminate the shotgun marketing approach."
- "Pre-qualified prospects come to you. Prospects seek you out and are often people you don't know or haven't dealt with previously."
- "You can reinforce your entire marketing program by utilizing the exposition as a part of a campaign that includes other forms of promotional activities such as direct-mail, magazine advertising, promotional giveaways and electronic media."
- "The exposition, with its pre-qualified attendees, develops the substantial leads for future follow-ups that reduce overall sales and marketing cost."
- "The exposition is an action-oriented medium that enables your sales personnel to close the order *now*."

Perhaps the most compelling reasons for companies to choose exhibiting at trade shows as an element of their marketing program relate to costs. As seen as Exhibit 8.2, the comparative cost of an industrial sales call is becoming increasingly disproportionate to the cost of reaching a qualified exhibit visitor at an exposition. This disproportionate relationship commenced in 1979 and continues through the mid-1980s.

It can be said that a trade show or exposition combines elements under the general rubric of marketing, such as advertising, sales, promotion, publicity, personal selling, product demonstration, and analysis of competition, resulting in a "synthesis" of activities that creates an "artificial marketplace" (Young 1986, 2). As such, expositions are attractive to companies for other reasons in addition to, but related ultimately to, cost.

If a product is extremely complex or otherwise difficult to demonstrate in print or electronic media, the exposition lends itself to putting potential customers in hands-on contact with a complicated product. Similarly, if the sales level associated with marketing a product represents high cost, companies will be inclined to look favorably upon expositions as arenas in which to market specific products. If a product is fairly young in its life cycle, or is a new introduction, expositions and trade shows are an ideal event at which to introduce a product to potential clientele. Additionally, if potential customers

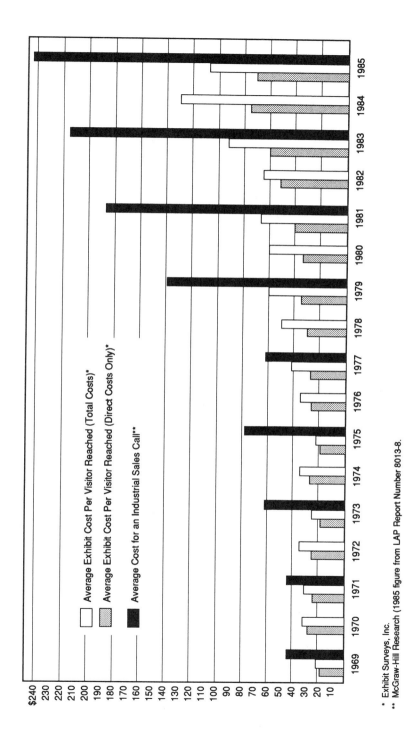

Exhibit 8.2 Average exhibit cost per visitor reached and average industrial sales call costs for seventeen years. *Source:* Greicus (no date, 2). Trade Show Bureau. Used with permission.

are widely distributed and not concentrated in any given geographical area, the cost factor comes into play in concentrating qualified buyers in this artificial marketplace (Lilien 1983, 29).

Other factors that are important in influencing a company's decision to use exhibiting at trade shows involve those related to the quality of the audience that might be attracted to that particular trade show. Elements of audience quality depend on the number of decision makers among the attendees, along with the proportion of those decision makers in the company's targeted market. If attendees at the trade show are highly qualified corporate executives who can make purchase decisions regarding equipment and products, either on the show floor or with minimal consultation with others after the show, these become high-quality attendees. At the same time, if, through their marketing efforts, show managers or meeting planners do a good job of screening and qualifying attendees, corporate exhibiting decisions become easier. Companies deciding on trade show participation will also consider carefully the number of attendees that will be at the convention or trade show, along with the location their exhibit will have on the show floor (Bello 1986; Dickinson and Faria 1984).

There is some evidence that the aggressiveness of the company in its market arena influences the decision-making process regarding participation in trade shows (Lilien 1983, 27). Aggressiveness can be related to some of the other decision criteria, but perhaps the one that it most properly reflects is the level of competition in which a company is engaged. A recent example from among the highly competitive sport and casual shoe market has NIKE, Reebok, and L.A. Gear unveiling their 1990 models of athletic shoes at the National Sporting Goods Association's World Sports Expo at Chicago's McCormick Place in September 1989. NIKE invested the resources necessary to design and erect an exhibit at McCormick Place that took up a total of 75,000 square feet (Buck 1989, E7). Commitments at this level provide a dramatic example of corporate aggressiveness within a competitive environment.

THE EXHIBIT MANAGER

Once the decision process has been completed at corporate levels to participate in exhibiting at expositions, under most circumstances, the subsequent decisions related to the exhibiting process fall to the individual designated as the exhibit manager. This individual may have other titles such as advertising manager, communication manager, or marketing manager (Young 1986, 7). In most circumstances, however, this person has as a central part of his or her professional activities the management and execution of the corporate exhibit program.

The exhibit manager, in turn, becomes responsible for the primary decisions and management activities on behalf of the corporate exhibit program. In general, these decisions involve selecting shows, budgeting, setting trade show and exhibit objectives, selecting and training booth personnel, and evaluating trade show exhibit and personnel performance (Young 1986, 18).

Exhibit 8.3 outlines the major responsibilities and activities of the exhibit

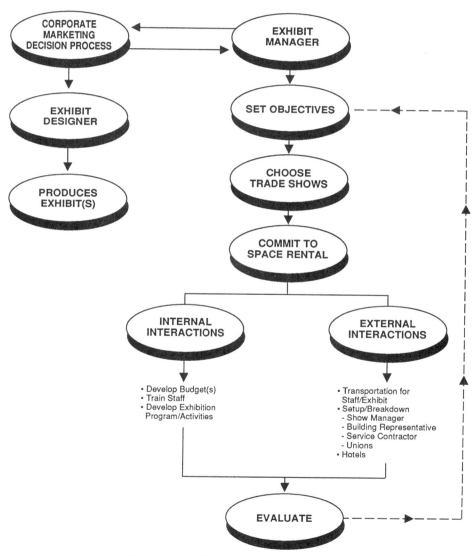

Exhibit 8.3 Diagram of exhibit manager activities.

manager. Note that the corporate marketing decision process is an interactive process utilizing and drawing upon the expertise of the exhibit manager in making high-level corporate decisions. Similarly, the relationship between corporate officers, the exhibit manager, and the designer and producer of the exhibit is also a cooperative effort in order that the exhibit that eventually carries the marketing message of the company is designed and executed in a way that most effectively fulfills the company's goals in exhibiting. It is also important that the exhibit can be effectively utilized and managed by exhibiting staff. A large exhibit of the NIKE class, for instance, is a dubious investment if exhibit personnel cannot work it efficiently and effectively.

The remainder of responsibilities and activities outlined in Exhibit 8.3 are vested in the authority of the exhibit manager.

It is shown in Exhibit 8.3 that a primary or initial responsibility of the exhibit manager is to set objectives for participation in trade shows and expositions. It is at this point that the exhibit manager demonstrates his or her knowledge and understanding of corporate marketing goals by setting priorities to accomplish them at any given trade show or exposition. The objectives most frequently cited as playing important roles in an exhibit program are:

- Generate qualified sales leads
- Develop interest in company and/or products
- Maintain an image
- Intensify awareness
- Establish a presence
- Introduce a new product
- Generate immediate sales

These seven exhibiting objectives were those most often cited by 316 exhibit managers in one study (Young 1986, 24) and are presented here in rank order indicating managers who "always" use these objectives in their exhibit program. In this instance, generating qualified sales leads ranks as the number one or most often used objective. In addition to the first, the next four objectives strongly suggest that exhibit managers couch their objectives in terms that are not very quantifiable, at least in immediate analysis. Clearly, however, the objectives indicate that managers see their presence at trade shows and expositions as being more than unidimensional sales activities.

Show selection will be based on many of the same factors that corporate managements use to decide to exhibit initially. A target audience needs to be identified, and through the objectives, the manager needs to determine what sorts of responses the company is anticipating from participation in the trade show. Data produced by show managements and meeting planners regarding demographics and characteristics of convention and exposition attendees will also be analyzed.

Once the appropriate trade shows and expositions have been chosen, the exhibit manager then sets the program in motion by committing to space rental. Exhibit space is typically assigned by the show manager or convention management to potential exhibitors according to one of four methods (Nichols 1985, 230–232):

- **First-come, first-served:** The classic method—the offering of exhibit space at a given show is made and booth space allotted based on the order in which requests are received.
- **Point system:** Exhibit space assignments are awarded on some previously established criteria that award points to exhibiting firms based on number of years an exhibitor has participated, amount of booth space used, and other factors that suggest some reward associated with establishing a long-term relationship between the exhibitor and the exposition.
- **Lottery system:** Under a lottery system of booth assignment, exhibitors will draw numbers for a position in selecting their exhibit space, and then selection is made in a numerical progression from lowest to highest lottery number, or vice versa.
- **Advance sales:** Under this method, booth assignments are made for the upcoming exposition during the run of the current exposition. Trade show management canvasses exhibitors and encourages them to sign up and commit to space for the coming year.

Whichever allocation system exhibit managers confront once they have committed to space rental, they must then seek confirmation and the finalization of financial arrangements. The manager can then turn organizational attention to the internal and external interactions that are critical to participation in the event. Since many of these interactions occur simultaneously, they will not be discussed in separate sections, but will be woven together to suggest their relationships.

Among the predominantly internal activities and interactions in which the exhibit manager participates are the very important tasks involved in developing the trade show budget. Most exhibit managers have authority to develop and execute the trade show budget, and perhaps the best way to view the budgeting responsibilities is to consider an inventory of the major budget variables to which the exhibit manager must allocate resources.

Exhibit 8.4 displays the five major budget variables along with the elements of those variables that influence the final size of resources allocated to each.

Exhibit Design & Construction	• New Construction • Exhibit Preparation & Refurbishing
Space Rental Costs	
Freight Transportation	• Common Carrier • Van Lines • Air Shipments • Drayage, Warehouse to Booth & Out • Drayage, Dock to Booth & Out
Show Services	• Installation & Dismantle Labor • Electrician Labor Per Hour • Electrician Labor Per Outlet • Plumbing Labor • Janitor Labor • Guard Service • Floral Service • Furniture Rental • Audio/Visual Rental • Projectionist Labor • Photography Service • Telephone • Utilities, Compressed Air • Utilities, Electricity • Utilities, Gas • Utilities, Water
Other	• Presenters/Models/Live Talent • Hotel Accommodations • Air Travel • Specialty Advertising • Exhibit Staff Training

Exhibit 8.4 Exhibitor budget expense categories. *Source:* Abstracted from IEA (1989, 4). Used with permission.

While exhibit design and construction is not a budget function that is associated with every show, elements of construction make up a significant portion of annual direct exhibit expenses (see, for instance, Exhibit 8.1). When refurbishing exhibits is added to this, it represents an area of controllable expense to which the exhibit manager has to pay careful attention.

Space rental costs are generally out of the hands of the exhibit manager, but may be varied by the amount of space to which the manager commits in any given exposition. Transportation expenses does not include the outlay of funds that managers have to allocate relative to air and ground transportation for exhibit personnel and staff. The components of this budget category, as displayed here, may not be pertinent to every show, but represent the universe of possible exhibit transportation expenses.

Show services that may be contracted for with either the exposition service contractor (ESC) or the building are presented here to show the potential inventory. These services may have varying degrees of influence on individual exhibitor budgets, and while it is unlikely that very many exhibits will require all of these, some do and most require at least some. It must, therefore, be kept in mind that the exhibit manager has significant potential outlays of expense dollars to service contractors and buildings for show-related services.

Other expenses can include staff-related travel and training expenses, entertainment, special promotional or advertising expenses, and allocations dedicated to casual labor of special staff that are hired on a nonrecurring basis to enhance the exhibit and its message.

The precision with which exhibit managers can predict the level of any of these budget variables will be one test by which the fiscal integrity of the exhibit management program is judged. The key to success here is often associated with knowing what has gone on in past budget periods and engaging in the kinds of research necessary to predict expenses with accuracy (Millikin 1988, 30).

One good source of budget information on potential charges that will impact budgeting decisions are the "exhibitor's service kits" typically compiled and distributed by show management or ESCs relative to participation in a particular exposition. These kits are informational packets containing data on materials and services important to exhibitors, and they are available through show management (Nichols 1985, 235–236). Among these data are information about booth position, information on the site and facility, information and regulations about payment policies and union activities, and price lists and ordering information for all potential decorating and show service charges (Corcoran 1989, passim). Millikin (1988, 30) recommends the further tactic for exhibit managers to call service contractors and product vendors directly and ask for and receive exact quotes on services required during the run of the show.

When it becomes necessary for exhibit managers to tighten or restrict budgetary expenses, a number of strategies exist from which managers can choose. First of all, exhibit space can be reduced. Second, the number of shows to which the exhibit is committed may be reduced or limited. A manager can choose not to participate in first-time shows, for instance, going only to shows with which the company has had significant and successful experience. Other specific cost reductions may be made in utilities and other services such as cleaning, photography, and audiovisual (Knight 1988).

Because virtually no exhibit in and of itself sells the product, a critical component of the exhibit manager's job is choosing and training staff and booth personnel to advance the goals of the company and help achieve the exhibit manger's objectives. Booth personnel represent and enhance the image designed into the exhibit.

There are four important considerations in selecting staff (Chapman 1987, 202–203):

1. The interests of the audience of trade show attendees should be matched by the interest and capabilities of the staff.
2. The site of the show: As audiences tend to be regional, staff should be selected to be representative of the region in which the trade show is held. In that way, they can more closely identify with their clientele.
3. Booth and exhibit personnel should also have outgoing personalities and be politely and expeditiously aggressive in qualifying booth visitors as prospects and potential sales leads.
4. Finally, if the products being exhibited are technically sophisticated, the exhibit manager needs to seriously consider employing individuals on the exhibit staff who have the requisite technical knowledge and skills to demonstrate products. They must also be able to answer involved and intricate technically oriented questions.

There is some reason to believe that simply assigning field sales staff to the exhibit booth or display is not necessarily the most effective method by which to choose booth personnel. It has been suggested that rather than field sales people who have traditionally traveled a territory, people who have an inclination or training towards on-premise retail-type sales may be better suited for the activities required of an effective exhibit staff on a trade show floor (Conlin and Seidenberg 1986, 51).

Exhibit staff need to be trained not only in sales skills, but in dealing with circumstances that are unique to exposition exposures. They need to be able to anticipate the sorts of questions that attendees will ask and should be trained in what to expect from attendees in terms of their background, demographics, and job titles.

Training exhibit staff also entails instruction in various company or exhibit rules and regulations on professional comportment. These may include regulations about attire; prohibitions against smoking, drinking, or eating in the booth; and specific ways to approach and qualify potential clientele. Show management, in many instances, has assisted exhibitors in qualifying attendees by issuing different colored or bordered badges that, at a glance, let exhibit staff know what type of attendee they are dealing with. A badge with a green stripe, for instance, may identify a purchasing executive; a badge with a blue stripe may be allotted to marketing executives.

The selection and training of exhibit personnel and their management is a critical aspect of the exhibit manager's job. The quality of the staff will have a significant impact on the ability of exhibit management to achieve their objectives for a given exposition.

Other aspects of the exhibit manager's job during the exposition involve the various interactions relative to managing the exhibit and its staff and other activities during the course of the show. The manager schedules exhibit personnel; provides meal breaks, support equipment, and supplies; arranges for housing, travel, and meals; assures that the exhibit's security needs are met; and is generally available on the floor of the exposition to support, back up, manage, and lead the exhibit personnel activities.

One very important job of the exhibit manager is "lead management." This involves setting up the systems and methods to organize, classify, allocate and follow up on sales leads generated at the show (Jones, 1989). Some shows are now offering exhibitors sophisticated electronic lead tracking systems where attendees' individual data and audience characteristics are encoded at registration on magnetic stripes (like a credit card) on show attendance badges. Booth personnel simply "swipe" the card through a reader and a computer generates a report for the exhibit manager to use in "lead management."

Another aspect of exhibit management that may be required by individual exhibitor programs is the sponsorship, planning, and execution of ancillary events that serve to buttress and enhance the corporate image and participation in the show. Among the events in which exhibitors may participate are the financial sponsorship of meal functions, receptions, parties, or technical sessions associated with the convention or exposition. Another typical and popular ancillary activity that exhibitors traditionally provide is the hospitality suite, where they provide food and beverage for a selected clientele in a hotel room designed to allow exhibit personnel to more closely interact with highly qualified potential clients. A recent development in this area has been the practice of exhibitors renting meeting rooms in a convention facility, furnishing them through an ESC, and contracting with the facility's caterer for foodservice—all to provide a private hospitality room on the show premises. Other exhibitors have arranged for catered food and beverage service right in the exhibit booth. In each case, these hospitality activities are designed to enhance the image of the exhibitor, build goodwill, and provide additional sales opportunities.

Other exhibitors have found ways to evidence their support for the convention or show attendees by sponsoring an element of ground transportation or some sort of entertainment event. Still other activities may include the sponsorship of a road race or some other type of athletic contest. All of these activities are designed to enhance the reputation of the exhibitor and provide an avenue by which the exhibitor has more reason to more closely interact with the highly qualified segments of attendees (Young 1986, 30, 42).

EXHIBIT EVALUATION

Evaluation of an exhibit's effectiveness at a trade show should be closely linked to the objectives set forth for that trade show. Exhibit managers will, therefore, try to develop quantifiable measures and gather data during the course of the exposition in order to judge how well their exhibit achieved its objectives.

Among the most frequently used performance measures, in order of usage, are (Kerin and Cron 1986, 14):

- Subsequent sales force feedback
- Number of leads generated
- Number of people visiting the exhibit
- Total attendance at the trade show
- Quantity of actual sales from leads

The data that are related to the sales measures in the foregoing list are usually expressed in terms of actual sales by field staff or exhibit personnel. Similarly, some attendees may indicate buying plans as highly likely and request that they be contacted after the show. The number of people visiting the booth can be seen as a measure of exhibit efficiency by the simple measurement of booth visits per day as a percentage of daily show attendance (Bellizzi and Lipps 1984, 51). These figures are then used to gain a measure of booth effectiveness through the cost per visitor reached. Exhibit managers can also use the total number of booth visits as a percentage of total attendance at the trade show, or a daily, hourly, or other incrementally divided measure to judge how well the booth achieved its attendance objectives. Booth visits and sales leads may also be expressed as ratios to various booth budget expense categories as evaluative measures.

WHO IS THE EXHIBIT MANAGER?

According to data developed in one recent study (Kerin and Cron 1986), the modern exhibit manager is college-educated, having majored in some aspect of business administration; is 39 years old; and is typically a male. This may be changing, though, for 70% of the female exhibit managers are less than 40 years old, and 55% of the male exhibit managers were, in this study, in excess of 40 years old. These exhibit managers have been discharging exhibit manager duties for less than five years and, typically, have less than ten years of business experience. Before moving into the exhibit management job, they held some other position in the company.

Gross salary across all types of job titles that have exhibit management responsibilities, in 1987, averaged US$35,927 (Knight 1987, 31).

This typical exhibit manager faces a number of major challenges in discharging all of the responsibilities of his or her office. Those challenges are (Kerin and Cron 1986, 28):

- Coordinating people and functions within the company
- Gaining top management's support
- Operating within budget constraints
- Coordinating multiple shows at one time
- Creating successful, impressive exhibits
- Managing relations with vendors and show management

Because some companies still do not have a clear and unambiguous commitment to trade show exhibiting, it becomes a particular challenge for the exhibit manager to marshal the resources available within any given company to support the efforts of exhibiting at trade shows and expositions.

A similar and concomitant challenge exists in gaining and retaining top management's support for the exhibiting function because, as pointed by Bonoma (1983, 76), many executives have a view that trade show participation is nothing more than a fairly useless perk that is only designed to benefit some exhibiting company executive and long-time customers.

Other challenges listed here are variously rated by exhibit managers and are displayed in order of their importance to the exhibit managers studied. Creating successful and impressive exhibits is a challenge that has not only creative and aesthetic aspects associated with it, but also incorporates most traditional managerial functions.

The picture of an exhibit manager that emerges from the analysis and research reported here is one of an individual whose coordinative talents are probably foremost among the managerial functions he or she needs to master. Being able to balance competing demands on the exhibit manager's time from both internal and external sources highlights the implicit challenges associated with the job of exhibit manager.

The profession of exhibit manager and the tasks associated with corporate exhibiting programs are critical and integral components of the CEMI.

EXHIBIT DESIGN AND PRODUCTION

For the purposes of this discussion, we must assume that when NIKE commits to a 75,000-square-foot piece of McCormick Place, the company is not just simply filling it up with racks of shoes. Rather, that sort of financial commitment would seem to call for a marketing display and sales area designed to accomplish most of the corporation's goals, and in a dramatic way. It can be said, therefore, that three major influences operate in the design and production of trade show and exposition exhibits:

- The firm's image and marketing objectives
- The exhibitor's product
- Exhibiting criteria

Each exhibitor participating in a trade show requires an exhibit that accomplishes its marketing purposes. According to Bob Francisco, executive vice president of an exhibit design firm (1986, 58), "An exhibit's role is not to be an attractive series of product stands, but to market a product or service. An exhibit's form, therefore, must follow that marketing function in order to be successful."

The question that needs to be asked in this context is: How can the exhibit's design contribute to the staff's ability to accomplish whatever the company's marketing objectives may be? As discussed in the previous section, whether trade show participation is designed to enhance the company's image, keep track of competition, accomplish direct sales or establish new sales leads, or achieve any of the other objectives commonly set by exhibitors, the exhibit itself must contribute to their achievement.

The design should be an integral part of the entire corporate message. It is of no use to mount large sophisticated advertising and promotional campaigns designed to attract potential clientele to the company's exhibit at a trade show and have them find a low-budget pipe-and-drape booth with a basic skirted table and piles of unorganized brochures and promotional materials.

The exhibitor's product, of course, has a significant influence on design. According to Chapman (1987, 141–147), four categories of products have differing influences on the form the display design eventually takes:

- **Small products that have to be displayed,** whether a single product or a number of different types, need an exhibit that effectively presents them in a retail type of environment. It must be remembered, though, that under trade show circumstances, attendees need to be able to see, touch, and interact with the products, so they cannot be locked away behind glass or other inaccessible sorts of display cases.

- **Small and medium-sized products that need to be demonstrated** require demonstration stations distributed around the display area that will encourage circulation and, at the same time, allow people to view demonstrations by exhibit personnel without crowding the display or aisle areas. This type of display must be designed to permit obstruction-free, over-the-shoulder viewing and allow exhibit staff to interact with and answer questions from booth visitors.
- **Services** present unique problems because under most circumstances, they cannot be displayed or demonstrated in the same ways a product can, for services are neither tangible, nor can they be inventoried. The exhibitor, therefore, is faced with the problem of how to sell or demonstrate a concept or a promise. Audiovisual equipment, graphics, computer-based interactive experiences and other "high-tech" productions need to utilize the classic service production philosophy of involving the customer in the service delivery system.
- Finally, **large products** also present unique problems. Everything from air-conditioning units to petroleum-drilling equipment to full-size trucks and trailers are routinely exhibited at various heavy-equipment and industrial trade shows. In these contexts, items on display often cannot be demonstrated but, again, audiovisual and graphic representations of the products performing their tasks may serve to answer most of the questions potential clients may have. It is also an opportunity for exhibit personnel to line up their clientele for off-premise demonstrations based on the interest generated through the floor display of the product.

The form of the product will, therefore, influence to a significant degree the final form of the exhibit's design.

The third major influence of exhibit design has to do with the exhibiting program the exhibit manager chooses to advance the marketing objectives of the firm. What these amount to, in many cases, are physical realities of the exhibit that influence the exhibit manager's job and how the exhibiting program is executed.

Among the major managerial considerations in this context are those that have to do with the number of shows to which the exhibit needs to be transported and the shows' relative proximity. The exhibit manager is also concerned with how much of the exhibit will be used in every venue to which it is committed. In some cases, companies may require exhibit designs that, for certain expositions, need not be present in their entire form. NIKE, for instance, cannot count on using 75,000 square feet in every venue at which the firm exhibits.

Other reality-based managerial considerations have to do with the time of the year of the show, whether significant numbers of products need to be shipped to each exposition site to stock the exhibit, and what the company's competitors are doing and how they exhibit.

Once these major issues have been resolved, exhibiting firms can then choose designers based on what the design firms do. Among the services provided by exhibit designers are (Chapman 1987, 155–156):

- Exhibit and graphic sign design
- Physical production of exhibits and graphic signs
- Development of booth space layout and exhibit setup drawings
- Exhibit storage and freight management service
- Supervision of exhibit setup and teardown at shows
- Crate design and manufacture
- Exhibit repair and refurbishing
- Exhibit marketing plan development
- Booth sales training
- Hospitality and special event management
- Live or audiovisual show production and management
- Development and production of show literature
- Show-related direct-mail or promotion management
- Research management
- Sales lead distribution and tracking

The design firm may provide some or all of these services, but under most circumstances, individual firms will offer a selected inventory from the above comprehensive list. Exhibiting firms can choose product and service suppliers based on the requirements of their particular program. At the very least, exhibit design, graphics, and the physical production of exhibits are fundamental requirements for most exhibiting companies. An increasingly important aspect of design and production is the provision of custom-made crates for ease of storage and shipment.

From this list of potential services, it can be seen that exhibiting companies have available to them a rich selection of choices that cross many other functional lines represented within the CEMI. Some of the services potentially offered by exhibit design and production firms have traditionally been the province of service contractors, destination management companies, or the exhibiting firms themselves. The fact that exhibit design and production firms have expanded the range of products and services to this extent is indicative of the importance that exhibiting plays in the CEMI. Exhibiting companies need a total design of their corporate exhibit that reflects the role it plays in reinforcing corporate image, delivering marketing messages, and generating sales.

There are various types of designer firms that discharge some or all of the duties inventoried above (abstracted from Chapman 1987, 155–157):

- Design and production can be done **in-house by the exhibiting company,** and in many instances, companies have the creative talent and production capabilities within their marketing departments to accomplish their own exhibit design and production.
- A **full-service exhibit house** is one that will provide all services, from initial consultation, market analysis, and design and production services through, on the above list, exhibit repair and refurbishing. They may also provide selective services relative to the actual use of the exhibit at the event.
- An **independent or custom designer** may or may not involve production, but many firms will utilize the talents of an independent creative design firm to produce the design, and then seek production and construction of the exhibit elsewhere.
- **Advertising agencies,** particularly those with large and sophisticated media production departments, have become increasingly involved in the production of exhibits as trade show and exposition media. This follows logically on some advertising firms' desire to blend all marketing media in a complete, cohesive, and related message on behalf of their corporate clients.
- **"Off-the-shelf" manufactured exhibits** of a generic, modular, and flexible nature represent another source of exhibit materials for exhibiting firms. Exhibitors can purchase from an inventory of displays, shelving, tables, and other furniture and display units that are portable, flexible and lend themselves to personal customization by the exhibiting company. Firms can, in effect, create their own physical presence by utilizing products, their own graphics, and exhibit staff to effectively present a unique presence on the show floor.
- **Exposition service contractors** (ESCs) also offer a variety of exhibit design and construction services to their clients. ESCs may also rent modular displays as part of their service and product inventory.

INTERACTIONS

Exhibit designers and producers interact primarily with exhibiting company clients. In addition, through their professional group, the Exhibit Designers and Producers Association (EDPA), they maintain linkages with show services firms and personnel, show managers, and transportation companies.

Obviously, the more deeply the exhibit designer is involved in the display of the exhibit at the exposition, the more closely he or she will also interact with other members of the CEMI, such as hotels, buildings, and meeting planners.

FUTURE AND CONCLUSION

At this stage of industry development, it is possible to predict that exhibits will probably become more sophisticated. The sophistication will, in many cases, increase costs, but exhibitors will capture savings in more flexible exhibits that have a longer life. There will also be a trend toward more interactive exhibits, which will possibly decrease exhibitors' costs by requiring fewer staff personnel. Exhibits will also have to be safety-engineered because fire and liability considerations are a major source of legal and financial concern to exhibitors, show managers, and buildings.

Exhibits, their management, and their design have been shown in this chapter to play a major and valuable role in the CEMI. Exhibit managers and their staffs participate in a range of activities through their exposition presence that impact most other members of the industry. Additional insights about exhibiting may be gained through references listed in the bibliography or directly from the Trade Show Bureau, IEA, or EDPA.

REFERENCES

Ball, Don, Conference Chair. 1986. *International Exhibitors Association Directory and Program*. Montreal, Canada: International Exhibitors Association Annual Conference and The Trade Show About Trade Shows, 91 pp.

Bellizzi, Joseph A., and Delilah J. Lipps. 1984. Managerial Guidelines for Trade Show Effectiveness. *Industrial Marketing Management* 13:49–52.

Bello, Daniel C. 1986. Attendee Purchase Behavior at an Industrial Trade Show. *Research Report #1070*. East Orleans, Massachusetts: Trade Show Bureau.

Bonoma, Thomas V. 1983. Get More out of Your Trade Shows. *Harvard Business Review* January–February: 75–83.

Buck, Richard. 1989. Northwest Stocks. *The Seattle Times* September 17: E6–E7.

Chapman, Edward A., Jr. 1987. *Exhibit Marketing: A Survival Guide for Managers*. New York: McGraw-Hill.

Conlin, Joseph, and Robert Seidenberg. 1986. Making the Sale at Trade Shows. *Successful Meetings* June: 50–52.

Corcoran, Thomas C. 1989. *Official Exhibitor Kit* (Manual). Chicago: National Restaurant Association.

Dickinson, John R., and A. J. Faria. 1984. Trade Show Organizers Take Note: Exhibitors Rank Participation Criteria. *Marketing News* 18(5):3.

Exhibit Surveys, Inc. 1988a. Exhibitors: Their Trade Show Practices. *Research Report #2050.* East Orleans, Massachusetts: Trade Show Bureau.

Exhibit Surveys, Inc. 1988b. Trade Show Exhibit Cost Analysis. *Research Report #2060.* East Orleans, Massachusetts: Trade Show Bureau, 14 pp.

Francisco, Bob. 1986. Booth Form Should Follow Marketing Function. *Successful Meetings* June: 58–59.

Greicus, Mike. (No date.) *Expositions: They Mean Business* (pamphlet). East Orleans, Massachusetts: Trade Show Bureau, 12 pp.

IEA. 1989. *1989 Budget Guide* (booklet). Annandale, Virginia: International Exhibitors Association, 8 pp.

Jones, Art. 1989. Private Communication

Kerin, Roger A., and William L. Cron. 1986. The Exhibit Manager Function—Perceptions of Exhibit Management and Marketing Executives. *Research Report #2040.* East Orleans, Massachusetts: Trade Show Bureau.

Knight, Lee. 1987. Exhibit Managers: Who Earns How Much. *Exhibitor* July: 27–56.

Knight, Lee. 1988. Budget Cutting in Lean Times (Parts One & Two). *Exhibitor* March and April. (Reprinted in *NAEM Inform-A-Gram #133*).

Lilien, Gary L. 1983. A Descriptive Model of the Trade Show Budgeting Decision Process. *Industrial Marketing Management* 12:25–29.

Millikin, Nancy A. 1988. Budget or Bust. *Tradeshow* February: 29–30.

Nichols, Barbara, ed. 1985. *Professional Meeting Management.* Birmingham, Alabama: The Professional Convention Management Association.

Walter, Donald J. 1989. Why Expositions Are a Vital Part of Your Marketing Plan. *Meeting Manager* June: 36, 39.

Young, Gary C. 1986. Exhibiting Practices: Setting Objectives and the Evaluation of Results. *Research Report #2010.* East Orleans, Massachusetts: Trade Show Bureau.

9

Transportation

CHAPTER OBJECTIVES

1. To describe the roles of the various forms of transportation important to the CEMI
2. To introduce the major implications of airline deregulation to the CEMI
3. To overview the tasks of convention, meeting, and exposition managers relative to event transportation requirements
4. To explore the linkages of transportation channels among CEMI components

INTRODUCTION

As introduced in Chapter 1, the concept of examining transportation relative to its role in the CEMI is more complex than the one-dimensional role airlines play in moving event attendees to and from their destination within the time frame of the convention, meeting, or trade show.

Realities of modern transportation systems and their interactions with each other complicate the picture. So does the role of airline deregulation and the subsequent changes in air routes, airports, airport hospitality environments, and ground transportation systems. These all combine in an increasingly complex equation within which the meeting planner, convention manager, or show manager must work to effectively manage this phase of his or her professional responsibilities.

Corporate meeting planners reported that expenditures for air transportation accounted for 22% of funds committed to meeting components, and added that ground transportation accounted for an additional 6% (M&C 1988, 24). The fact that nearly one-third of meeting expenses are attributable directly to transportation costs demonstrates the significance of the role transportation plays in a planner's decision criteria.

But it is not simply costs that have implications for interactions between CEMI components and transportation firms. The ease of transporting attendees (57%), transportation costs (46%), and distance from individual attendees (44%) were three of the top four factors considered important in destination selection for a corporate meeting planner (M&C 1988, 38).

The predominant importance of airlines, however, can be demonstrated by the fact that among corporate planners, 90% use commercially scheduled airlines frequently or sometimes for transportation to and from corporate meetings (M&C 1988, 42). Sixty-eight percent of corporate meeting planners have decision-making responsibility for airline travel, and 62% of those planners spend a moderate amount of time on various aspects of travel planning (M&C 1988, 44).

While there are no dollar figures available for association meeting planners, air transportation was considered very important by 65% of association meeting planners who plan national and international conventions and meetings (Myers 1989, 38), and ranked fourth in a list of ten factors considered important in site selection in another study of association meeting planners (ASAE 1986, B15).

Transportation *cost* for attendees was slightly less important for association meeting planners because between 87% and 90% of planners stated that attendees pay their own way even though the association may make broadly based travel arrangements available to meeting and convention attendees (M&C 1988, 77). However, ease of transportation to and from the convention and meeting location were ranked second in a 1987 *Meetings and Conventions* magazine study (M&C 1988, 74). Between 78% and 83% of association meeting planners execute meetings and conventions that involve air transportation (M&C 1988, 77).

It is therefore easy to see that transportation in general, and air travel specifically, play major roles in both corporate and association planners' professional activities relative to executing meetings and conventions.

AIR TRAVEL

It was perhaps the introduction of the jumbo or wide-body Boeing 747 aircraft in 1970 that had the earliest recognizable significant impact on the form that group movements, particularly those related to the CEMI, took.

The availability of the jumbo jets and, to a lesser extent, the proliferation of the smaller 727, made possible the transportion of groups from as few as a half dozen to more than 250 persons (Hosansky 1986, 52).

Prior to that, the interaction between meeting and convention planners (still a fledgling profession in the late sixties and early seventies) and the highly regulated airline transportation industry relied primarily upon individuals making their own travel arrangements. All that changed, however, beginning in 1978 with the introduction of the concept of airline deregulation. Its full implementation in the early 1980s has led industry members such as the Convention Liaison Council (CLC) to state:

> Never has it been more important to be knowledgeable about air travel, and never has it been more difficult to acquire that knowledge. With the deregulation of airlines . . . there has been a bewildering array of new air fares, changing regulations, emerging and vanishing air routes, and even airlines. Keeping abreast of these changes is not easy. (McGee 1985, 16)

Deregulation has clearly become one of the most important variables that govern the relationship of the various segments of the CEMI to the airline industry. It has become incumbent upon meeting planners and show managers to acquire knowledge and techniques in negotiating air travel arrangements on behalf of members and attendees planning to fly to events.

Because most of the major carriers in the United States and Canada fully recognize the importance of group-related travel, they have established divisions of their marketing effort to deal with convention, incentive, and charter sales exclusively. This division will typically be headed by a director or vice president and have a staff formulated and structured of account executives who are familiar with the conventions and meetings market and the needs, wants, and requirements of convention, exposition, and meeting planners.

Most airlines will participate in fare negotiations and other possible considerations, many of which are displayed in Exhibit 9.1. It should be remembered that group reservation policies will vary from carrier to carrier depending on a number of variables (McGee 1985, 17):

- Type of meeting (international or domestic)
- Time of year
- Passenger load factors
- Frequency of service
- Meeting site in relation to hub city

- Discounted Fares

- Complimentary Tickets for Staff (ratio negotiable)

- Toll-Free Telephone Reservations for Attendees

- Special Departure Lounges

- Early Boarding

- Assist Planners in Destination Cost Analysis

- Convention Desk at Facility

- Assistance in Promotional Efforts

- Purchase of Advertising in Group Media,
  Convention Program

- Arrival/Departure Manifests

Exhibit 9.1 Negotiation points for planners: airlines. *Source:* Abstracted from Convention Liaison Council Manual (1985, 53); and Nichols (1985, 157). Used with permission.

PLANNER/AIRLINE NEGOTIATIONS

Depending on which of the above variables (or combination thereof) is in play during a planner's pre-event activities, the planner may find varying levels of willingness on the part of the airlines to enter into significant negotiations. Negotiations can involve a number of potential points, the most common of which are abstracted from planning literature and displayed in Exhibit 9.1.

Fare negotiations will usually be manifested by a percentage reduction off published full-fare round-trip coach fares for a particular destination. Increasingly, airlines will participate in negotiations to provide complimentary tickets for use by planners and managers on some ratio basis related to how many attendees take advantage of the discounted convention fare. This, too, will vary from carrier to carrier, but in 1989 will normally be one complimentary round-trip ticket for every 40 to 50 attendee-paid round-trip tickets.

Most of these arrangements will include the airline's provision of a toll-free telephone number for attendees to call and a special account number to mention when making travel arrangements with the designated carrier. The designated carrier may also provide special departure lounges or access to VIP lounges at airports, early boarding for convention attendees, and other amenities designed to convey the airline's welcome to the convention or meeting attendee.

Planners may negotiate assistance from the airlines in analyzing relative travel costs and patterns from one potential site to another. Airlines may also participate on the floor of the convention, meeting, or trade show by having a visual presence in the form of a travel desk. Airlines may also financially support the organization by purchasing advertising in association magazines or convention programs, or by providing brochures that are useful in promoting attendance at the meetings.

Other services that may be available through the airline group marketing staff include the provision of arrival and departure passenger name manifests directly to the meeting planner so that he or she will have up-to-date daily information on attendee numbers. This helps the meeting planner or convention manager in judging utilization of ground transportation, housing requirements, and other attendance-related details of the event.

Planners may have requirements that demand extraordinary efforts on the part of airlines. At any given meeting or convention, there may be VIPs such as corporate or association top management, honored guests and speakers, or other program participants who require special travel arrangements, including first-class air travel. Airlines can usually help by assisting planners with travel arrangements consistent with those expected by the VIP.

Clearly, not only has airline deregulation changed the way in which not only airlines do business, but most components of the CEMI who traditionally book large volumes of traffic with airlines also find that their business relative to the airlines has been significantly changed. Perhaps two major effects of airline deregulation have had the most impact on members of the CEMI.

The first effect is the well-documented **restructuring of airline fares.** In the early to mid-1980s, airline fares dropped considerably and competition from new, restructured, and merged airlines kept fares at fairly low levels compared to levels as recently as 10 to 15 years ago. As the airline industry has restructured itself, fares will probably stabilize and then start to rise as more mergers result in fewer individual carriers and larger airlines operationally organized around geographic hubs.

Hubs are a second effect of airline consolidation. Certain airport facilities are singled out as the airlines' major operational emphasis in one area. At each airline's hub, the airline concentrates arriving and departing flights to permit the greatest number of cross-connections from feeder airlines and connecting flights from other destinations in the airline's own flight network (Glab 1985, 28).

Out from these hubs radiate the so-called spokes of airline route networks.

As a result of this new configuration, each airline has turned many former nonstop routes into one-stop flights. For instance, in the southeast United States, because so many major airlines have hubs concentrated in Atlanta, it is almost impossible to fly from the Gulf Coast directly to New York without a layover or plane change in Atlanta. Similar circumstances exist in Chicago, Denver, Los Angeles, St. Louis, New York, and Dallas/Ft. Worth, among others.

While this has created some inconvenience for travelers in terms of limiting nonstop flights, it has substantially increased the number of cities between and among which travelers can fly.

In addition to the establishment of hubs, most ". . . major carriers have also started signing marketing partnership agreements with regional and commuter airlines. These agreements, designed to feed traffic from the flights of the smaller carrier onto the larger one, and vice-versa, result in the smaller carriers benefitting from the nationwide reservations network of the larger partner . . ." (Glab 1985, 28). Because this has the effect of expanding the flight opportunities for larger numbers of people, the obvious impact on the CEMI results from the increased attractiveness of holding meetings at airline hubs to take advantage of travel arrangements and discounts that can be made with those hub airlines.

There is also some evidence that airlines are opening what are now termed "mini-hubs" in newer or secondary markets because the hub activities in primary markets have become saturated with flights (Beauchine 1986, 14). This has clear implications for meeting planners who prefer to site meetings, conventions, and expositions in secondary cities. They can now avail themselves of the same advantages associated with travel planning to primary city markets.

A further impact on the meetings market of airline hub development has been the rapid expansion of meeting and hospitality facilities at hub airports. A perfect example of this is the serious consideration now being given to the construction of a new convention center at Los Angeles International Airport after the present Los Angeles Convention Center has completed expansion in 1991 (McGee 1988, 81–82). The importance of airline and hub-related travel and hospitality business to a city like Denver is evidenced by the fact that the population of Denver recently voted to invite firms to bid on the construction of an entirely new airport by the mid-1990s.

Because of construction and travel activity patterns at airport hubs throughout the country, new and improved meeting sites and facilities at locations convenient to the air traveler will provide the meetings market in the coming decade with a significant increase in the range of choices of meeting sites depending, of course, on the type of meeting. Airport hotel facilities are still not close to garnering the majority of meeting planner convention activity, ranking fourth in the types of facilities used by corporate planners. Association meeting planners also had airport facilities ranked as fourth; however, when looking at the difference between facilities used for conventions and facilities used for association meetings, airport hotel facilities enjoyed more association meeting activity than convention activity (M&C 1988, 40, 76).

In the past, planners have avoided airport hotels for any but the shortest of meetings whose attendees required easy access to meeting facilities that they could fly into and out of on the same day. With the considerable construction of luxury-class hotel rooms and meeting facilities at hub airports, however, it becomes arguable that the attractiveness of combining preferential airfares, close proximity to meeting facilities, and convention-quality overnight lodging will mandate more careful consideration of airport area hotels on the part of meeting planners and convention managers. It appears that for certain events, the economics of scale that can be realized through utilizing hub locations may be very attractive to cost-conscious planners.

TRAVEL AGENTS

Another component of the transportation industry whose role needs to be introduced in these CEMI contexts is that of the travel agent. Historically (prior to deregulation), meeting planners and travel agents did business in much the same way as independent travelers and travel agencies. Planners mainly used travel agents as de facto ticket agents for the airline travel requirements of their groups. There is some reason to believe that these relationships are changing in a fundamental way.

Some travel agencies are now offering meeting planning activities on behalf of major corporate clients as a part of their travel service inventory. While some meeting planners see this as a threat (Leo 1986), most travel agencies will probably continue to do what they do best—provide specific services to all travelers. However, some agencies will continue to offer meeting planning services if they are successful and profitable ventures. As Doug Heath, executive vice president of Meeting Planners International, points out, while travel agencies moving into meeting planning is "a natural progression . . . [those] who perform well will survive." It may be that travel agency services will evolve more along the lines of destination management companies (Chapter 11), serving as adjuncts to planners on-site, as opposed to competition for planners for off-site activities.

Whatever becomes of this particular controversy, there is one aspect of the travel agent/meeting planner relationship in the travel distribution system that has the potential for fundamentally altering the structural relationship between planners and agencies. In 1982, in what was called the Competitive Marketing Case, the Civil Aeronautics Board analyzed and investigated agreements between airlines and travel agencies, which are, in effect, one of the most important distribution systems for airline ticketings. The purpose of this investigation was to determine if airline–travel agency agreements were anticompetitive. One of the major findings of this case was to allow airlines to appoint nonaccredited travel agents (outside agencies or individuals) to sell on-line point-to-point tickets (Bitner and Booms 1986, 106). Because of the prevalence of automated airline ticketing reservations systems, many of which handle ticketing and reservations for a number of affiliated airlines, planners may be doing meeting-related ticket booking directly with airlines, bypassing travel agencies altogether (Conte 1986, 79).

It appears likely, however, that travel agencies and meeting planners will continue to interact within the realm of the travel agency's primary function—that of providing airline tickets, especially for corporate planners. Whereas 58% of corporate meeting planners use travel agents, only 28% of association meeting planners normally use travel agency services (M&C 1988, 43, 80).

The data displayed in Exhibit 9.2 clearly demonstrate that even for those who use travel agencies, the primary relationship centers on airline ticketing. As might be expected, corporate planners accessed more travel agency services than association planners, reflecting association planners' convention planning management experience. For most services other than ticketing, association planners' knowledge of the market and willingness to enter into their own negotiations obviate the need for travel agents as intermediaries.

It seems clear from these data that the primary relationship between planners and travel agencies will remain airline ticketing, with some importance attached to hotel bookings, particularly for corporate planners.

GROUND TRANSPORTATION

Whether the event is a city-wide convention linking a score of hotels with a convention center, or a single meeting for eight marketing executives in one centralized location, it is axiomatic that on-site people need to be moved, if in no other context, at least from the airport to lodging facilities or the meeting site. It is a rare occurrence when the majority of attendees at any given meeting or event all arrive by personal transportation. Whatever the configuration of the event, however, knowledge about the capabilities,

TRAVEL AGENT SERVICE	CORPORATE PLANNERS	ASSOCIATION PLANNERS	
	All Types of Meetings	Conventions	Association Meetings
Airline Ticketing	97%	98%	98%
Hotel Room Reservations	55%	19%	28%
Hotel Recommendation	36%	7%	13%
Producing Itineraries	28%	12%	10%
Provide Maps, Brochures	22%	9%	16%
Destination Recommendation	22%	6%	7%
Hotel Selection	21%	4%	8%
Site Inspection	19%	16%	12%
Destination Selection	14%	3%	3%
Other	8%	3%	1%
Multiple Mentions BASE	(422)	(122)	(100)

Exhibit 9.2   Travel agency service usage (if planner used travel agent). *Source:* Meetings and Conventions. 1988. *Meetings Market '87.* Reed Travel Group: Secaucus, NJ (43, 80). Used with permission.

capacities, and types of ground transportation available at the meeting site are critical to the success of the event (McGee 1985, 18).

A characteristic mix of ground transportation in any given locale will be available from city or municipal bus lines, airport service buses, hotel proprietary buses, regular or group fare taxis, and private limousine and coach services (Nichols 1985, 158). The factors that govern which services will be chosen from which particular operators to handle ground transportation for an event will depend on a number of variables, the most common of which are cost, service, and performance reputation. The number and availability of the vehicles, their condition, and the planner's requirements for any special services may also be major considerations.

Some transportation companies provide integrated packages of services, including city and regional tours, nightclub packages, and sightseeing service tie-ins with tour boats and local air or helicopter transportation.

To gain perspective on the intricacies of ground transportation, consider a city-wide convention in Chicago that has 100,000 attendees, fills up virtually every first-class hotel room in the entire metropolitan area, and hosts a trade show at McCormick Place. The arrangement of the details relative to buses alone requires nothing less than professional transportation management. Buses will be hired and scheduled from a number of sources, most likely using all of the private service operators, in addition to chartering off-peak city buses. The hotel community will be zoned to facilitate round-trip regular schedules to and from hotels and McCormick Place. Due consideration has to be given to trade show hours, from 10:00 A.M. to 6:00 P.M., and normal urban rush hours. With up to 100,000 people in attendance on each show day, it can be clearly seen that special attention must be given to coordinating ground transportation for such an event, and significant costs must also be anticipated.

The requirement for shuttle service from hotels to convention centers in meetings larger than the one described above may require that the sponsoring organization defray their cost of service at this level. Among the ways this may be accomplished is to charge a nominal fee for each ride, sell books of shuttle tickets to attendees, defray the shuttle cost by including it in the registration fee, or seek sponsorship from industry members in the form of donations or grants (Nichols 1985, 159).

Conversely, transporting eight marketing executives who arrive on five different flights at San Francisco International Airport to a hotel on Union Square entails significantly less planning challenges. Requirements for high-quality service are no less apparent, however, in this context. It may be that one of the marketing executives is a senior vice president who expects limousine transportation. Under these circumstances, it is important that those arranging for ground transportation also pay particular attention to the personal and professional requirements of those for whom the service is being planned.

Exhibit 9.3 displays the basic information that meeting planners, convention managers, and exposition managers need from ground operators in order to plan ground transportation for any event, from the small eight-executive meeting to the city-wide convention.

Note that there are a number of variables included here that take arrangements for ground transportation out of the realm of simply renting a bus and propel this activity into an important aspect of the planner's event-related duties. Something as mundane as where buses are to be parked can have a significant effect on the perceptions of success of any given event or element of an event. If ground transportation suffers failures, attendees will carry away a negative impression of at least that aspect of the event.

- Minimum Rental Periods

- Minimum Rental-Period Costs

- Overtime Availability of Vehicles

- Vehicle Capacities

- Handicap Easements on Vehicles

- How Vehicles Are Dispatched

- Condition of Vehicles

- Availability of Backup Equipment

- If Vehicles Are Air-Conditioned

- Where They Can be Parked

- Hours of Operation

- Possible Routes

- Insurance Coverage

- Status of Drivers' Contracts

- Negotiability of Costs

- Applicable Surcharges

Exhibit 9.3   Ground transportation information. *Source:* Convention Liaison Council Manual (1985, 19). Used with permission.

Nothing is so frustrating to a convention attendee in a strange town as a breakdown in event transportation.

MATÉRIEL

A major CEMI role is also played by firms that specialize in transporting cargo instead of humans. In general, these activities occur within two contexts:

- Office supplies, equipment, and materials necessary for the management of the meeting
- Crated exhibits and displays to be erected at the trade show or exposition

It is said that sometimes just one lost package can spoil a whole meeting (McGee 1985, 35). If the box of computer disks loaded with registration data is lost, or if the crate of registration packets is late, carefully devised meeting plans can start to unravel in a hurry. It is important that planners and managers make careful provision for the shipping, handling, and storage of that material and equipment that is essential to management of the event on-site. Planners have learned that certain critical items may need to be shipped in duplicate or triplicate just to guard against inadvertent loss or destruction.

The key elements of successful remote-site operations for meeting and convention management are embedded in the quality of planning and attention to details that is exercised during the pre-event activities at the home office. Displayed in Exhibit 9.4 is a comprehensive checklist covering shipping procedures and the details attendant thereto.

Note the provision for setting up a "control sheet" that gives the manager easily accessible data on everything that has been shipped so that, if something does go wrong, tracing procedures can be commenced with full information at hand. Additionally, having at-hand information about the facility's personnel and procedures is important so the planner can retrieve previously shipped and stored items.

In the current atmosphere of easily accessible overnight shipping channels, losing a shipment may be less than a fatal blow to a planner's event than it was ten years ago. However, there is no substitute for having a complete inventory of management materials on-site at the precise time needed. Even a delay of 24 hours can present significant difficulties to the execution of most major and many smaller events. The key here, as in many other contexts within the CEMI, is to recognize the possibilities of certain contingencies arising and plan for their management.

Even though it is exclusively the responsibility of exhibiting firms at trade shows and expositions, transportation plays a significant role in the CEMI through shipping and handling of exhibitors' booths and displays from exposition to exposition around the country. As pointed out in Chapter 8, many exhibiting companies follow a schedule of shows to which the exhibit travels and, as such, have a major transportation requirement as part of their budgeting process.

Data developed for the Trade Show Bureau (Exhibit Surveys 1988, 1) indicate that transportation costs amount to 13% of exhibitors' budgeted annual expenses. This is an exhibitor's fourth largest expenditure after space rental, exhibit construction, and show services, and represents a significant outlay of revenues on behalf of major exhibitors. Think for a moment of the implications of shipping a display such as NIKE's 75,000-square-foot trade show presence alluded to in Chapter 8.

Choose Best Shipping Method	• Parcel Post • Rail • Truck • Air • Private
Set Up Control Sheet	• Item Number • How Shipped • Date Shipped • Waybill • Date Received • Contents • Value • Copy to Facility
Find Out From Facility	• Who Receives Shipments • Where Stored • Labeling Instructions • Liability Policy • Maximum Weight & Size • Method for Notifying Receipt • Unpacking, Repacking Assistance; Charges • Billing for Shipping Charges
Plan All Shipments For Arrival at Least a Few Days Before Meeting	
Instruct Staff	• Proper Labeling • Packaging • Shipment Schedules • On-Site Re-Packing Policies
Insurance Information	• Amount • Type: Damage, Loss, Theft • Policy Numbers • Receipts • Contact

Exhibit 9.4   Checklist for shipping procedures. *Source:* Convention Liaison Council Manual (1985, 36). Used with permission.

Exhibitors have to arrange transportation details for their exhibits and effectively plan itineraries to coincide with exposition commitments. This will also involve seeking out and securing storage facilities at or near the exposition site should the exhibit arrive there significantly prior to move-in days. After the show, exhibitors may have to arrange additional storage prior to shipping their matériel to the next exposition site or back to the home office.

The importance of the role of transportation in this context is demonstrated by the fact that several major nationwide transportation companies and common carriers have dedicated divisions or parts of divisions that have as their main marketing and operational focus the transportation of exhibits to and from trade shows and expositions around the country.

CONCLUSION

When considering the role of transportation in the CEMI, it is important to understand the interrelationships that exist between moving people inbound, outbound, and on-site, and effectively performing the same services on behalf of matériel. Transportation is, therefore, more than a simple airline reservation or bus ride. It becomes a complex interaction of factors before, during, and after any given event that must be managed properly in order for the event to succeed.

REFERENCES

ASAE. 1986. *Association Meeting Trends*. Washington, D.C.: American Society of Association Executives and the International Association of Convention and Visitors Bureaus, 58 pp.

Beauchine, Fay. 1986. U.S. Airlines Woo Convention Business. *Convention World* January/February: 14.

Bitner, Mary J., and Bernard H. Booms. 1989. *Channels of Distribution in the Tourism Industry* (prepublication manuscript). Seattle: Washington State University, mimeo of Section V, 116 pp.

Conte, Maria. 1986. Travel Agents Change with the Times. *Successful Meetings* October: 78–79.

Exhibit Surveys, Inc. 1988. How the Exhibit Dollar Is Spent. *Research Report #2060*. East Orleans, Massachusetts: Trade Show Bureau.

Glab, Jim. 1985. The Airline Industry: Is Stability Gone Forever? *Medical Meetings* September/October: 28–30.

Hosansky, Mel, et al. 1986. The Evolution of An Industry. *Meetings and Conventions* June: 48–67.

Leo, Darrell. 1986. The Travel Agent . . . Wolf at the Door? *Meetings and Conventions* February: 39–43, 113.

M&C/Meetings and Conventions Magazine. 1988. *Meetings Market '87*. Secaucus, New Jersey: Reed Travel Group.

McGee, Regina, ed. 1985. *The Convention Liaison Council Manual.* Washington, D.C.: The Convention Liaison Council.

McGee, Regina. 1988. Hub Airports Rev Up for Tomorrow. *Successful Meetings* September: 71–85.

Myers, Elissa Matulis. 1989. The Lion's Share of Meetings Business. *Association Management* February: 34–38.

Nichols, Barbara, ed. 1985. *Professional Meeting Management.* Birmingham, Alabama: The Professional Convention Management Association.

10

Exposition Service Contractors

CHAPTER OBJECTIVES

1. To define and describe the role of the exposition service contractor (ESC)
2. To overview the interrelationships between the ESC and key CEMI members
3. To explain the organizational structure of the ESC segment of the CEMI
4. To inventory services offered by ESCs
5. To overview the role of ESC involvement in event production

INTRODUCTION

ESCs were originally and are sometimes still referred to as decorators. This term was applied because they literally "decorated" an empty space with carpet, pipe-and-drape booths, furnishings, and other amenities for exhibitors and show managers (Nichols 1985, 215).

As trade shows and expositions have become more complex and sophisticated, ESCs have expanded their service inventories to include not only these original services, but many others necessitated by the requirements involved in move-in, setup, and move-out of a show (Black 1986, 10). These services will be discussed in more detail in subsequent sections of this chapter.

With the growth in size and sophistication of trade shows, there has been a parallel growth in the size, service inventories, and importance of ESCs. The major interactions between an ESC and other members of the CEMI focus on the meeting planner/trade show manager, the exhibitors, and the convention center or hotel.

Whether an exposition is hosted and managed by an association meeting planner, or privately managed by a trade show manager, the quality of meeting support services and available equipment is critical to the success of most events (Elliot 1985, 32). Meeting support services were ranked third in a hierarchy of 16 factors considered very important by corporate meeting planners in the selection of a facility or hotel. Association planners ranked such services fifth in planning for conventions, and seventh relative to association meetings on the same hierarchy (M&C 1988, 39, 75).

In the corporate case, this represents a climb in the ranking from fifth in the 1985 survey. Association planner figures reflect a modest rise (from sixth) for conventions and no change for other association meetings (Market Probe 1986, Tables 20 and 66), and suggest increased importance placed on planners' relationships with ESCs.

This relationship between the meeting planner or show manager and the ESC is a critical and close one. On behalf of the planner, the ESC lays out floor plans; helps assign booth space; provides and supervises move-in, setup, and move-out labor; and serves as focal point for most exhibitor services.

To the exhibitor, the ESC represents not only the provider of critical services such as drayage, booth furniture, signage, and perhaps utilities, but through these and other services, one of the exhibitor's major expenses. For the three-year period ending in 1987, Trade Show Bureau figures put show services at 22% of cost reported by exhibitors for that period (Exhibit Surveys 1988, 1). This may also represent one of the most controllable of exhibitor expenses, for the 22% figure is only a 1% increase over the previous three-year period, significantly lower than the inflation rate average of about 4% per year. This indicates that exhibitors are limiting their purchases of show services in order to hold down overall exhibit costs.

The relationship between ESCs and hotels/convention facilities is in a state of change. ESC managers will say that among their most difficult events to service are those that are held in hotels because hotels are not typically configured to receive shipments of exhibits. This is usually due to lack of convenient loading dock space and easy access to the show location, usually the hotel's ballroom.

An additional complicating factor is the suspicion with which hotel managements in general view use of ballroom and banquet space for anything other than foodservice events. Because of this, hotel managements can have unrealistic expectations about the amount of time ESCs need for move-in and move-out activities. On balance, for those hotels that are not set up to host exhibits on anything more than on an extremely modest scale, the relationship between ESCs and hotels has to be carefully managed or it can deteriorate quickly.

The relationship between ESCs and convention center facilities is almost always of a professional nature that recognizes the limitations, expectations, and capabilities of both parties. This relationship is going through a process of change in some buildings which, because of political pressure or legislative mandate to break even or show a profit, have begun internalizing services that previously were the exclusive domain of the ESC.

A recent research project (Rutherford 1989) found that a majority of major centers in North America now sell and operate the following services that have traditionally been in inventories of most ESCs:

- Electrical services
- FAX transmission and receiving
- Plumbing, drain, and compressed air
- Sound services
- Stage construction/lighting services
- Telephone service

Additionally, more than 25% of the respondents also indicated they offer booth cleaning, major audiovisual service, pipe and drape setup, audio recording, and cable TV directly to building users, bypassing the ESC as an intermediary.

While in some instances this may have strained relationships between ESCs and convention facilities, the major effect that has grown out of this phenomenon is that ESCs have concentrated more heavily on providing other services from within their inventories and on developing new services that have the potential to provide additional revenues.

SERVICES

As suggested above, the amounts and types of services that may be offered by any given ESC firm are probably limited only by the needs of the market and the creative capabilities of individual firms. Most, however, will offer a basic selection of services that are fairly common across ESC firms. The spectrum of these services is displayed in Exhibit 10.1.

It should be noted that the 22 services listed here represent typical offerings, and any given ESC firm may offer some or all of them. It should also be noted that several of these services may also be the province of specialty service

- Drayage/Warehousing
- Crate Storage/Retrieval
- Furniture, Floor Coverings, Accessories
- Pipe & Drape Erection
- Utilities
- Labor Planning/Supervision
- Move-In/Move-Out Logistics
- Floor Plans/Layouts
- Signage
- Audio Visual Equipment and Personnel
- Flowers & Plants, Rental/Service
- Cleaning Services
- Security Equipment & Personnel
- Modular Exhibit Rentals
- Exhibit Design & Construction
- Lighting Design/Rental
- Sound Systems
- Photographic Services
- Business Service Centers:
  Secretary, Copying, FAX, Computers, etc.
- Postal & Package Services
- Catering, if not building exclusive
- Consulting: Helping exhibitors maximize
  their exposition presence.

Exhibit 10.1   Typical services offered by ESCs.

contractors who provide only that service to a number of different types of clientele and events.

There are other items on this list that are further evidence of the growing difficulty of drawing distinctions between certain members of the CEMI. The aforementional internalization of utility services provision by convention centers is one obvious example. From this list, there may be other services that are competitively offered by destination management companies, subsidiaries of ESCs, or other private entrepreneurs.

On this list, however, the first nine services are generally most commonly offered through ESCs themselves. These basic services form the bulk of ESC activity as it relates to the planning, move-in, setup, and move-out of any given exposition or trade show event.

Perhaps the least familiar of this inventory of services to those not familiar with all aspects of the CEMI is that of drayage. Drayage refers to the fee for the hauling of a load of material. As it applies to the CEMI, drayage is the service and the charge for that service that an ESC levies on an exhibitor's display. It typically involves a two-tiered pricing structure:

- The first occurs when the exhibitor ships the crated exhibit directly to the convention center at the time the ESC is there to move it in and set it up.
- The other price applies when the exhibitor has shipped the exhibit long enough in advance of the show that it requires the ESC or drayage company to warehouse the exhibit for up to 30 days prior to the show.

In either case, the exhibitor pays a set fee per 100 pounds of weight (usually with a 200-pound minimum) for round-trip carting of the exhibit from the truck to the exhibit booth site on the convention floor and, at the show's conclusion, return to the truck loading dock. Drayage costs will also include the movement of empty crates into and out of the convention hall and storage of those crates while the show is in session.

Drayage costs have become so important to exhibitors that the International Exhibitors Association (IEA) has produced a drayage action plan for its membership to help members identify ways in which they can control drayage costs. Drayage has become a key profit center for ESCs, and as such, it is also recognized as a cost center to exhibitors. So, the relationship between ESCs and exhibitors, as discussed above, has to be viewed in the context of what are one firm's profits are another firm's costs.

A typical ESC firm will have a large inventory of available furniture, floor coverings, and accessories to enhance exhibitors' booth space or to completely furnish hospitality suites or other areas of the facility at the request of show management or exhibitors.

Among the most important services rendered on behalf of show managers, convention planners, and exhibitors by the ESC is that of planning and supervision of labor. This is an area that few people outside the CEMI totally and completely understand, because there is a confusing array of labor organizations that have carefully defined jurisdictional authority over certain aspects of a trade show moving in, setting up, and being moved out. Exhibit 10.2 lists a number of typical labor unions with brief descriptions of the services they provide on behalf of the event.

It must be remembered that due to the way labor contracts are written and managed, in any given community there may be very little flexibility on the part of building users in what they can and cannot do relative to the setup of individual exhibits. It is this aspect of ESC services where their value is highlighted. ESC managers and supervisors know and understand union rules, regulations, and jurisdictions, and are organized to dispatch the various crafts and skills in line with a carefully orchestrated set of plans to accomplish the event manager's objectives (Vaughn 1985, 370).

TRADE	SERVICE FUNCTION
Carpenters	• Display uncrating, installation, dismantling, recrating.
Decorators	• Draping and cloth installation, non-electric sign installation.
Electricians	• All electrical equipment, including signs, lights and television/VCR.
Pictoral Artists	• Sign painting and graphics.
Plumbers & Gas Fitters	• All plumbing, drain and gas fittings and installation.
Porters	• Sweeping, cleaning, dusting.
Stagehands	• Projectionists.
Millwrights	• Machinery installers, repair.
Teamsters & Riggers	• Material handling in and out of building premises. Machinery uncrating, unskidding, positioning, leveling and reskidding.

Exhibit 10.2 Typical labor unions and their exposition functions. *Source:* ESCA (1986, 23). Used with permission.

In a typical circumstance, exhibitors will order union-provided services in advance through forms included in their exhibitor service kits (Chapter 8). If they neglect or choose not to order in advance, they must settle for first-come, first-served on the show floor after advance orders are filled. The ESC is the only person who has authority to resolve union problems (ESCA 1986, 23), and ". . . all negotiations and discussions regarding labor should be handled between the trade show manager, the service contractor and the union agent" (Vaughn 1985, 372).

Problems typically occur where there are union rules against exhibitors performing tasks that, according to union contract, should be done by a labor union member. In some union jurisdictions, this can mean that something as simple as plugging in a television or VCR cannot be done by an exhibitor but must be done by a member of the electricians union. As part of their coordinative management function, ESCs are familiar with these rules and supervise labor in a way that best utilizes them and diminishes opportunities for misunderstanding and confrontation.

This list of labor organizations should not be considered exhaustive or exclusive. In some jurisdictions, it may be that exhibitors and ESCs are only required to deal with a minimum number of these labor organizations. In other jurisdictions, it may be that many more union members have contractually defined areas of responsibility. It is up to the ESC to manage these skilled workers.

The remainder of services offered by any given ESC will depend upon the market, the talent pool available to the ESC, competition, and ESC company policy. The services inventoried in Exhibit 10.1 represent the universe of possibilities for any given ESC, but it should be recognized that under most circumstances, only the largest firms with a national focus will generally come very close to offering a selection as comprehensive as this. Specialty contractors, under most circumstances, will fill any service voids left by an area's ESCs.

ESC ORGANIZATION

In order to provide the ranges of services discussed above, the organizations of ESC firms evolved to reflect the categories of expertise they can marshal to perform services. A typical functional organizational chart for a full-service ESC firm is presented in Exhibit 10.3.

In a large firm, sales will generally have both a national and a local focus. National sales leads are generated through convention and visitor bureau membership, recommendations of convention services managers or event managers, and research and prospecting on the part of the ESC sales staff. Referrals from show managers and meeting planners who have used that particular ESC firm in the past can also assist in securing future business.

On the local side, ESC firms work with destination management companies as well as individual meeting and party planners in the production, design, and execution of local events. These can potentially represent the entire spectrum of local corporate, cultural, and social activities.

Whether there is a separate department or not, some ESC employees will have logistics work as a responsibility. This will include planning and scheduling of personnel for given events, dealing with shipping problems, working with labor unions on planning the assignment of contracted labor, and

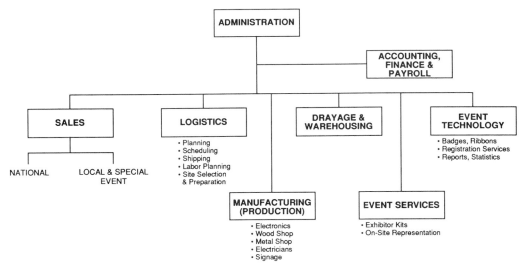

Exhibit 10.3   ESC functional organization chart.

working with meeting planners and show managers on site selection and site preparation.

Drayage and warehousing, if a part of the ESC's service inventory, calls for personnel, warehouse space, and trucks and other equipment to be assigned to locations relative to the individual time lines of events. Typically, an ESC will own its own fleet of trucks and equipment for these purposes, in addition to owning or leasing warehouse facilities.

Increasingly, an important part of ESC services are those that are lumped under the category of event technology. This division will produce customized badges and ribbons, provide registration services, and from those registration activities, generate reports and statistics for meeting planners and show managers. This function may also involve the rental of equipment to exhibitors that allows them to qualify sales leads directly from imprinted show badges during exhibit visits by attendees.

Responsibilities for event services may also be a separate functional division or a subfunction of another department. In either event, the thrust of event services activities is to manage the relationships between the ESC and exhibitors. This may include the production and mailing to exhibitors of an official exhibitor kit that ". . . provides each exhibitor with . . . information on the materials and services that are available for the physical erection of a display, as well as other order forms" (Nichols 1985, 235).

Exhibitor kits will normally include information on the following topics (Corcoran 1989, passim):

- Name of exhibition
- Facility, city, and state of the exhibition site
- Time line of dates, including move-in and move-out dates
- Assigned move-in and move-out target dates
- General information, rules, and regulations about the exhibition
- Some reference to promotional activities on the part of the show manager or association
- Product sampling, storage, and services policies
- Labor and utility services
- Booth furnishings
- Order forms for all additional services that may be required

The official exhibitors kit may also include basic policy information on payment, union rules and regulations, an outline of CEMI relationships, and statistics about previous shows.

Additionally, it is the responsibility of events services people to have on-site representation for the ESC on the show floor. In the event of extremely large shows, this may be "zoned" representation where the floors of the show will be divided into zones, with a representative of the ESC staff responsible for a given number of booths on the exhibit floor. Since the ESC is usually the official (only) service contractor for a particular event, it is the responsibility of the ESC to interface between the exhibitors and all of the trade union workers involved in the show.

For any given show or event, a full-service ESC may be required to physically manufacture or construct exhibits, stages, displays, sets, and signs. These are services that assist the show managers, planners, and exhibitors in achieving their goals for exposition participation. A full-service ESC will have a manufacturing or production department that has the capability of this sort of production.

ESC ACTIVITY OVERVIEW

Under most circumstances, a single ESC will be chosen by the show manager or association planner as an "official service contractor" for the exposition part of the convention. The selection of an official service contractor may be based on a number of information sources available to the show manager, but usually involve referrals from the building, hotel, or other show managers. In some markets, there may only be one ESC in the area (Hoyle, Dorf, and Jones 1989, 324–325), which limits local choices, but with the national operating focus of some ESC firms, a show manager's choices are not as limited as in the past.

Once the official service contractor designation has been made, the ESC will work with the planner or show manager on setting up floor plans of the facility (Nichols 1985, 218). These floor plans will become a fundamental part of the prospectus that the show manager uses to market the rental of space to potential exhibitors.

The service contractor will then commence planning for activities relative to the event. This planning begins with logistic work, labor scheduling, and production of event documents such as the official exhibitor kit (McGee 1985, 46).

Immediately prior to the show, utilizing the floor plan and logistic arrangements for labor and equipment, the ESC arrives at the building and proceeds to mark the exposition floor according to the guidelines of the floor plan. This is usually done with tape to outline aisles and booths. Registration areas are set up and furnished, and the pipe and drape that delineate individual booths are erected.

Working with the drayage supervisor, the ESC floor manager supervises the arrival of freight from either the ESC warehouse, other warehouses, or shipments dropped directly at the facility loading dock by common carriers. At that point, a wide variety of fairly confusing activities commence simultaneously. Freight and equipment begin moving into and out of the building according to the schedules worked out in advance. Crates have to be moved to exhibit locations, equipment has to be unpacked and erected, and empty crates have to be removed from the exhibit floor and stored according to their position in the move-out plan.

During this period, exhibits continue to be unpacked and set up, booth furnishings and carpet are installed in exhibitor booths, utilities and telephones are connected, and signs are hung.

Once all the heavy moving is in the concluding phases, final activities include the laying of aisle carpet, last-minute cleaning, and the setting of security perimeters and badge control for exhibit floor access. Then the show opens.

During the show, the ESC personnel, through their service desks and floor managers, resolve disputes, troubleshoot, and fill last-minute service orders. The ESC will work with exhibitors and show management to manage the entire process of show execution, and then prepare for move-out.

Move-out activities are the reverse of those involved in move-in, with critical components being security of booth furnishings and products, crate delivery, repacking, and drayage to the loading dock. Carpets are rolled up; pipe, drape, and signage are dismantled; and the building is cleaned and turned back to the facility owners to prepare for the next event.

CONCLUSION

In a brief overview, the above are the primary activities of the ESC before, during, and after any given event. The critical relationships to remember about this segment of the CEMI are those between and among the ESC, the meeting planner or show manager, the building, and the exhibitors.

REFERENCES

Black, Robert. November 19, 1986. *The Trade Show Industry: Management and Marketing Career Opportunities.* Lecture to Cornell University. East Orleans, Massachusetts: Trade Show Bureau.

Corcoran, Thomas C. 1989. *Official Exhibitor Kit 1989.* Chicago: National Restaurant Association.

Dotson, Penny C. 1988. *Introduction to Meeting Management.* Birmingham, Alabama: The Professional Convention Management Association.

Elliot, Sara. 1985. Site Selection and Evaluation. In *Fundamentals of Association Management: Conventions,* ed. Steven H. Blackwell, Peter R. Turner, and Debbie L. Wolfe. Washington, D.C.: American Society of Association Executives.

ESCA. 1986. *Annual Guide to Exposition Service,* 1st ed. Los Angeles: Exposition Service Contractors Association, mimeo.

Exhibit Surveys, Inc. 1988. How the Exhibit Dollar Is Spent. *Research Report #2060.* East Orleans, Massachusetts: The Trade Show Bureau.

Hoyle, Leonard H., David C. Dorf, and Thomas J. A. Jones. 1989. *Managing Conventions and Group Business.* East Lansing, Michigan: The Educational Institute of the American Hotel and Motel Association.

IEA. 1986. *The IEA Drayage Action Plan.* The International Exhibitors Association, mimeo.

Market Probe, International. 1986. *The Meetings Market '85.* Seacaucus, New Jersey: Murdoch Magazines Research Department.

M&C/Meetings and Conventions Magazine. 1988. Meetings Market '87. Secaucus, New Jersey: Reed Travel Group.

McGee, Regina, ed. 1985. *The Convention Liaison Council Manual.* Washington, D.C.: The Convention Liaison Council.

Nichols, Barbara, ed. 1985. *Professional Meeting Management.* Birmingham, Alabama: The Professional Convention Management Association.

Rutherford, Denney G. 1989. Convention Centers and Their Managements. Research in progress. Seattle, Washington: Washington State University.

Vaughn, Don. 1985. Trade Show Management. In *Fundamentals of Association Management: Conventions,* ed. Steven H. Blackwell, Peter R. Turner, and Debbie L. Wolfe. Washington, D.C.: American Society of Association Executives.

11

Destination Management Companies

CHAPTER OBJECTIVES

1. To define the concept of destination management companies (DMCs)
2. To trace the growth of DMCs
3. To explain how DMCs are organized
4. To describe the relationship between DMCs and other CEMI components
5. To inventory typical services offered by DMCs

INTRODUCTION

In the not-too-distant past, CEMI members that are now becoming universally known as destination management companies (DMCs) were primarily involved only with the coordination of on-site ground transportation for visiting groups and conventions. Because of this, these companies were called *ground service operators* and typically provided transportation services for meeting planners and associations while their groups were "on the ground" at the convention or meeting site.

EVOLUTION

Commencing in the early seventies, these companies started to evolve into what we now term DMCs. One reason suggested for this is that, in the past, most meeting attendees and convention delegates were men, and for the most part, entertainment and activities were planned with that particular demographic in mind. It has been suggested that as the women's movement increasingly influenced all aspects of North American life, more and better-educated spouses with greater expectations began attending conventions and meetings; at the same time, more women were entering the managerial work force and beginning to attend meetings and conventions as delegates. One effect was that traditional programs once created at the convention or meeting site to provide distractions and entertainment for spouses had to be changed. Increasingly, the spouses who accompanied convention and meeting delegates were men accompanying their wives. As a result, ground service operators who had typically arranged for "ladies luncheons, fashion shows and cooking demonstrations" found an increasingly strong demand for collateral convention activities that appealed to a broader demographic audience and that demanded programs of more substance (Hosansky 1986, 64).

Because meeting planners seldom knew all the capabilities of local entertainment and attraction suppliers well enough to find such activities from their home offices, they increasingly came to reply upon the expertise of companies in the local area. These firms not only knew the suppliers, but were creating the organizational infrastructure to assemble and produce programs of entertainment and informational programs custom-designed to appeal to event attendees and their guests.

SERVICES

As the relationship between planners and DMCs has evolved, planners have recognized that DMCs, in one sense, have become "planners for planners." Because planners often have only a limited number of site visits prior to any given event, they have come to contract with and rely upon local DMCs to devise what can become a complex inventory of services.

Exhibit 11.1 displays an inventory of potential and typical services operated by full-service DMCs. In this exhibit, the services have been divided into four broad and fairly general categories of entertainment, tours, ground services, and convention and meeting services.

These represent the range of potential services that can be offered by a DMC, but it should be noted that any given DMC will probably specialize in a selection of these services. Most of them, however, perhaps revealing the short period of time that they have been evolving into DMCs, still pay tribute to their roots by offering comprehensive ground services based on transportation.

Increasingly, however, DMCs have come to offer a wide variety of enter-

Entertainment	• Theme Parties/Meals • Dining Tours • Theatre Arrangements • Sports Event Tickets • Attraction Ticket Service
Tours	• Pre/Post-Event Tours • Sightseeing • Air & Water Tours • Museums, Other Cultural & Educational • Guides
Ground Services	• Meet & Greet • Baggage Handling • Airport Transfer • Shuttle Bus Service • Hospitality Desk Staff • VIP Transportation • Spouse/Youth Activities
Convention/Meeting Services	• Registration Personnel & Services • Models, Booth Personnel • Exhibitor Entertaining • Site Selection Assistance • Special Effects • Production Planning • Prop Rentals • Audio Visual Services • Graphic Arts • Translators • Parlimentarians • Gifts & Mementos • Speakers, Entertainers • Package Delivery, Office Services • Program Evaluation • Press/Media Events

Exhibit 11.1   Destination management service inventory.

tainment-related events and tours that highlight cultural, educational, theatrical, or sporting themes.

One important addition to DMC services is the provision of on-site personnel to meetings and conventions. These are local people who are not only familiar with the area, but also trained in various convention- and meeting-related tasks that provide for the planner or manager a cadre of experienced personnel. Meeting planners can thus save the considerable expense of transportation and living expenses for a large group of people from the home office to handle office, clerical, and registration duties.

In these four general categories will be found most of the activities provided for events by DMCs as they are currently managed. It can be seen from a number of these specific activities that there exists a blurring of service responsibility between DMCs and other members of the CEMI. In some areas and in some instances, audiovisual services may be provided by a specialty service contractor, the convention or hotel facility, or the exposition service contractor. But the provision of audiovisual services is one product that some DMCs have made a specialty. Therefore, in any given metropolitan area that hosts a substantial number of meetings or conventions, there may be active competition for the planners' services dollar from among convention centers, hotels, specialty service contractors, exposition service contractors, and DMCs.

RELATIONSHIP WITH OTHER CEMI COMPONENTS

The DMC has evolved into an *intermediary* between the planner and a number of different local suppliers of services to convention and meeting event attendees. The role of DMCs has grown to be of such importance to many planners that DMCs have been described as "our salvation" (Hosansky 1986, 63).

The relationship between the activities of the DMCs, their clients, and local suppliers of services is depicted in Exhibit 11.2. The typical circumstance would find a member of the DMC staff working directly with a planner, show manager, or convention manager on, for instance, a boat cruise, cocktail party, and barbecue package. The local supplier of such services would make available to the DMC exclusive use of both party and dinner facilities (depending on numbers) for the convention delegates or meeting attendees. The DMC would charge the planner the commercial rate of the supplier, and the supplier, in turn, would pay a commission to the DMC. The planner's funds come from registration fees paid by delegates or funds contributed by sponsoring organizations or industries. Where the DMC's margins on the provision of service are relatively small—for instance, when the DMC expends more energy and resources on setting up the event than it garners in commissions—to cover expenses and profits, the DMC management will add a fee to the charge passed along to the planner.

ORGANIZATION

DMCs are typically small businesses that may have had their genesis in the ideas and creative talents of one or two individuals who had been allied with

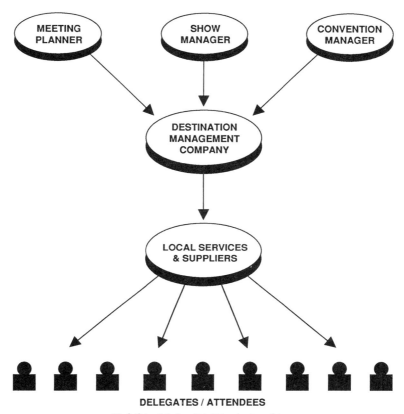

Exhibit 11.2   DMC relationships.

the CEMI in some other form. Sometimes hotel convention services managers or meeting planners themselves have ventured into the entrepreneurial activities that result in a DMC. DMCs can, however, also become quite large depending on the range and scope of activities and the amount of potential business in a given convention or meeting destination. Referring back to Exhibit 11.1, few if any DMCs will offer all of these services; however, increasingly, it is possible to identify companies that include a fairly comprehensive list of most of these in their service inventory.

To accomplish these tasks and because DMCs are, in most instances, no longer one-person offices, they have had to organize along traditional lines, reflecting a diversity of specialization. Exhibit 11.3 presents a typical functional organization for such a company.

The chief executive is normally the individual who is the founder and creative force in the business. Typically, such a business will require the

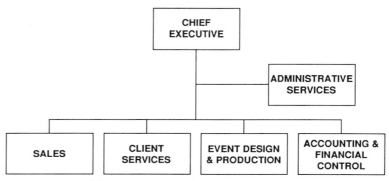

Exhibit 11.3   DMC functional organization.

services of someone to handle administrative, secretarial, and clerical functions. Line employees, those who are in normal direct contact with clients, include sales, client services, and event design and production.

The sales function involves those activities that normally result in developing business. Sales leads, much the same as for exposition service contractors, are developed through membership in the CVB and referrals from hotel or convention center personnel. An important source of DMC business derives from referrals among the meeting planner network and advertising in planner periodicals. DMCs will also hold memberships in local chapters of national planner organizations.

Client services is directly analogous to the functions performed within a hotel by the convention services manager, and within a convention center by the event services staff. In other words, while the company is in contact with and working on behalf of the client, one person will have direct responsibility for the management of those events on behalf of the client. Also on behalf of clients, client services staff members plan and manage events to their conclusion.

Some DMCs include in their inventory an emphasis on entertainment, theme parties, and other events that require multistep production. Some of these may include provisions for props and sets, requiring someone to be in charge of and responsible for the physical production and assembly of creative talent to effect such events. This may be done in-house, contracted to a specialty supplier, or done by an ESC.

Finally, with revenues coming in and being disbursed in a number of different directions depending on the number of clients, types of events, and number of suppliers for whom the DMC is serving as a broker, financial and accounting control is a critical and essential function in a DMC's organizational framework. Like many small businesses, a DMC may operate on fairly close margins, and it requires careful attention to accounting practices, financial control, and cash flow. This function may also include personnel records and payroll.

Because the concept of DMC-type companies is still in the early phases of the evolutionary process, there is much discussion within the meeting planning and convention literature about the range and quality of services offered by companies calling themselves DMCs (Conte 1989, 33). As a result, it is important for meeting planners and convention managers to carefully assess the quality of service they expect from relationships with DMCs. Because, in effect, DMCs have become "planners for the planners," meeting planners have come to rely upon the talents, organizational skills, and creative expertise of DMCs to produce significant types of convention and meeting events.

Because, according to some estimates, 60–70% of all U.S. groups use DMCs (Hosansky 1986, 65), there are broad implications for meeting planners. Careful research will go a long way toward assuring planners that the relationship they establish with a DMC will be a successful one.

Exhibit 11.4 outlines the sorts of information planners need about a DMC before entering into a contractual relationship. In many ways, these categories of background information about DMCs parallel the sorts of information any experienced manager would ask about a potential employee. Obviously, not all of these items will necessarily apply if a planner is only entering into a simple bus/shuttle transportation agreement, but the more involved that the planner and the DMC become in designing and producing multiple events, the more important these questions about the DMC's capabilities become.

- Local Headquarters & Staffing

- Longevity: Length of time in destination management

- Size & Depth of Operations Staff

- Professional Affiliations Within Community

- Nationa/International Professional Affiliations

- Computerization; Facsimile Capability

- Good Insurance Policy Structure

- Financial Stability

- Price Structure

- Multiple Client Capability

Exhibit 11.4 Destination management reference points. *Source:* Abstracted from Zauzmer (1987, 27); Wilson (1987, 158).

The growing inventory of companies that are classifying themselves as DMCs has led to the inevitable formation of a professional association to lend structured legitimacy to their activities, promote CEMI recognition, and provide educational and professional services to its members. The International Destination Management Association (IDMA) has been formed to advance these types of interests on behalf of their DMC membership (Conte 1989, 51).

Additionally, selected DMC's have formed national and international referral organizations of affiliated independent companies to network and promote the services of their membership from location to location. These operate much the same way a hotel referral organization such as Best Western operates, with a membership fee to join, plus annual dues. The membership pays additional money for specific professional services such as advertising, newsletters, promotional brochures, and maintenance of a central information distribution system.

While it is still true that many meeting planners assign a lot of program arrangements discussed in this chapter to office staff or accomplish them themselves, increasingly it is recognized that a professional DMC ". . . can save hours of time and countless telephone calls . . . to create and manage special events and tours. Many companies offer services beyond transportation and guides; for example, theme party organization, airport greetings, staffing of hospitality rooms and registration areas" (Nichols 1985, 256).

CONCLUSION

As the potential value of DMC-type services becomes more widely recognized within the meeting planer and convention manager community, these businesses will continue to enter the competitive environment of the CEMI as more locales become recognized as convention destinations. Because meeting planners continue to require "something more" in the way of site assistance to make their meeting and convention events more attractive, memorable, and successful, the development within the CEMI of DMCs have become, indeed, ". . . a new breed of site professionals who offer the traditional services of a ground operator and much more" (Roscoe 1985, 133).

REFERENCES

Conte, Maria C. 1989. Destination Management Companies: How They Lighten the Planner's Load. *The Meeting Manager* June: 33–34, 51–52.

Hosansky, Mel, et al. 1986. The Evolution of an Industry. *Meetings and Conventions* June: 48–67.

Nichols, Barbara, ed. 1985. *Professional Meeting Management.* Birmingham, Alabama: The Professional Convention Management Association.

Roscoe, Patricia L. 1985. What's a Destination Management Company, Anyway? *Successful Meetings* May: 133.

Wilson, Pamela J. 1987. Checklist for Hiring a Destination Management Company. *Meeting News* December 4:158.

Zauzmer, Debra. 1987. How to Choose the Right DMC. *Meeting News* October 15:8, 27.

12

Food and Beverage

CHAPTER OBJECTIVES

1. To establish the role food and beverage service (FBS) plays in the CEMI
2. To outline the importance of FBS to the CEMI
3. To describe the relationships between providers of FBS and others in the CEMI
4. To establish the structure of convention- and meeting-related FBS activities
5. To overview the types of FBS commonly purchased by the CEMI
6. To discuss issues important to FBS as it relates to the CEMI

INTRODUCTION

The providers of FBS to convention, exposition, and meeting attendees are generally considered a component of the leisure, sports, and recreational foodservices market. Among the inventory of such types of FBS are (Warner 1989, 10–14):

- Convention centers
- Stadiums
- Coliseums
- Amusements parks and attractions
- Parimutuel wagering facilities (horse and dog tracks)
- Fairs and expositions

- Theater lobbies
- Miscellaneous activities (golf tours, auto racing, other one- or two-day sports or leisure-oriented events)

While the various leisure, sports, and recreational foodservices have been clearly established as a component of the total foodservice market, the specific provision of FBS to the CEMI demonstrates unique attributes that make it possible to examine this type of FBS as a separate activity. Previous chapters have documented that leisure and recreational types of activities are an important part of most meeting and convention agendas, but the primary focus of such events has always been and will continue to be on the business-related activities fundamental to all processes in the CEMI.

A common thread linking all types of leisure, sports, and recreational FBS is that it is "event-oriented," where each event presents different challenges to management that arise from different and sometimes unique variables. It is the concept of event-oriented foodservice that allows us to single out hotel-provided event FBS and examine it together with the similar services provided through convention center facilities and by independent caterers as a separate segment of the leisure, sports, and recreational market that is specific to the CEMI.

Because all hotels that host convention and meeting activities have built into their organizational structure full-time food and beverage components, a portion of which is dedicated to catering to group-related events, this chapter will focus on event-oriented FBS as it is structured, operated, and managed in convention center facilities.

As established in Chapter 4, food and beverage revenues for convention facilities represent either the first or second largest profit center for the facility. This depends on three major variables:

1. Size of the facility
2. Type of FBS contract
3. Facility management and policy

Whether one of these variables, or some combination of them, is the predominant influence, the importance of FBS revenues to convention center facilities is well established. A recent study by Laventhol and Horwath (1988, 2) established that *net* food and beverage income varied from 10% to 50% of *gross* rental incomes for the 80 exhibit halls contacted in their annual survey. Clearly, food and beverage provides the outstanding potential as a profit center for convention facilities to reduce operating deficits (Laventhol and Horwath 1988, 1).

Meeting planners also place a high order of importance on the quality of foodservice provided by a convention facility. Eighty percent of corporate planners in the *Meetings Market '87* survey considered quality foodservice to be very important when considering selection of a facility or hotel. This ranked as the number one factor for the 16 in the survey inventory. A similar level of importance was attached to quality of foodservice by association planners, with 80% finding it a very important factor in convention planning and 63% finding it very important in association meeting arrangements (M&C 1988, 39, 75).

The quality of foodservice at convention facilities and the importance it plays in the success of the meeting cannot be overemphasized as it relates to the decision processes of meeting planners. According to Bloom (1981, 47), of the recommendations and resources used to choose meeting sites, input from other meeting planners and suggestions from others in their organizations ranked one and two among the aggregate corporate and association planners contacted in the survey. Because meeting planners have their own annual professional meetings and conventions (for example, Meeting Planners International, the Professional Convention Management Association, the Society of Government Meeting Planners, and the National Association of Exposition Managers), the opportunities for such networking are enhanced. Experiences at facilities are a common topic of conversation in both formal and informal sessions, with foodservice often a central issue. Meeting planners recognize that nothing is more memorable to their memberships than outstanding or terrible FBS. It is, therefore, critical to them that everything possible be done to assure that the events for which they are responsible have high-quality food and beverage activities.

Because so many convention and visitors bureaus (CVBs) are closely associated with marketing strategies for convention facilities and are similarly involved in selling hospitality amenities for an entire area, as a marketing tool, FBS is also important to CVB managements and sales forces as well. It has been suggested (Anonymous 1985, 4) that CVB officials could even pressure facility managers to produce quality food that will help attract conventioneers. In light of the formal and informal information exchanges outlined among meeting planners above, dispatching bureau sales people to a well-informed market without high confidence in FBS as a marketing edge is a difficult proposition at best.

While it may not be immediately obvious, other members of the CEMI have an interest in the provision of quality FBS to their constituencies. Exposition managers have a deep interest in keeping convention and trade show delegates within the facility to maximize potential exhibit visits by attendees. Exhibitors themselves have similar objectives. Marginal or poor foodservice that literally drives convention and trade show attendees out of the building in search of better value or variety diminishes the opportunities to generate maximum show utilization.

STRUCTURE OF CONVENTION- AND MEETING-RELATED FOODSERVICE

One way in which to view the structure of FBS as it relates to the CEMI is displayed in Exhibit 12.1. In this view, the total market of event-driven FBS activities is divided between those in which the main theme is dominated by leisure activities and those in which the main theme of the event is dominated by business-related activities.

On the leisure side of the diagram are those events that are primarily produced to encourage attendance at a sporting or other pleasurable activity. For the patron, this may include attending a play or ballet, or betting on a horse race, watching a favorite team, or wandering the exhibits at a state or county fair. On the other hand, business-dominated activities are identifiable as unique events. Even though they may have, as a component to their execution, leisure, sporting, or recreational types of activities, the primary focus of the event is some activity or structure of activities specifically related to attendees' business or professional lives.

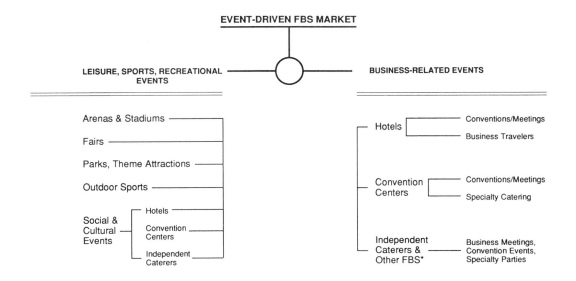

* Often using Destination Management Company (DMC) and Exposition Service Contractor (ESC) as intermediaries or service providers.

Exhibit 12.1   FBS market.

Because of economies of scale that can be achieved during 24-hour year-round operations, hotels are uniquely suited to count, as part of their organizational and marketing mix, full-time banquet and catering services. This allows hotels to compete effectively for all but the largest potential group business.

Independent caterers traditionally have sought markets that are locally oriented, generally smaller, and more socially focused than those sought by hotels or convention facilities. This, however, is changing with the advent of more flexible potential catering venues that provide for foodservice access by other than exclusively contracted catering companies. Many catering companies now have the personnel and equipment to execute catered events in venues as varied as museums, train stations, aquariums, and zoos in addition to more traditional facilities. Independent catering contractors are also becoming more involved in providing FBS for business organizations of all kinds, whether it be the socially oriented office party or FBS for corporate meetings. City-wide conventions and out-of-town tour groups may find their parties served by an independent caterer through the efforts of destination management companies. It is in these contexts that the independent caterer has been successful in carving out a niche in providing FBS to convention- and group-related markets.

Because of the requirement to provide a wide range of types of FBS on the premises for any given event, convention center facilities perhaps offer the best case for study in the world of event-driven FBS. Depending upon the

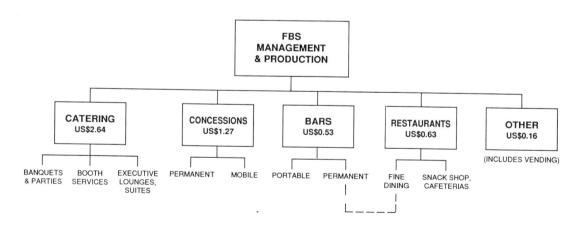

Note: Dollar figures are *average per capita* figures for all buildings surveyed in Exhibit Hall Industry 1988 Annual Report (Laventhol & Horwath 1988, 2) and *excludes* consumer shows.

Exhibit 12.2   Convention center facility FBS structure.

central focus, theme, or type of event, convention center managements may find themselves involved in any or all of the potential FBS displayed in Exhibit 12.2.

The numbers displayed parenthetically here are average per capita figures for all convention centers and exhibit facilities, and are included in this exhibit to demonstrate the relative importance of each component of the convention center facility FBS structure in delivering food and beverage income revenues.

CATERING

By definition, "Catering generally refers to the business of supplying food, goods and services to public and private functions of all types" (Warner 1989, 266–267) This generally holds true for catering services provided by convention facility food and beverage operators with the provision that, under most circumstances, public functions are limited to local events or consumer (paid attendance) shows.

According to these data and general industry consensus, catering is clearly the primary source of food and beverage income for convention and exposition events at these facilities. Catering can take a number of different forms—banquets, theme parties, and receptions primarily come to mind. Additionally, FBS operators are seeking out novel and unique ways in which to deliver FBS to previously unrealized segments of the FBS potential market.

Increasingly, exhibitors will purchase food or beverage services from caterers for both personnel and convention attendees as part of the total marketing and entertainment package. In a similar context, exhibitors and associations may rent meeting rooms, lounge areas, or executive suites and have them decorated by a service contractor to serve as hospitality or entertainment facilities for the entertainment of VIPs and important potential clients. Convention center FBS operators are encouraging the developments of these sorts of new markets. Modern convention center caterers will be organized and equipped to deliver FBS to any part of the facility and under almost any circumstances.

There are also significant opportunities for catering FBS to large local events whose requirements for sit-down banquets and other catered events may exceed the capacity of any single provider from the hotel community.

Whatever the marketing mix of a specific foodservice organization at a convention center, the activities involved in delivering catering services are fundamentally the same. Exhibit 12.3 outlines what is called the "catering cycle" (Warner 1989, 267), which highlights the major steps in selling, planning, executing, and concluding any particular catering event.

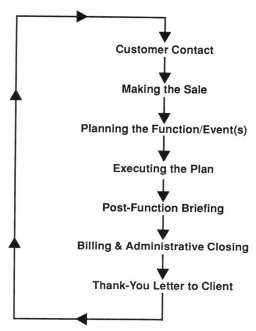

Exhibit 12.3   The catering cycle. *Source:* Warner (1989, 267) @ Van Nostrand Reinhold, NY. Used with permission.

Customer contact may come from a local group, but most often is related to the booking of a facility by a convention or exposition manager. The facility's catering capabilities are outlined and, in some instances, demonstrated during the booking process.

It is important to remember that at a major convention, there may be multiple meal functions in several areas of the building at any given time—breakfast, lunch, or dinner. Add to this the potential for coffee and refreshment breaks for perhaps dozens of meetings, foodservices to exhibitors on the trade show floor, receptions and parties, and executive lounge and suite catering, and the complexity of planning a function or event becomes obvious.

Planning, of course, is the key to the execution of the event, and in many instances, it is incumbent upon catering management to educate the client in the best ways to take advantage of the caterer's facilities, people, and creative potential.

At the conclusion of the event, most catering managements participate in evaluative activities, ending with billing and other financial arrangements. FBS managers can then lay the groundwork for future sales activities by acknowledging gratitude to the client.

CONCESSIONS

While concession stands are the most common form of foodservice for other recreational food and beverage organizations, at convention centers they take a secondary, but still important, role relative to FBS operations. In the past, concessions at convention centers were limited and unimaginative. There is, however, evidence that concessions have undergone significant change in the modern era. Concessions today are not necessarily permanent, nor are they necessarily tied into the beer, popcorn, and hot dog style of menu, although these still may account for significant sales.

Concession menus generally consist of the quick service of "hand-held" food from limited menus. Much of this food is pre-prepared and packaged to facilitate service. This offers the customer the opportunity to spend limited time standing in line, maximizing opportunities to visit trade show exhibits and other convention-related attractions.

Classic concession menus are constructed of six generally recognized categories of food and beverage groups (Warner 1989, 123):

1. Hot dogs and other sausage items
2. Popcorn and peanuts
3. Cold drinks, primarily soda and beer
4. Hot drinks, primarily coffee
5. Novelty items, including such "fun foods" as cotton candy, snow cones, and pretzels
6. Standard fast-food fare, such as hamburgers, french fries, pizza, and nachos

With the well-documented trend toward more a more healthful American diet that currently emphasizes less sodium, lower fat, higher fiber, and so forth, concessions menus at convention centers and elsewhere are adapting to include deli-type sandwiches other than hot dogs. Salads, yogurt, and other foods designed to appeal to a more health-conscious clientele are also showing up on menus.

As suggested in Exhibit 12.2, it is no longer necessary for concession stands to be affixed to permanent locations. Increasingly, convention centers are finding custom-designed or modular equipment available that allows food and beverage managements to take the concession operation to any part of the building or its grounds. This allows the center to be flexible in providing concession service to a wide variety of activities attendant to any given event.

While concession FBS generally accounts for less than one-half of the per capita net income to facilities that catered events produce, they are inherently more profitable. Because there is less labor and capital involved in concession FBS, their collective contribution to profit structure may be proportionately larger. It is for this reason that centers and their FBS managements are aggressively seeking ways to enhance their reputations for quality concession service.

BARS, RESTAURANTS, OTHER

Bars and restaurants represent comparatively minor revenue generator components of FBS at convention center facilities. Most centers will accomplish the vast majority of liquor service through the portable bars that are used throughout the facility to support catered events. Some facilities now have permanent beverage service associated with a fine dining restaurant that may be open when there is no event in the building. One convention facility that has a public operation open year-round is the Riverfront Convention Center in New Orleans (Warner 1989, 6). While this is not a unique circumstance, it is still relatively rare.

Given the amount of financial commitment that foodservice companies and convention facilities devote to food production, it may be that fine dining in the form of a public access restaurant will become more common in the near future. This will allow facility and catering managements to obtain further productive usage out of not only equipment, but key food management and service personnel. Convention center restaurant-type operations may also include snack bars offering limited seating, cafeterias, and specialty restaurants that are only open during events.

Other food and beverage revenues may be generated through prepackaged food sales and vending, but under most circumstances, they represent only a minor portion of FBS revenue generated at convention and exposition facilities.

MANAGEMENT OF CONVENTION FACILITY FBS

Because of the importance of FBS to the financial health of the convention facility, how FBS is organized and managed to maximize benefits for the facility and its clientele takes one or a combination of three different forms:

1. In-house operation
2. Caterer
   • Exclusive catering contract
   • Open contract with authorized list of caterers
3. Other, usually public use and access for local events

While any given convention facility may use any of these forms of FBS organization and management, the majority of leisure market and convention center facilities have some sort of contractual arrangement with an outside caterer as an exclusive provider of FBS at that facility. Nationally, leisure market facilities average nearly 60% that are contract-operated, with the remainder being either self-operated or some combination of the two (Warner 1989, 12). Recent research on major convention facilities in the United States and Canada found 81% of foodservice contracted to an outside company, with 16.5% handled in-house by facilities staff and the remainder through some other form of catering management (Rutherford 1989).

Building-operated FBS, although not a common occurrence, still exists in some markets. Some, though, have even considered in-house catering to be totally impractical (Bany 1977). This bias against in-house catering has its historical roots in the reluctance of public facilities to participate in the investment required to design and construct food production and service facilities. A similar reluctance on their part to hire, train, and retain the specialized production management and service staff necessary to produce high-quality FBS is an additional factor that keeps such facilities out of the FBS business. Other disadvantages are usually considered to be the relative lack of purchasing power of an individual municipal caterer compared to a national contract caterer and the specialized accounting systems unique to major FBS activities (Stotereau 1977, 1–2).

There is some evidence, however, that at least in secondary markets, new facilities are rethinking these historical prejudices. These facilities' managements may be more likely to do their own foodservice because nationally focused catering companies can be reluctant to invest the amount of money required to equip a kitchen in a market where financial returns may be less than their corporate requirements (Quinn 1985, 14). Because many new convention center facilities are being constructed in secondary markets (see Chapter 4), it may be a signal that more facilities may be willing to attempt to handle foodservice on their own. Facility-operated foodservice, however, remains a relatively minor actor in the national picture.

Public access is another relatively minor circumstance that may exist only in certain small, locally focused markets. This arrangement allows charitable, educational, municipal, and other nonprofit organizations and individuals to use public assembly facilities with low charge and to bring in their own food. While this is not very common, it does assist the facility in being a good community citizen and encourages a wide variety of building use by all segments of the local public market.

The downside of public use arrangements involves intensified demands on facilities staff for inspection, supervision, maintenance, and security activities. There is also a very real possibility of damage to equipment and facilities. Increasingly, there are also potential problems with insurance, liability, and other legal issues (Bany 1977, 2).

The other two forms of FBS management normally found in convention centers involve contractual arrangements with outside catering companies. Of the 81% of centers that indicated their FBS facilities were managed through outside contracts, fully 87.5% of those were exclusive catering contract arrangements (Rutherford 1989). The remainder stipulated an "open" catering contract wherein the facility marketing staff and event coordinators helped user groups choose from a list of approved foodservice management companies. Each of the operators on the list so stipulated is certified as being familiar with the facility, meets certain food quality and staffing criteria specified by the facility, and agrees to specified contractual arrangements.

The major advantage of this type of arrangement is that each firm may offer specific advantages that can be tailored to customers' individual needs or desires. Major disadvantages involve an increase in facility management time for inspections, maintenance, repair, and supervision. In addition, responsibility for equipment, fixtures, flatware, stemware, and so forth presents particularly troublesome control problems. The final disadvantage is that, for all practical purposes, most multigroup foodservice events are virtually eliminated (Bany 1977, 2) because it is unlikely that more than one caterer can use the premises at one time. In the case of an exclusive caterer, several events may be simultaneously scheduled, with the caterer producing all meals.

The exclusive caterer arrangement remains as the most popular and, from most observers' standpoint, the most practical of the arrangements discussed here. Contracts to become an exclusive caterer at a public assembly or convention center facility are usually awarded after some sort of competitive bidding process, with one management company being designated to provide all food and beverage services at the center for a specified period of time.

The biggest advantage of such an arrangement involves the economies of scale that a large, often national, FBS company can bring to the facility. The exclusive caterer can help to maximize use of all facility areas because of the ability to produce simultaneous food events in different areas or multiple food events on any given day. This also contributes to maximizing the potential for revenue production.

Contract caterers with a national focus can bring teams of professionals to the facility that can enhance the capability of the facility in its FBS activities. Another aspect of that advantage is the ability of the company to bring into the facility, for any given event, additional talent from other facilities within the firm's system. These persons may come from buildings that are between events or not particularly busy. Such additional staff will assist in production, management, and service supervision.

Sophisticated national catering and foodservice firms will also provide specialized accounting, reporting, and control systems to assist the facility in achieving revenue goals under terms of the contract. Additionally, the foodservice company will hire and train all personnel and may be required by the contract to invest capital in facilities and/or production equipment.

In some instances, contractual arrangements with exclusive caterers have been criticized because under guaranteed financial arrangements, incentive and motivation to produce at competitive levels may be diminished. This has been known to grow out of managerial complacency under the terms of long (often ten-year) contracts. This, in turn, leads to reputation problems for the facility because, under most circumstances, the facility bears the brunt of the criticism for poor food and service. It does not matter if it was provided by the contractor; the informal information exchange documented earlier will inextricably link the poor FBS and the facility whether the contract caterer is named or not.

These sorts of difficulties can lead to legal problems and the attendant bad publicity that can result from public legal processes of this nature. The disadvantage in this circumstance is the difficulty of "firing" a contractor who enjoys the benefits of an "ironclad" ten-year deal. Public assembly facilities, in executing such contracts, need to provide for a stipulated program of quality assurance that includes incentives, punishments, and contract dissolutions in the event of noncompliance on the part of the catering contractor.

With the predominance of exclusive catering arrangements for FBS at convention facilities, the terms of the contract allowing such exclusivity become very important. Contracts can vary in length, from 2 years to 20 years, with an increasing emphasis on shorter terms that help preclude the problems inherent in long-term relationships. Other variables that commonly influence the final form exclusive contracts take include the type of facility and its predominant market, the provisions for participation with capital investments, and legal or charter restrictions that may attach to public assembly facilities through enabling legislation.

There are two major types of contracts commonly enacted between convention facilities and providers of FBS management and operations. In the first, called a **profit-and-loss contract,** the building receives a percentage or flat dollar amount of the caterer's gross revenues. The percentage is affected by capital investment participation and may also be affected by length of contract.

The second type of contract is the **management fee contract,** in which the building is responsible for all costs of operation and pays directly to the caterer a stipulated amount of money as administrative overhead and a percentage of the profits based on capital investment participation in the facility by the caterer.

OVERVIEW OF FBS EVENTS

Food and beverage events at conventions, expositions, and meetings are more than just the provision of basic human needs. In a very real sense, "They serve as the primary social mechanism by which . . . attendees meet new associates, renew old acquaintances, develop positive feelings about the overall convention experience, and exchange ideas and solutions to mutual problems" (McGee 1985, 57). It is at these social occasions that business that cannot be accomplished at formal sessions is conducted. In many ways, these FBS events further the cause of the formal sessions through informal interpersonal processes.

The key variables affecting the success of these adjuncts to the meeting process are:

- Planner knowledge of his/her group
- Type and length of event
- Goals/objectives of the meeting/convention
- FBS management's ability to respond to planner requests
- Time, budget, and logistics constraints

Within this framework, and recognizing the limitations on both parties, the planner and FBS manager need to participate in a mutual education process that matches facility capabilities with event requirements.

Common event-related food and beverage functions are usually chosen from or custom-designed from the following inventory (Nichols 1985, 145–154; Warner 1989, 293r, 297):

- Breakfast

  —Sit-down, served
  —Buffet
  —Continental

- Brunch
- Coffee/refreshment breaks
- Luncheon

  —Sit-down, served
  —Buffet
  —Boxed, carry-out

- Receptions
- Cocktails and hors d'oeuvres
- Dinners

  —Sit-down, served
  —Buffet
  —Theme (entertainment may be involved)

- Parties
- Late suppers

Catering menu selections at convention centers usually can be characterized as comprehensive, extensive, and flexible. They are typically well produced, may include pictures, and are designed as merchandising sales tools (Warner 1989, 292). They will offer a range of prices and selections designed to fulfill the needs of a broad segment of the center's market.

Another major factor that is often overlooked in the planning of an FBS event and menu selection is the purpose of the event itself. With a clear idea of the planner's, purpose, FBS management will be better able to assist in menu design. A reception for new members, for instance, may be enhanced by a different menu design than a retirement function for an outgoing executive (Jones 1984, 144).

Referring to the inventory of convention- and meeting-related food events above, it must be recognized that the word *traditional* is difficult to apply to any list of food events for any given group. Attitudes and habits about food, its composition, presentation, and consumption, are undergoing a significant change from 10 to 20 years ago. While morning, noon, and evening meals are still typical for most people, demographic, social, health, and budgetary influences are changing the way in which these particular events are being designed.

While the "power breakfast" may be *in*, in certain metropolitan areas when attendees are at meetings and conventions, for the most part, heavy morning meals are becoming less the rule and more the exception (Juergens 1988, 46). Increasingly, planners are taking the option of providing morning meeting attendees with buffets or continental breakfasts that feature a variety of lighter, more health-conscious foods such as granola, bran muffins, yogurt, dry cereals, fruit, and low-fat dairy products. These sorts of morning meals are less labor-intensive, are generally less costly, and lend themselves easily to conducting business sessions in conjunction with meals.

Refreshment breaks are also being designed to be unique and more memorable than the traditional coffee and danish of the past. While coffee is still a fundamental staple, and its absence or unavailability widely and negatively commented upon, planners and FBS managers are now dressing up the traditional coffee break with imaginative serving selections. These can include fruit, juices, soft drinks, flavored popcorn, and other popular "finger foods" that have previously been the staples of only the evening cocktail party.

Formal, sit-down luncheons and dinners are also less popular than in the past. From the ranges of possibilities available to planners, convention facility and hotel FBS managers can now design meals to appeal to a broad range of individual tastes and still achieve relatively dramatic presentations, especially at lunch, that will not impede afternoon business sessions by being too heavy or rich. Planners with budgets are also finding that flexibility can be achieved through the utilization of lunch portions at evening meals, saving money that perhaps can be more effectively invested in receptions, desserts, or a dramatic dinner accompaniment such as a vintage wine (Juergens 1988, 47, 51).

Alcohol service at cocktail parties and receptions has also undergone significant changes as planners and FBS managers alike recognize the potential legal problems associated "over-serving" alcoholic beverages. Planning strategies in this context involve time limitations on open bars, portion control, or limited number of drink coupons per attendee. Circulating servers with champagne or wine in lieu of hard liquor and the provision of hor d'oeuvres, food items, and soft drinks also limit alcohol consumption. In this way, planners and managements alike are able to directly monitor liquor consumption and stay within facility policy guidelines.

While it may be a contradiction, the health consciousness of many people seems to evaporate in the face of rich, luscious, and beautifully presented dessert items. In spite of this contradiction, planners and FBS managers often find that dramatic dessert presentations are the most memorable portion of an event meal function. Desserts, therefore, can become an important focal point in both planners' and attendees' judgments on the success of the event. So, while planners may be choosing more health-oriented breakfasts, luncheons, and dinners, facilities may find themselves providing increasingly rich and complex dessert items up to, and including, formal multiple-item dessert buffets that may cap off an evening of dancing or entertainment.

Within budget constraints, creativity on the part of the planner and FBS management appears to be unlimited. The importance of foodservice has increased the willingness of planners and facility managements alike to meet the challenge implicit in this critical element of a meeting's success.

ISSUES AND CONCLUSION

The issues and challenges that are facing hotel and facility owners, FBS managements, and CEMI planners and managers, individually and collectively, represent a blend of old problems and new contingencies.

A traditional challenge has always been the quality of the food and beverage product, which, with its price, must reflect some cost-value relationship to the ultimate purchaser and consumer. As discussed in this chapter and elsewhere, a reputation for poor food or service can be a haunting burden a hotel or facility may have difficulty resolving. The issue of quality is inextricably related to price, for in the minds of the ultimate consumer, even a well-prepared inexpensive meal in a banquet environment can seem mediocre by restaurant or home standards. Similarly, a high-priced meal that fails from a culinary standpoint will also have negative impacts. It is managing the quality-price relationship that presents a large and enduring challenge to FBS managers and planners alike.

Legal issues are becoming more important to facility operators and their FBS partners. When a contract exists between the convention facility and a catering company, the issues of contract compliance have attached to them vast potential for legal disputes. Avoiding such confrontations is in the best interests of both facility owners and FNS managers. They key, perhaps, is in designing a contract that obligates both parties to adhere to criteria of performance standards that are as objectively drawn as possible. The ability to measure performance against evaluative criteria will obviate most of the potential for legal adversity.

Another area that presents legal challenges is that of liability for liquor service. Within the laws of any state or municipality, the terms of contracts between facilities and FBS providers will include insurance requirements and liquor service policies that are becoming industry-wide standards. The same potential threats exist for hotel-based liquor service. Most major hotel companies have designed and implemented policies and training to insulate them from the vast majority of potential liquor liability problems. It is up to the facilities and food managers alike to educate planners and convention managers as to legal responsibilities and requirements relative to liquor liability.

The final general family of issues facing the CEMI's relationships with its FBS providers involves the management of the FBS function. A facet of this issue also common to hotel companies is that of turnover. Meeting planners experience frustrations in dealing with sales, catering, and food production staffs who are often long-gone in the interim between the sale and the execution of the event. A key to the resolution of this particular issue is consistency in policies over the long term. In a convention facility, the central focus of the challenge is on experience and longevity of a caterer's management and production executives, along with corporate support and resources to individual on-site management at the convention facility.

These and as yet unidentified future issues will continue to provide challenges to the world of foodservice as it relates to the CEMI. The importance of FBS to the success of group events is fundamental and serves to underscore the critical relationship between and among FBS providers and key members of the CEMI.

REFERENCES

Anonymous. 1985. Reexamining Food and Beverage Service (editorial). *Facility Manager* 1(2):4.

Bany, John B. 1977. Catering Options for a Municipal Facility. In *Facility and Operations Manual*. Chicago, Illinois: International Association of Auditorium Managers (edited collection of operational position papers, mimeo).

Bloom, Heidi. 1981. Marketing to Meeting Planners: What Works? *The Cornell Hotel and Restaurant Administration Quarterly* 22(2):45–50.

Jones, James E. 1984. *Meeting Management: A Professional Approach*. Stamford, Connecticut: Bayard Publications, Inc.

Juergens, Jennifer. 1988. F&B: When to Scrimp and When to Splurge. *Meetings and Conventions* October: 45–51.

Laventhol and Horwath. 1988. *Exhibit Hall Industry Annual Report Vol. IV*. Tampa, Florida: Laventhol & Horwath.

M&C/Meetings and Conventions Magazine. 1988. Meetings Market '87. Secaucus, New Jersey: Reed Travel Group.

McGee, Regina, ed. 1985. *The Convention Liaison Council Manual*. Washington, D.C.: The Convention Liaison Council.

Nichols, Barbara, ed. 1985. *Professional Meeting Management*. Birmingham, Alabama: The Professional Convention Management Association.

Quinn, Lawrence R. 1985. Everything **and** and Kitchen Sink. *Facility Manager* 1(2):14–19.

Rutherford, Denney G. 1989. Convention Centers and Their Managers. Research in progress. Seattle, Washington: Washington State University.

Stotereau, Edwin J. 1977. In-House vs. Contracted Caterers. In *Facility and Operations Manual*. Chicago: International Association of Auditorium Managers (edited collection of operational position papers, mimeo).

Warner, Mickey. (No date.) Recreational Foodservice Module 13 in *Foodser-

vice: A Segmented Industry. Chicago: International Foodservice Manufacturers Association, mimeo. (Proprietary document.)

Warner, Mickey. 1986. Recreational Food Service Management: A New Academic Challenge. *Florida International University Hospitality Review* 4(1):62–72.

Warner, Mickey. 1989. *Recreational Foodservice Management.* New York: Van Nostrand Reinhold.

Appendix 1

1989 Convention Center Manager Survey and Results

PART ONE

Respondent Information

1. How old are you? <u>28–65</u> x = 46.2 (80)

2. Your sex: 91.<u>3</u>% Male   7.<u>0</u>% Female (80)

3. Your race: 2.5% Black/Negro/Afro-American (80)
   1.<u>3</u>% Hispanic or Spanish surname
   <u>-</u> Asian/Pacific Islander
   93.<u>8</u>% White/Caucasian
   2.<u>5</u>% Native American
   <u>-</u> Other / specify _____

4. What is your marital status? (80)
   2.<u>5</u>% Never married   8.<u>8</u>% Divorced
   88.<u>8</u>% Married, living w/spouse   <u>-</u> Widowed
   <u>-</u> Married, separated from spouse

5. Do you have children? 93.<u>6</u>% Yes / How many? <u>1–9</u>
   (78)   6.<u>4</u>% No   x = 2.4

6. Are you a U.S. Citizen? 91<u>%</u> Yes   9.<u>0</u>% No (78)

7. What is your basic salary before deductions for the
   current year? (79)
   2.<u>5</u>% Below $40,000   8.<u>9</u>% $70,000 to $74,999
   6.<u>3</u>% $41,000 to $44,999   11.<u>4</u>% $75,000 to $79,999
   7.<u>6</u>% $45,000 to $49,999   1.<u>3</u>% $80,000 to $84,999
   12.<u>7</u>% $50,000 to $54,999   2.<u>5</u>% $85,000 to $89,999
   7.<u>6</u>% $55,000 to $59,999   3.<u>8</u>% $90,000 to $94,999
   17.<u>7</u>% $60,000 to $64,999   1.<u>3</u>% $95,000 to $99,999
   6.<u>3</u>% $65,000 to $69,999   10.<u>1</u>% Over $100,000

Please choose the **academic** degree(s) you hold from the list
at the left, and place in blanks below. Leave blank if no
academic degree:

CHOOSE FROM THIS LIST
AA   MA   8. ____ 1st Degree
AAS   MS   9. ____ 2nd Degree
BS   MBA   10. ____ 3rd Degree
BA   OTHER/specify _____   11. ____ No Degree

12. If you hold a degree, please choose the discipline in which
    the highest degree was awarded (earned); otherwise, go to
    question #13. (56)
    33.<u>9</u>% Business Administration
    66.<u>1</u>% Other/specify _____

13. How long have you been employed in the conventions and
    meetings industry? <u>2–39 years</u>   x = 15.93 (80)

14. How long have you been employed at your present
    facility? <u>1–25 years</u>   x = 8.15 (80)

15. How long have you been employed in your present
    position? <u>1–25 years</u>   x = 6.17 (80)

16. In comparison to others in the conventions and meetings
    industry, has your own economic position improved,
    worsened or stayed roughly the same over the past five
    years? (79)
    34.<u>2</u>% Improved markedly   1.<u>3</u>% Worsened somewhat
    47.<u>4</u>% Improved moderately   <u>-</u> Worsened significantly
    15.<u>2</u>% Stayed the same

17. In comparison to professionals such as yourself who are
    employed **outside** the conventions and meetings industry,
    has your own economic position improved, worsened or
    stayed roughly the same over the past five years? (78)
    15.<u>4</u>% Improved markedly   21.<u>8</u>% Worsened somewhat
    52.<u>6</u>% Improved moderately   <u>-</u> Worsened significantly
    10.<u>3</u>% Stayed the same

18. Comparing yourself with other facility professionals of your
    age and qualifications, how successful do you consider
    yourself to be in your career? (80)
    56.<u>3</u>% Very successful   <u>-</u> Fairly unsuccessful
    42.<u>5</u>% Fairly successful   1.<u>3</u>% Very unsuccessful

19. Do you think you would be more satisfied or less
    satisfied with life outside the conventions and meetings
    industry? (80)
    7.<u>5</u>% More satisfied   48.<u>8</u>% Less satisfied
    43.<u>8</u>% Equally satisfied

20. During the past two years, have you ever considered
    leaving the conventions industry permanently? (80)
    31.<u>3</u>% Yes, I've given it consideration
    27.<u>5</u>% Yes, I've considered it, but not seriously
    41.<u>3</u>% No, I've not considered it

21. Within the past two years, have you sought or made a
    serious inquiry about another position? (80)
    31.<u>3</u>% Yes, I have sought another position
    27.<u>5</u>% Have not sought, but made a serious inquiry
    41.<u>3</u>% Neither

22. Within the past two years, have you received an offer of
    another job, or a serious inquiry about your availability for
    another position? (80)
    47.<u>5</u>% Yes, an offer   8.<u>8</u>% Neither
    43.<u>8</u>% Not an offer, but a serious inquiry

23. Is your current position: (79)
    19.<u>0</u>% Civil service
    20.<u>3</u>% A contract arrangement / How long? _____
    50.<u>6</u>% Employed at will
    10.<u>1</u>% Other/specify _____

24. What are the average number of hours you work per
    week? (80)
    22.<u>5</u>% 40-50 hours   3.<u>8</u>% 71-80 hours
    48.<u>8</u>% 51-60 hours   3.<u>8</u>% 81+ hours
    21.<u>3</u>% 61-70 hours

PART TWO

Facility Information

SIZE OF FACILITY

25. Gross sq. ft. of EXHIBITION space 15,000–999,999   (80)
    x = 199,028
26. Gross sq. ft. of MEETING ROOM space 1,200–250,000 (77)
    x = 48,121
27. Gross sq. ft. of DINING AREA   3,000–365,000   (56)
    x = 43,083
28. Gross sq. ft. of CONCESSION AREA(S)   24–40,000   (54)
    x = 7,340
29. Gross sq. ft. of FOOD PREP/KITCHEN AREA 1,500–40,000
    (68)   x = 8,487

EMPLOYMENT

30. Number of FULL-TIME staff persons   4–99   (78)
    x = 48.78
31. Number of PART-TIME call-in staff (assume full utilization
    of exhibit, meeting and food service space)   5–99   (74)
    x = 73.15

REPORTING STRUCTURE

32. Do you report to: (80)
    37.5% Board of Directors   7.5% County Executive
    3.8% City Council   8.8% City Manager
    2.5% County Council   3.8% State Legislatue
    8.8% Mayor   12.5% Municipal Authority
                                        or Commission
    _-_ City or County Department Head/
        specify _____
    15.0% Other/specify _____

33. Is your facility: 95.0% Publicly owned   (80)
                          5.0% Privately owned

34. Is your facility: (72)
    87.5% Publicly managed by public-sector employees
    12.5% Privately managed by a management company

FOOD SERVICE

35. How is your food service handled?   (79)
    16.5% In-house by facility staff
    81.0% Contracted to outside company
          If contracted: 87.5% Exclusive catering contract
                         14.0% Open catering contract
    2.5% Other/specify _____

36. Average number of events per year:
    Conventions with exhibits   2–158   x = 26.86   (64)
    Trade shows   2–50   x = 15.49   (59)
    Non-profit groups   0–193   x = 32.06   (48)
    Consumer shows   1–130   x = 18.26   (61)
    Local group events   0–500   x = 110.55   (56)
    Local food & beverage events 0–250   x = 66.74   (54)

LIST OF SERVICES

Please circle the appropriate response for each service as
follows:
    Circle **B** — if BUILDING OPERATED
    Circle **C** — if OUTSIDE CONTRACTOR is used
    Circle **I** — if INCLUDED IN RENT

If you do offer the service to clients for a fee, RATE the
service on a scale of 1 (of little importance)
to 5 (of great importance) to you as a revenue source.

GENERAL	B %	C %	I %	MEAN	
37. Audio recording	24.7	74.0	1.3	2.23	(77)
38. Booth cleaning	37.7	55.8	6.5	2.64	(77)
39. Cable tv	31.3	64.2	4.5	2.06	(67)
40. Electrical services	64.6	32.9	2.5	4.32	(79)
41. Entertainment or talent buying	21.4	77.1	1.4	1.80	(70)
42. FAX transmission/receiving	71.0	26.1	2.9	1.96	(69)
43. Major audio-visual service	25.6	74.4	-	3.20	(78)
44. Pipe & drape set-up	28.0	72.0	-	3.38	(75)
45. Plumbing/drain/compressed air	73.1	21.8	5.1	3.05	(78)
46. Satellite downlinks (dish access)	13.4	86.6	-	2.00	(67)
47. Satellite uplinks	6.3	92.2	1.6	1.96	(64)
48. Sign making	23.0	75.7	1.4	2.29	(74)
49. Sound services	64.9	31.2	3.9	3.04	(77)
50. Stage construction/lighting services	62.3	37.7	-	3.18	(77)
51. Telephone service	57.0	43.0	-	3.25	(79)
52. Video recording	14.5	85.5	-	2.13	(76)
53. Post-event packaging/mailing	15.9	84.1	-	1.76	(69)
ADVERTISING & MARKETING					
54. Marquee services	65.2	4.3	30.4	2.45	(69)
VIDEO & INFORMATION SERVICES					
55. In-house services	51.6	38.7	9.7	2.63	(62)
56. Hotel services & information	30.0	55.0	1.5	1.96	(60)
57. Tourism trip information	28.3	58.3	13.3	2.17	(60)
58. Restaurant/entertainment info.	32.3	51.6	16.1	2.24	(62)

OTHER

59. Does your facility utilize computerized meeting and event
    planning software? 50.6% Yes   49.4% No   (77)

60. If yes, on a scale of 1 (unsuccessful) to 5 (very successful),
    how has this software worked?   x = 3.58   (33)

PART THREE
Issues

Listed below are a number of issues and topics culled from past meetings, private conversations and various publications that face conventions and meetings managers. Please evaluate each issue in two contexts:

1. **TIME** — The time you spend on these issues annually
2. **IMPORTANCE** — The amount of importance you place on these issues

Please rank each issue on a scale of 1 (virtually no time or of no importance) to 5 (a great deal of time or of utmost importance)

TIME		ISSUE	IMPORTANCE	
MEAN	SD		MEAN	SD
2.71	1.2	61. Personal contributions/work toward professionalism of convention managers	3.43	1.27
1.93	1.1	62. Professional contributions/work toward certification for convention managers	2.62	1.34
2.62	1.1	63. Professional contributions/work toward education for convention facility managers	3.65	1.13
2.53	1.1	64. Staff recruiting	3.82	1.19
3.29	1.1	65. Staff training	4.38	.86
3.93	1.0	66. Staff quality	4.65	.70
3.71	1.08	67. Relations with convention & visitor bureaus	4.05	1.07
3.86	1.0	68. Creation/generation of additional revenue sources	4.41	.84
4.05	.96	69. Budgeting responsibilities	4.44	.85
3.41	1.08	70. Relations with tradeshow managers	4.04	1.04
2.19	1.3	71. Labor negotiations/unions	2.92	1.52
2.82	1.3	72. Problems with show managers	3.65	1.27
2.84	1.2	73. Problems with meeting planners	3.68	1.21
2.57	1.2	74. Problems with service contractors	3.42	1.24
1.62	.89	75. Problems with transportation companies	2.17	1.36
3.34	1.2	76. Relations with politicians	3.88	1.18
2.87	1.17	77. Dealing with security issues	3.57	1.15
2.89	1.32	78. Working with hotels	3.56	1.3
3.61	1.09	79. Public & community relations	4.29	.86
4.03	.92	80. Managing facility personnel	4.44	.85
3.87	.98	81. Dealing with operations manager	4.27	.75
3.53	1.1	82. Managing director of event coordination	3.99	1.01
3.55	1.07	83. Working with chief accountant	3.90	.98
3.67	1.14	84. Dealing with sales managers	3.91	1.09
2.65	1.03	85. Managing chief engineer	3.12	1.17
2.41	1.02	86. Dealing with operations foreman	2.99	1.25
3.44	1.13	87. Working with food service director	3.93	1.01
2.82	1.14	88. Consumer shows	3.23	1.18
2.84	1.16	89. Rate schedules	3.64	1.12
3.51	1.21	90. Strategic marketing (18 months and out)	4.04	1.07
3.46	1.12	91. Tactical marketing (inside of 18 months)	3.87	1.11
3.24	1.37	92. Changing/improving building design	3.65	1.38

Appendix 2

Sample Job Description: Convention Service Manager

PRIMARY DUTIES

The convention service manager or director of convention services is in charge of and responsible for representing the property to the convention and corporate meeting officials, to their organizations' staffs and leadership, and to their meeting attendees, once the booking has been made and confirmed.

This person's basic responsibilities are to ensure that schedules are maintained and that services are rendered to the customer by the facility in accordance with the written and signed agreements or contracts made with the buyer at the time the convention or meeting was booked.

This position involves continuous corrdination with the various operating departments to make certain that quality service standards are maintained. It also ensures that all elements of the convention or meeting, from the time of attendee arrival through the setup to billing and departures, run smoothly and efficiently.

The director of convention services is the chief liaison between the property and the convention or meeting group. In addition to these public relations and service roles, the director of convention services has a sales responsibility to the facility for rebooking the group by providing the best service and follow-through.

In addition to these primary functions, the director of convention services has tasks in the following areas:

- **Administrative Responsibilities**

  1. Develop objectives, goals, and policies relating to the group business servicing philosophy and procedures of the property, for approval by the director of marketing and the property's management committee.

2. Develop administrative procedures relating to the daily servicing operations of the facility; establish a procedure for daily review of each convention or group in the house.
3. Maintain the necessary records and filing systems to provide detailed information about the servicing requirements of each group.
4. Maintain an inventory of necessary equipment and supplies for the setup of meeting and function rooms; ensure that proper maintenance and replacement programs are followed.
5. Work with outside audiovisual companies for the securing of special equipment not carried by the property.
6. Work with the local convention bureau and with counterparts in other properties in situations where multiple housing or use of outside meeting facilities is needed.

- **Working Relations with Sales/Marketing Department**

  1. Work with the director of marketing and the sales/marketing staff to develop and implement sales and servicing programs relating to the development, servicing, and retention of conventions and group business.
  2. Coordinate directly with the account executive responsible for each booking to ensure the smooth transition of the handling of the account between the time of the booking and the arrival of the group.

- **Interdepartmental Relations**

  1. Work with the rooms division manager concerning the allocation and assignment of guest rooms, especially VIP and hospitality suites.
  2. Work with the catering manager on allocating function space and ensure proper entries in the function book.
  3. Work with the food and beverage manager on matters relating to food production, theme parties, and other meal functions.
  4. Work with the housekeeping department to handle special housekeeping requirements, such as servicing VIP accommodations and hospitality suites.
  5. Work with maintenance and engineering to ensure proper meeting and function room climate control, special utility requests for meeting rooms and exhibit areas, and general maintenance operations.
  6. Work with security to ensure that proper procedures are followed for securing the registration desk, exhibit areas, and storage space used by each group.
  7. Work with the accounting department to ensure that proper billing procedures are followed and that a system is established for a daily review of the group's master account.

8. Coordinate the activities of all property departments participating in the servicing of each convention and meeting, and ensure on an event-by-event basis that all servicing details by all departments are carried out.
9. Prepare and distribute detailed requirements memoranda to all department heads well in advance of each convention or meeting.

- **Customer Service Responsibilities**

1. Take over each account after confirmation of booking and contact the group's meeting planner or other representative to establish a schedule of communications.
2. Meet with association executives, corporate meeting planners, and other convention officials to finalize plans concerning details of meetings, food and beverage functions, and recreational/entertainment activities that are part of the program; offer assistance, ideas, and creative input to help showcase the program activities.
3. Maintain a checklist of services available from both the property and outside local firms, including audiovisual equipment, exhibit management services, security, printing, registration desk personnel, photography, and entertainment.
4. Inform convention representatives of local fire regulations, room occupancy limitations, exhibit area floor load allowances, drinking age and beverage servicing restrictions, and other legal requirements.
5. Check on behalf of convention or meeting representatives with the property's operating departments to ensure that rooms, food, reception, meeting, and exhibit space have been blocked and that servicing requirements are understood in accordance with the contract or letters of agreement.
6. Periodically inform the operating departments of any changes, additions, or deletions concerning meeting requirements.
7. Working with the meeting planner, prepare a detailed servicing memorandum on a daily, event-by-event basis.
8. Schedule a preconvention briefing session with the convention and meeting representatives and the property department heads the day prior to the opening session to review all details and record any last-minute changes.
9. Greet convention representatives upon arrival and show them locations of meeting and exhibit areas, food and beverage outlets, and other features of the property.
10. Check daily on each meeting and function room, exhibit area, and registration area to ensure that proper room setup, audiovisual equipment, supplies, and other servicing details have been taken care of in accordance with the customer's requirements.

11. Ensure that the time and location of each event is posted daily on reader boards, and in elevators, and is distributed as a daily events sheet to all departments; check to make sure that function signs are placed around appropriate doorways and that directional signs are properly placed.
12. Maintain close communication with the customer to coordinate any last-minute changes.
13. Contact convention officials at the end of the program to discuss their plans for future events and issue invitations to return.
14. Prepare a detailed critique at the end of the convention comparing forecasted room pick-ups and meeting/function guarantees with the actual figures.
15. Schedule a postconvention briefing between the convention officials and property department heads to discuss the results of the convention on a department-by-department basis.

Source: Hoyle, Leonard H., David C. Dorf, and Thomas J. A. Jones. 1989. *Managing Conventions and Group Business.* East Lansing, Michigan: Educational Institute of the American Hotel and Motel Association. pp. 156–157. Used with permission.

Appendix 3

Convention Industry Organizations

Air Transport Association of
America (ATAA)
1709 New York Avenue, N.W.
Washington, DC 20006
(202) 626-4000

American Hotel and Motel
Association (AHMA)
888 Seventh Avenue
New York, NY 10019
(212) 265-4506

American Society of Association
Executives (ASAE)
1575 Eye Street, N.W.
Washington, DC 20005
(202) 626-2723

Association of Conference and
Events Directors—International
(ACED)
Colorado State University
Rockwell Hall
Fort Collins, CO 80523

Association for Convention
Operations Management (ACOM)
1819 Peachtree Street N.E.,
Suite 560
Atlanta, GA 30309
(404) 351-3220

Association of Independent
Meeting Planners (AIMP)
5103 Wigville Road
Thurmont, MD 21788
(301) 271-4222

Convention Liaison Council
(CLC)
1575 Eye Street, N.W.
Washington, DC 20005
(202) 626-2764

Council of Engineering and
Scientific Society Executives
(CESSE)
2000 Florida Avenue, N.W.
Washington, DC 20009

Exhibit Designers and Producers
Association (EDPA)
611 E. Wells Street
Milwaukee, WI 53202
(414) 276-3372

Exposition Service Contractors
Association (ESCA)
400 South Houston
Union Station, Suite 210
Dallas, TX 75202
(214) 742-9217

Health Care Exhibitors
Association (HCEA)
5775 Peachtree-Dunwoody Road
Building D, Suite 500
Atlanta, GA 30342
(404) 242-3663

Hotel Sales and Marketing
Association International
(HSMAI)
1400 K Street, N.W., Suite 810
Washington, DC 20005
(202) 789-0089

Institute of Association
Management Companies (IAMC)
5820 Wilshire Boulevard,
Suite 500
Los Angeles, CA 90036

Insurance Conference Planners
Association (ICPA)
8721 Indian Hills Drive
Omaha, NE 68114
(402) 390-7300

International Association of
Auditorium Managers (IAAM)
4425 W. Airport Freeway,
Suite 590
Irving, TX 75062
(214) 255-8020

International Association of
Conference Centers (IACC)
362 Parsippany Road
Parsippany, NJ 07054
(201) 887-3505

International Association of
Convention and Visitor Bureaus
(IACVB)
P.O. Box 758
Champaign, IL 61820
(217) 359-8881

International Association of Fairs
and Expositions (IAFE)
P.O. Box 985
Springfield, MO 65801
(417) 862-5771

International Communication
Industries Association (ICIA)
3150 Spring Street
Fairfax, VA 22031
(703) 273-7200

International Exhibitors
Association (IEA)
5103-B Backlick Road
Annandale, VA 22003
(703) 941-3725

Meeting Planners International (MPI)
1950 Stemmons Freeway
Dallas, TX 75207-3109
(214) 746-5250

National Association of
Exposition Managers (NAEM)
710 Indiana Avenue
Indianapolis, IN 46202
(317) 638-6236

Professional Convention
Management Association (PCMA)
100 Vestavia Office Park,
Suite 220
Birmingham, AL 35216
(205) 823-7262

Religious Conference Management
Association (RCMA)
One Hoosier Dome, Suite 120
Indianapolis, IN 46225
(317) 632-1888

Society of Company Meeting
Planners (SCMP)
2600 Garden Road, Suite 208
Monterey, CA 93940
(408) 649-6544

Society of Government Meeting
Planners (SGMP)
1213 Prince Street
Alexandria, VA 22314-9998

Society of Incentive Travel
Executives (SITE)
271 Madison Avenue
New York, NY 10016
(212) 889-9340

Trade Show Bureau
P.O. Box 797
8 Beach Road
East Orleans, MA 02643
(508) 240-0177

Travel Industry Association of
America (TIAA)
2 Lafayette Center
1133 21st Street, N.W.
Washington, DC 20036
(202) 293-1433

Appendix 4

Selected Annotated Bibliography

Astroff, Milton T., and James R. Abbey. 1988. *Convention Sales and Service,* 2nd ed. Cranbury, New Jersey: Waterbury Press. The second edition of one of the standard reference and management books regarding the selling and servicing of the conventions market. Includes extensive pro forma examples and samples.

Blackwell, Steven H., Peter R. Turner, and Debbie L. Wolfe, ed. 1985. *Fundamentals of Association Management: Conventions.* Washington, D.C.: American Society of Association Executives. Edited collection of essays on managing conventions for associations. A good "readings" companion for *Professional Meeting Management* (Nichols 1985).

Brown, George R., and Kenneth W. Medley. 1975. *Principles of Association Management.* Washington, D.C.: American Society of Association Executives and the United States Chamber of Commerce. Previous edition of the similarly titled Ernstthal and Jefferson book. While some of the material is out of date, the book still presents a good overview of issues, structure, and management of volunteer associations.

Chapman, Edward A., Jr. 1987. *Exhibit Marketing: A Survival Guide for Managers.* New York: McGraw-Hill. The only book published specifically about the exhibiting function. Includes checklists and advice to help the exhibit manager achieve greater effectiveness.

Dotson, Penny C. 1988. *Introduction to Meeting Management.* Birmingham, Alabama: Professional Convention Management Association. Introductory textbook; a companion to *Professional Meeting Management* (Nichols 1985). Provides overviews of all aspects of meeting planning with exercises, quizzes, and discussion questions.

Ernstthal, Henry, and Vivian Jefferson, ed. 1988. *Principles of Association Management: A Professional's Handbook*. Washington, D.C.: American Society of Association Executives. A complete reference work of edited essays by experts in various aspects of association management.

Gartrell, Richard B. 1988. *Destination Marketing for Convention and Visitor Bureaus*. Dubuque, Iowa: Kendall/Hunt. Complete book for designing and managing a convention and visitor bureau (CVB). Includes discussion and application of extensive data developed by IACVB and appendix with model bylaws, job descriptions, organization charts, and budget materials, among others.

Hoyle, Leonard C., David C. Dorf, and Thomas J. A. Jones. 1989. *Managing Convention and Group Business*. East Lansing, Michigan: Educational Institute of the American Hotel and Motel Association. Written to provide broad and deep coverage of the conventions and meetings market for hotel sales staffs, this book focuses specifically on selling and servicing the group market. Extensive use of pictures, forms, and displays to illustrate text discussions.

Jones, James E. 1984. *Meeting Management: A Professional Approach,* 2nd ed. Stamford, Connecticut: Bayard Publications. A "how-to" book by a professional meeting manager. Includes checklists and examples.

McGee, Regina M., ed. 1985. *The Convention Liaison Council Manual*. Washington, D.C.: The Convention Liaison Council. A practitioner's handbook. Includes brief overviews and discussions of all aspects of meetings management. Good selection of charts, diagrams, and checklists.

Nichols, Barbara C., ed. 1985. *Professional Meeting Management*. Birmingham, Alabama: Professional Convention Management Association. In-depth, detailed coverage of every aspect of meetings management. Prepared by professional practitioners, it includes discussion, examples, charts, forms, and pictures.

Peterson, David C. 1988. *Convention Centers, Stadiums and Arenas*. Washington, D.C.: Urban Land Institute. The author is a partner in the national accounting firm of Laventhol and Horwath, specializing in sports and convention facilities consulting. The book covers facility development topics from conception, planning, and design through operations and finances. Included are nine case studies of recent convention center projects.

Warner, Mickey. 1989. *Recreational Foodservice Management*. New York: Van Nostrand Reinhold. The only comprehensive treatise on the leisure, sports, and recreational foodservice segment of the industry. Includes a case study on convention center food and beverage operations.

Wolfe, Debbie L., ed. 1984. *Fundamentals of Association Management: Organization*. Washington, D.C.: American Society of Association Executives. Edited collection of readings on all aspects of association management. Makes a good "readings" companion to Brown and Medley.

M&C/Meetings and Conventions. 1988. *The Meetings Market '87*. Reed Travel Group. Secaucus, New Jersey: Meetings and Conventions Magazine. A systematic survey of the readership of *Meetings and Conventions* magazine yielded completed instruments from 803 corporate and 488 association meeting planners. The study yielded data on planners' practices and opinions on a broad range of questions, from site selection to travel agent usage.

Glossary

ABA American Bar Association.

ACOM Association for Convention Operations Management.

ASAE American Society for Association Executives.

Association An organized body that exhibits some variety of volunteer leadership structure, which may employ a staff, that serves a group of people who share some interest, activity, or purpose. The association is generally organized to promote and enhance that common interest, activity, or purpose.

Breakouts Small group meetings conducted within the overall topic context of a general meeting. Several concurrent breakout meetings are usually held following a general session (general meeting attended by all delegates or attendees to a convention).

CEMI Conventions, expositions, and meetings industry.

CEO Chief executive officer.

CHRIE Council on Hotel, Restaurant and Institutional Education.

CLC Convention Liaison Council.

CSE Chief staff executive.

CSM Convention services manager.

CVB Convention and visitors bureau. A coordinating body that exists to sell a city as a convention and tourism destination.

DMC Destination management company.

Drayage Handling of cargo/freight into and out of a convention, meeting, or exhibition facility.

EDPA Exhibit Designers and Producers Association.

ESC Exposition service contractor.

ESCA Exposition Service Contractors Association.

Exposition See *Trade show.*

FAM trip Familiarization trip organized by convention and visitor bureaus; designed to familiarize meeting planners and association executives with local facilities and services and market them as viable destination considerations.

FAX Facsimile transmission.

FBS Food and beverage service.

FIT Free independent traveler.

Fly-in See *FAM trip.*

Hotel room tax Tax levied to visitor hotel bills based on a percentage of the room rate paid. Also known as *bed tax* or *pillow tax.*

HRA Hotel and restaurant administration.

HSMAI Hotel Sales and Marketing Association International.

Hub airport Airline consolidation of operations whereby a single airport facility is designated as its central operating point in a given area or region.

IACVB International Association of Convention and Visitors Bureaus.

IEA International Exhibitors Association. Formerly the National Trade Show Exhibitors Association (NTSEA).

INET Database network available to members of the International Association of Convention and Visitors Bureau (IACVB) which provides system-wide information on conventions booked and hosted by members.

Leaking An economic term that refers to money spent outside the local economy for goods, services, and raw materials.

License agreement A detailed legal document (contract) that outlines the rights, duties, and obligations of both "user" and "provider" relative to the rental of space in a convention facility.

Loss leader The practice of pricing a product below production cost to "lead" customers to make other purchases.

Market-driven organization An organization whose operating structure evolves according to conditions and preferences of its solicited market(s).

Meeting facilitator A planner with authority and responsibility for *specific* (as opposed to all) details attendant to any given meeting.

Meeting manager The "principal" planner for an organization, responsible for policy, budget, implementation, evaluation, and all other aspects of meeting planning.

Meeting planner The individual in an organization whose duties consist, in whole or in part, of planning the details attendant to meetings of various types and sizes.

MPI Meeting Planners International.

NAEM National Association of Exposition Managers.

No-shows Reservations not used.

NRA National Restaurant Association.

NSF Net square feet; usually the basis by which exhibit space is rented.

NTSEA See *IEA*.

PAC Political action committee.

PAF Public assembly facility.

PCMA Professional Convention Management Association.

PEC Political education committee.

Pipe and drape The most common means of delineating individual exhibit booth space on an exhibition floor. Pipes are configured to serve as an overall frame over which are *draped* fabric or other materials which serve as the "walls" of the booth.

Profit center Organizational component that generates revenues in excess of expenses.

SGMP Society of Government Meeting Planners.

Teardown The move-out phase of an exhibition; the breaking down and crating of exhibit booths and the overall clearing of the exhibition area.

Trade show A group of product suppliers, assembled by a show manager, who set up physical exhibits in an exhibition hall of some type to appeal to a specific group or market.

Turnaround time The total time involved relative to the move-in and move-out of a convention, trade show, or exposition; or, the total time involved relative to meeting room preparation and setup from function to function.

VIP Very important person.

WARF Washington Association Research Foundation.

WSAE Washington Society of Association Executives.

Index